Psychology and Religion

Margaret Gorman, R.S.C.J., editor

Psychology and Religion

A Reader

paulist press   *new york/mahwah*

Margaret Gorman, a Religious of the Sacred Heart, and former Chair of the Department of Newton College of the Sacred Heart, is at present Adjunct Professor of Theology and Psychology at Boston College. Her research interests lie in the areas of adolescent and adult faith and moral development.

Library of Congress
Catalog Card Number: 84-62151

ISBN: 0-8091-2684-2

Published by Paulist Press
997 Macarthur Boulevard
Mahwah, N.J. 07430

Printed and bound in the United States of America

Contents

Margaret Gorman
Preface 1

I. THEOLOGIANS ON FAITH

1. *Karl Rahner*
   Unthematic Knowledge of God 7

2. *Paul Tillich*
   What Faith Is 12

3. *Avery Dulles, S.J.*
   The Meaning of Faith Considered
   in Relationship to Justice 28

II. PSYCHOLOGY AND RELIGION

4. *G. Stephen Spinks*
   Psychology and Religion 49

5. *William James*
   Conclusion *from* The Varieties
   of Religious Experience 63

6. *Sigmund Freud*
   The Future of an Illusion 74

7. *Carl G. Jung*
   Religion as the Counterbalance
   to Mass-Mindedness 81

8. *Ann Belford Ulanov*
   Psychology's Function for Religion 86

III. ADULT DEVELOPMENT—PSYCHOLOGICAL AND RELIGIOUS

9. *Daniel J. Levinson*
   Conception of the Adult Life Course 93

10. *Samuel Osherson*
    Reconstitution of Meaning in Adult
    Development 104

11. *D.W. Winnicott*
    The Search for the Self 108

12. *Ana-Maria Rizzuto*
    Conclusions *from* Birth of the Living God 116

13. *James Fowler*
    Stages of Faith Development 135

14. *William J. Bouwsma*
    Christian Adulthood 145

15. *Thomas Merton*
    Final Integration 160

IV. MORAL DEVELOPMENT—THEOLOGICAL AND PSYCHOLOGICAL PERSPECTIVES

16. *Charles E. Curran*
    The Christian Conscience Today 169

17. *Ronald Duska and Mariellen Whelan*
    Kohlberg's Moral Judgment Stages 181

18. *John A. Meacham*
    A Dialectical Approach to
    Moral Judgment and Self-Esteem 188

19. *Sigmund Freud*
    Some Psychical Consequences of the
    Anatomical Distinction Between the Sexes 199

20. *Carol Gilligan*
    Woman's Place in Man's Life Cycle 203

21. *John Michael Murphy and Carol Gilligan*
    Moral Development in Late Adolescence and
    Adulthood: A Critique and Reconstruction
    of Kohlberg's Theory 214

V. GUILT

22. *Karl Rahner*
    "Sins" and Guilt 229

23. *Louis Monden, S.J.*
    The Three Levels of Ethics 232

24. *Sigmund Freud*
    Civilization and its Discontents 242

VI. PRAYER, SYMBOL AND SPIRITUALITY

25. *Erich Neumann*
    Reflections on the Shadow 263

26. *Martin L. Hoffman*
    Development of Prosocial Motivation:
    Empathy and Guilt 270

27. *Jolande Jacobi*
    Individual and Collective Symbols 294

28. *Abraham H. Maslow*
    Comments on "Religions, Values,
    and Peak-Experiences" 301

29. *Walter Houston Clark*
    Mysticism as a Basic Concept
    in Defining the Religious Self 310

30. *Edward Kinerk, S.J.*
    Toward a Method for the
    Study of Spirituality 320

Acknowledgments

Unthematic Knowledge of God, from *Foundations of Christian Faith* by Karl Rahner. English translation copyright © 1978 by The Crossroad Publishing Company. Reprinted by permission.

What Faith Is, pages 1–5, 7–10, 16–18, and 22 from *Dynamics of Faith* by Paul Tillich. Copyright © 1957 by Paul Tillich. Reprinted by permission of Harper & Row, Publishers, Inc.

Psychology and Religion by G. Stephen Spinks. Reprinted with permission from Methuen & Company, Publishers.

Selection from *The Future of an Illusion* by Sigmund Freud, translated and edited by James Strachey, reprinted by permission of W.W. Norton & Company, Inc. Copyright © 1961 by James Strachey.

Religion as the Counterbalance to Mass-Mindedness (pages 16–18) from *The Undiscovered Self* by Carl G. Jung, translated from the German by R. F. C. Hull. Copyright © 1958 by C. G. Jung, reprinted by permission of Little, Brown and Company in association with the Atlantic Monthly Press.

Psychology's Function for Religion from *The Feminine in Jungian Psychology and in Christian Theology* by Ann Belford Ulanov, © 1971 by Northwestern University Press. Reprinted by permission.

Conception of the Adult Life Course by Daniel J. Levinson, from *Themes of Work and Love in Adulthood,* Neil J. Smelser and Erik H. Erikson, editors. Cambridge, Mass.: Harvard University Press. Copyright © 1980 by the President and Fellows of Harvard College. Reprinted by permission of the publishers.

Reconstitution of Meaning in Adult Development (pages 29–30) from *Holding on or Letting Go* by Samuel D. Osherson. Copyright © 1980 by The Free Press, a Division of Macmillan, Inc. Reprinted with permission.

The Search for the Self from *Playing and Reality* by D. W. Winnicott. Copyright © 1971 by Mrs. D. W. Winnicott. Reprinted by permission of Basic Books, Inc., Publishers.

The Birth of the Living God: A Psychoanalytic Study by Ana-Maria Rizzuto. Copyright © 1979 by The University of Chicago Press, Publishers. Reprinted with permission.

Christian Adulthood by William J. Bouwsma, pages 77–92, reprinted by permission of *Daedalus* (Vol. 105, Spring 1976), Journal of the American Academy of Arts and Sciences, Boston, Mass.

Final Integration, excerpted from *Contemplation in a World of Action* by Thomas Merton. Copyright © 1965, 1969, 1970, 1971 by the Trustees of the Merton Legacy Trust. Reprinted by permission of Doubleday & Company, Inc.

A Dialectical Approach to Moral Judgment and Self-Esteem by John A. Meacham, from *Human Development,* Vol. 18 (pages 69–74). Reprinted by permission of S. Karger, Basel, Publishers.

Some Psychical Consequences of the Anatomical Distinction Between the Sexes by Sigmund Freud, from *Collected Papers,* Vol. 5, by Sigmund Freud, edited by James Strachey. Published by Basic Books, Inc. by arrangement with the Hogarth Press Ltd. and the Institute of Psycho-Analysis, London. Reprinted by permission.

Woman's Place in Man's Life Cycle by Carol Gilligan, from *Harvard Educational Review* 1979, Vol. 49, pages 431–446. Copyright © 1979 by the President and Fellows of Harvard College. All rights reserved. Used by permission.

Moral Development in Late Adolescence and Adulthood: A Critique and Reconstruction of Kohlberg's Theory by John Michael Murphy and Carol Gilligan, from *Human Development,* Vol. 23 (pages 77–83). Reprinted by permission of S. Karger, Basel, publishers.

"Sins" and Guilt from *Opportunities for Faith* by Karl Rahner. English translation copyright © 1974 by S.P.C.K. Reprinted by permission of The Crossroad Publishing Company.

The Three Levels of Ethics, taken from *Sin, Liberty and Law* by Louis Monden. Copyright © 1965 by Andrews, McMeel & Parker. Reprinted with permission. All rights reserved.

Selection from *Civilization and Its Discontents* by Sigmund Freud, translated by James Strachey, used by permission of W.W. Norton & Company, Inc. Copyright © 1961 by James Strachey.

Reflections on the Shadow from *Depth Psychology and a New Ethic* by Eric Neumann, translated by Eugene Rolfe, copyright © 1969. Reprinted by courtesy of C. G. Jung Foundation for Analytical Psychology of New York.

Empathy, Role Taking, Guilt, and Development of Altruistic Motives by Martin L. Hoffman, from *Moral Development and Behavior,* edited by Thomas Lickona. Copyright © 1976 by Holt, Rinehart and Winston. Reprinted by permission of CBS College Publishing.

Individual and Collective Symbols by Jolande Jacobi, from *Complex/Archetype/Symbol in the Psychology of C. G. Jung,* translated by Ralph Manheim, Bollingen Series 57. Copyright © 1959 by Princeton University Press. Excerpt, pages 103–110, reprinted by permission of Princeton University Press.

Religions, Values and Peak Experiences by Abraham Maslow, from *The Farther Reaches of Human Nature.* Copyright © 1971 by Bertha G. Maslow. Reprinted by permission of Viking Penguin Inc.

Mysticism as a Basic Concept in Defining the Religious Self by Walter Houston Clark, from *From Religious Experience to a Religious Attitude,* edited by A. Godin. Reprinted with permission of Loyola University Press, Chicago. Copyright © 1965.

Toward a Method for the Study of Spirituality by Edward Kinerk, S.J., from *Review for Religious,* Vol. 40, No. 1, January 1981. Reprinted by permission.

Margaret Gorman

Preface

Theologians and psychologists have often been perceived as in conflict over their views as to the role of faith and/or religion in life. Some psychologists felt that religion was the cause of neurosis. In fact Freud classified religions as mass delusions. Theologians felt that psychologists reduced God to a mere psychological phenomenon. Recently, however, both groups are beginning to listen to each other. For example, Vatican II urged consultation with the social sciences. The American Psychological Association, after some delay, finally in 1978 accepted as one of their divisions (36) the division of Psychologists Interested in Religious Issues, called by some The William James Division.

Some psychologists are recognizing the religious dimension as an essential component of psychological health. Maslow said in 1970 that humanistic psychologists "would consider a person sick or abnormal in an existential way if he were not concerned with these religious questions." Rahner, too, recognized the psychological dimension in the expression of dogma when he said that faith must be perpetually reawakened by "breaking up crusts of custom formed by institutionalized formulations."

The readings selected for this book are an attempt to juxtapose the ideas of theologians with those of psychologists on areas of concern common to both groups: faith and religion as a dimension necessary for psychological health; human development in general and faith and moral development in particular; guilt, prayer and spiritual development.

While we present some of the psychological critiques of religion (especially that of Freud), for the most part the readings in psychology were chosen to illustrate the fact that psychology can contribute substantially, not to the understanding of the nature

1

of religion or of the transcendent itself, but to the understanding of the human experience of religion and the transcendent.

The section on human development concentrates on adult development where one important task is to integrate the religious concepts learned in childhood with experiences drawn from adult living. It is in adulthood that religious concepts can illuminate experience and life's experiences can flesh out religious concepts. The crisis of mid-life which has been presented as a search for meaning and self-identity might well be seen as a search for meaning in a transcendent or religious sense.

A theme underlying the selection of the articles in this book is that spiritual development is a kind of dialectic between growth in awareness of one's self—who one is—and growth in awareness of who God is. Faith development might well be seen as growth in the awareness of who one is for God and before God. As one becomes more aware of the depths of one's being, one becomes more aware of the God who created that being and is its ground. And increased insight into God as love (through prayer and reflection on the Scriptures), in turn, gives increased insight into one's self as loved by God. The selections from Winnicott and Rizzuto deal with the search for the self and the relationship between one's early relationships and one's image of God.

The writings on moral development build on Kohlberg's original theory. Meacham shows the value of self-esteem for the higher stages of moral development. Since Gilligan has shown that there is also a morality of care and responsibility, it seemed wise to juxtapose her view of woman's moral sense with that of Freud. The broader view of post-conventional moral judgment described by Gilligan and Murphy is quite consistent with the description of Christian conscience given by Charles Curran.

The psychological concept of guilt is closely related to moral judgment and moral maturity. Freud gives the classical description of neurotic guilt but it needs to be balanced by both theological (Rahner and Monden) and psychological (Neumann and Hoffman) views of healthy guilt.

The last section on prayer and spirituality begins with a consideration of symbol, since it is through symbol that we speak of God. Symbols evoke religious experiences, or peak experiences, as Maslow would call them. The section closes on the theme of the whole book—that spiritual growth is the growth of the authentic self in relationship with the Divine.

Thus, underlying the choice of these readings is the conviction that psychology can contribute greatly to the understanding of, not so much the nature of religion in general, but the experience of religion by each person. This experience includes an awareness of a transcendent and of one's own finiteness in relation to the transcendent. Religion also includes the dimension of community, a community of believers and a tradition of beliefs. Early writings on psychology and religion, especially those of Freud, concentrated on the negative aspects of institutional religion or on the "abnormal" aspects of conversion. Maslow in his article showed how he had to correct his former statements about institutions. The readings in this book are deliberately chosen to present the views of those psychologists who emphasize the positive, constructive and developmental aspects of the personal and social dimensions of religion.

Part I

THEOLOGIANS ON FAITH

Karl Rahner

1. Unthematic Knowledge of God

Karl Rahner, theologian and professor emeritus, died in Munich on March 30, 1984. The two selections that follow present a recurring idea in Rahner: that all persons have a non-reflective awareness of God. Some, as the second selection indicates, try to avoid reflecting on and appropriating consciously this awareness, by immersing themselves in busyness or by denying that the question has any relevance.

We shall be concerned later with showing that there is present in this transcendental experience an unthematic and anonymous, as it were, knowledge of God. Hence the original knowledge of God is not the kind of knowledge in which one grasps an object which happens to present itself directly or indirectly from outside. It has rather the character of a transcendental experience. Insofar as this subjective, non-objective luminosity of the subject in its transcendence is always orientated towards the holy mystery, the knowledge of God is always present unthematically and without name, and not just when we begin to speak of it. All talk about it, which necessarily goes on, always only points to this transcendental experience as such, an experience in which he whom we call "God" encounters man in silence, encounters him as the absolute and the incomprehensible, as the term of his transcendence which cannot really be incorporated into any system of coordinates. When this transcendence is the transcendence of *love,* it also experiences this term as the *holy* mystery.

We shall be going into this in detail later, but one thing which should be mentioned here in order to clarify what transcendence means is that if man is a being of transcendence towards the holy and absolutely real mystery, and if the term

7

and source of the transcendence in and through which man as such exists, and which constitutes his original essence as subject and as person, is this absolute and holy mystery, then strangely enough we can and must say: mystery in its incomprehensibility is what is *self-evident* in human life. If transcendence is not something which we practice on the side as a metaphysical luxury of our intellectual existence, but if this transcendence is rather the plainest, most obvious and most necessary condition of possibility for *all* spiritual understanding and comprehension, then the holy mystery really is the one thing that is self-evident, the one thing which is grounded in itself even from our point of view. For all other understanding, however clear it might appear, is grounded in this transcendence. All clear understanding is grounded in the darkness of God.

Hence upon close examination the mysteriousness of this term of transcendence is not simply the contrary of the notion of the self-evident. In our knowledge only that is self-evident for us which is self-evident in itself. But everything we understand becomes intelligible, but not really self-evident, only by the fact that it is derived from something else and thus resolved: into axioms on the one hand, and on the other into the elementary data of sense experience. But it is thereby derived and made intelligible either in the mute opaqueness of sense data, or in the half-light of ontology, and hence in the absolute and holy mystery.

What is made intelligible is grounded ultimately in the one thing that is self-evident, in mystery. Mystery is something with which we are always familiar, something which we love, even when we are terrified by it or perhaps even annoyed and angered, and want to be done with it. For the person who has touched his own spiritual depths, what is more familiar, thematically or unthematically, and what is more self-evident than the silent question which goes beyond everything which has already been mastered and controlled, than the unanswered question accepted in humble love, which alone brings wisdom? In the ultimate depths of his being man knows nothing more surely than that his knowledge, that is, what is called knowledge in everyday parlance, is only a small island in a vast sea that has not been traveled. It is a floating island, and it might be more familiar to us than the sea, but ultimately it is borne by the sea and only because it is can we be borne by it. Hence the existentiell question for the knower is this: Which does he love more, the small island of his so-called knowledge or the sea of infinite mystery? Is the little light with which he illuminates this island—we call it science and scholarship—to be an eternal light which will shine forever for him? That would surely be hell.

If a person wants, of course, in the concrete decisions of his life he can always choose to accept this infinite question only as a thorn in the side of his knowledge and his mastery and control. He can refuse to have anything to do with the absolute question except insofar as this question drives him to more and more individual questions and individual answers. But only when one begins to ask about asking itself, and to think about thinking itself, only when one turns his attention to the scope of knowledge and not only to the objects of knowledge, to transcendence and not only to what is understood categorically in time and space within this transcendence, only then is one just on the threshold of becoming a religious person. From this perspective it is easier to understand that not many are, that maybe they are not capable of being, that they feel that it demands too much. But anyone who has once raised the question about his transcendence and about its term can no longer let it go unanswered. For even if he were to say that it is a question which cannot be answered, which should not be answered, and which, because it demands too much, should be left alone, even then he would have already given an answer to this question, whether the right one or the wrong one is here beside the point.

THE POSSIBILITY OF EVADING THE EXPERIENCE OF TRANSCENDENCE

A person can, of course, shrug his shoulders and ignore this experience of transcendence. He can devote himself to his concrete world, his work, his activity in the categorical realm of time and space, to the service of his system at certain points which are the focal points of reality for him. That is possible in three ways:

1. Most people will do this in a naive way. They live at a distance from themselves in that concrete part of their lives and of the world around them which can be manipulated and controlled. They have enough to do there, and it is very interesting and important. And if they ever reflect at all on anything which goes beyond all this, they can always say that it is more sensible not to break one's head over it.

2. Such an evasion of this question and of accepting human transcendence can also take place along with the resolve to accept categorical existence and its tasks, recognizing and accepting the fact that everything is encompassed by an ultimate question. This question is perhaps left as a question. One believes that it can be postponed in silence and in a perhaps sensible scepticism. But when one explains that it cannot be answered, he is admitting that in the final analysis such a question cannot be evaded.

3. There is also a perhaps despairing involvement in the categorical realm of human existence. One goes about his business, he reads, he gets angry, he does his work, he does research, he achieves something, he earns money. And in a final, perhaps unadmitted despair he says to himself that the whole as a whole makes no sense, and that one does well to suppress the question about the meaning of it all and to reject it as an unanswerable and hence meaningless question.

We can never know unambiguously which of these three possibilities is the case in any given person.

From FOUNDATIONS OF CHRISTIAN FAITH, An Introduction to the Idea of Christianity, by Karl Rahner, translated by William V. Dych, pp. 21–23, 32–33. Reprinted by permission of the publisher, The Crossroad Publishing Company. © 1976 Verlag Herder Freiburg im Breisgau; English translation copyright © 1978 The Seabury Press.

QUESTIONS

1. Do you agree that we all do have some intuitive awareness that God is present in us and that this awareness is just not reflected upon?

2. What do you think Rahner means when he asks which we love more—the tiny island of one's so-called knowledge or the sea of infinite mystery?
3. Which type of evasion of the experience of transcendence is more common today?

SUGGESTED READINGS

McCool, G. (1975). *A Rahner Reader.* New York: Seabury.
O'Donovan, L. (1980). *A World of Grace.* New York: Seabury.
Rahner, K. (1978). *Foundations of Christian Faith.* New York: Seabury.

Paul Tillich

2. What Faith Is

Prussian-born Paul Tillich was an ordained minister of the Evangelical Lutheran Church and came to the United States in 1933. He taught theology in various universities in Germany and at Harvard University and Union Theological Seminary in New York City. In this selection, Tillich succinctly defines faith as the state of being ultimately concerned. Like Rahner, he sees faith as a fundamental human condition. Like Rahner, too, he sees that persons can avoid this concern by making other things such as success the ultimate. Of all three theologians presented in this section, Tillich is the one who explicitly incorporates psychological concepts into his discussion of faith, especially in his discussion of the relation between faith and doubt.

1. FAITH AS ULTIMATE CONCERN

Faith is the state of being ultimately concerned: the dynamics of faith are the dynamics of man's ultimate concern. Man, like every living being, is concerned about many things, above all about those which condition his very existence, such as food and shelter. But man, in contrast to other living beings, has spiritual concerns—cognitive, aesthetic, social, political. Some of them are urgent, often extremely urgent, and each of them as well as the vital concerns can claim ultimacy for a human life or the life of a social group. If it claims ultimacy it demands the total surrender of him who accepts this claim, and it promises total fulfillment even if all other claims have to be subjected to it or rejected in its name. If a national group makes the life and growth of the nation its ultimate concern, it demands that all other concerns, economic well-being, health and life, family, aesthetic and cognitive truth, justice and humanity, be sacrificed. The extreme nationalisms of our century are laboratories for the study of what ultimate concern means in all aspects of human existence, including the smallest concern of one's daily life. Everything is centered in the only god, the nation—a god who certainly proves to be a demon, but who shows clearly the unconditional character of an ultimate concern.

But it is not only the unconditional demand made by that which is one's ultimate concern, it is also the promise of ultimate fulfillment which is accepted in the act of faith. The content of this promise is not necessarily defined. It can be expressed in indefinite symbols or in concrete symbols which cannot be taken literally, like the "greatness" of one's nation in which one participates even if one has died for it, or the conquest of mankind by the "saving race," etc. In each of these cases it is "ultimate fulfillment" that is promised, and it is exclusion from such fulfillment which is threatened if the unconditional demand is not obeyed.

An example—and more than an example—is the faith manifest in the religion of the Old Testament. It also has the character of ultimate concern in demand, threat and promise. The content of this concern is not the nation—although Jewish nationalism has sometimes tried to distort it into that—but the content is the God of justice, who, because he represents justice for everybody and every nation, is called the universal God, the God of the universe. He is the ultimate concern of every pious Jew, and therefore in his name the great commandment is given: "You shall love the Lord your God with all your heart, and with all your soul, and with all your might" (Deut 6:5). This is what ultimate concern means and from these words the term "ultimate concern" is derived. They state unambiguously the character of genuine faith, the demand of total surrender to the subject of ultimate concern. The Old Testament is full of commands which make the nature of this surrender concrete, and it is full of promises and threats in relation to it. Here also are the promises of symbolic indefiniteness, although they center around fulfillment of the national and individual life, and the threat is the exclusion from such fulfillment through national extinction and individual catastrophe. Faith, for the men of the Old Testament, is the state of being ultimately and unconditionally concerned about Jahweh and about what he represents in demand, threat and promise.

Another example—almost a counter-example, yet nevertheless equally revealing—is the ultimate concern with "success" and with social standing and economic power. It is the god of many people in the highly competitive Western culture and it does what every ultimate concern must do: it demands unconditional surrender to its laws even if the price is the sacrifice of genuine human relations, personal conviction, and creative *eros*. Its threat is social and economic defeat, and its promise—indefinite as all such promises—the fulfillment of one's being. It is the breakdown of this kind of faith which characterizes and makes religiously important most contemporary literature. Not false calculations but a misplaced faith is revealed in novels like *Point of No Return*. When fulfilled, the promise of this faith proves to be empty.

Faith is the state of being ultimately concerned. The content matters infinitely for the life of the believer, but it does not matter for the formal definition of faith. And this is the first step we have to make in order to understand the dynamics of faith.

2. FAITH AS A CENTERED ACT

Faith as ultimate concern is an act of the total personality. It happens in the center of the personal life and includes all its elements. Faith is the most centered act of the human mind. It is not a movement of a special section or a special function of man's total being. They all are united in the act of faith. But faith is not the sum total of their impacts. It transcends every special impact as well as the totality of them and it has itself a decisive impact on each of them.

Since faith is an act of the personality as a whole, it participates in the dynamics of personal life. These dynamics have been described in many ways, especially in the recent developments of analytic psychology. Thinking in polarities, their tensions and their possible conflicts, is a common characteristic of most of them. This makes the psychology of personality highly dynamic and requires a dynamic theory of faith as the most personal of all personal acts. The first and decisive polarity in analytic psychology is that between the so-called unconscious and the conscious. Faith as an act of the total personality is not imaginable without the participation of the unconscious elements in the personality structure. They are always present and decide largely about the content of faith. But, on the other hand, faith is a conscious act and the unconscious elements participate in the creation of faith only if they are taken into the personal center which transcends each of them. If this does not happen, if unconscious forces determine the mental status without a centered act, faith does not occur, and compulsions take its place. For faith is a matter of freedom. Freedom is nothing more than the possibility of centered personal acts. The frequent discussion in which faith and freedom are contrasted could be helped by the insight that faith is a free, namely, centered act of the personality. In this respect freedom and faith are identical.

Also important for the understanding of faith is the polarity between what Freud and his school call ego and superego. The concept of the superego is quite ambiguous. On the one hand, it is the basis of all cultural life because it restricts the uninhibited actualization of the always-driving libido; on the other hand, it cuts off man's vital forces, and produces disgust about the whole system of cultural restrictions, and brings about a neurotic state of mind. From this point of view, the symbols of faith are considered to be expressions of the superego or, more concretely, to be an expression of the father image which gives content to the superego. Responsible for this inadequate theory of the superego is Freud's naturalistic negation of norms and principles. If the superego is not established through valid principles, it becomes a suppressive tyrant. But real faith, even if it uses the father image for its expression, transforms this image into a principle of truth and justice to be defended even against the "father." Faith and culture can be affirmed only if the superego represents the norms and principles of reality.

This leads to the question of how faith as a personal, centered act is related to the rational structure of man's personality which is manifest in his meaningful language, in his ability to know the true and to do the good, in his sense of beauty and justice. All this, and not only his possibility to analyze, to calculate and to argue, makes him a rational being. But in spite of this larger concept of reason we must deny that man's essential nature is identical with the rational character of his mind. Man is able to decide for or against reason, he is able to create beyond reason or to destroy below reason. This power is the power of his self, the center of self-relatedness in which all elements of his being are united. Faith is not an act of any of his rational functions, as it is not an act of the unconscious, but it is an act in which both the rational and the nonrational elements of his being are transcended.

Faith as the embracing and centered act of the personality is "ecstatic." It transcends both the drives of the nonrational unconscious and the structures of the rational conscious. It transcends them, but it does not destroy them. The ecstatic character of faith does not exclude its rational character although it is not identical with it, and it includes nonrational strivings without being identical with them. In the ecstasy of faith there is an awareness of truth and of ethical value; there are also past loves and hates, conflicts and reunions, individual and collective influences. "Ecstasy" means "standing outside of oneself"—without ceasing to be oneself—with all the elements which are united in the personal center.

A further polarity in these elements, relevant for the understanding of faith, is the tension between the cognitive function of man's personal life, on the one hand, and emotion and will, on the other hand. In a later discussion I will try to show that many distortions of the meaning of faith are rooted in the attempt to subsume faith to the one or the other of these functions. At this point it must be stated as sharply and insistently as possible that in every act of faith there is cognitive affirmation, not as the result of an independent process of inquiry but as an inseparable element in a total act of acceptance and surrender. This also excludes the idea that faith is the result of an independent act of "will to believe." There is certainly affirmation by the will of what concerns one ultimately, but faith is not a creation of the will. In the ecstasy of faith the will to accept and to surrender is an element, but not the cause. And this is true also of feeling. Faith is not an emotional outburst: this is not the meaning of ecstasy. Certainly, emotion is in it, as in every act of man's spiritual life. But emotion does not produce faith. Faith has a cognitive content and is an act of the will. It is the unity of every element in the centered self. Of course, the unity of all elements in the act of faith does not prevent one or the other element from dominating in a special form of faith. It dominates the character of faith but it does not create the act of faith.

This also answers the question of a possible psychology of faith. Everything that happens in man's personal being can become an object of psychology. And it is rather important for both the philosopher of religion and the practical minister to know how the act of faith is embedded in the totality of psychological processes. But in contrast to this justified and desirable form of a psychology of faith there is another one which tries to derive faith from something that is not faith but is most frequently fear. The presupposition of this method is that fear or something else from which faith is derived is more original and basic than faith. But this presupposition cannot be proved. On the contrary, one can prove that in the scientific method which leads to such consequences faith is already effective. Faith precedes all attempts to derive it from something else, because these attempts are themselves based on faith.

3. THE SOURCE OF FAITH

We have described the act of faith and its relation to the dynamics of personality. Faith is a total and centered act of the personal self, the act of unconditional, infinite and ultimate concern. The question now arises: what is the source of this all-embracing and all-transcending concern? The word "concern" points to two sides of a relationship, the relation between the one who is concerned and his concern. In both respects we have to imagine man's situation in itself and in his world. The reality of man's ultimate concern reveals something about his being, namely, that he is able to transcend the flux of relative and transitory experiences of his ordinary life. Man's experiences, feelings, thoughts are conditioned and finite. They not only come and go, but their content is of finite and conditional concern— unless they are elevated to unconditional validity. But this presupposes the general possibility of doing so; it presupposes the element of infinity in man. Man is able to understand in an immediate personal and central act the meaning of the ultimate, the unconditional, the absolute, the infinite. This alone makes faith a human potentiality.

Human potentialities are powers that drive toward actualization. Man is driven toward faith by his awareness of the infinite to which he belongs, but which he does not own like a possession. This is in abstract terms what concretely appears as the "restlessness of the heart" within the flux of life.

The unconditional concern which is faith is the concern about the unconditional. The infinite passion, as faith has been described, is the passion for the infinite. Or, to use our first term, the ultimate concern is concern about what is experienced as ultimate. In this way we have turned from the subjective meaning of faith as a centered act of the personality to its objective meaning, to what is meant in the act of faith. It would not help at this point of our analysis to call that which is meant in the act of faith "God" or "a god." For at this step we ask: What in the idea of God constitutes divinity? The answer is: It is the element of the unconditional and of ultimacy. This carries the quality of divinity. If this is seen, one can understand why almost every thing "in heaven and on earth" has received ultimacy in the history of human religion. But we also can understand that a critical principle was and is at work in man's religious consciousness, namely, that which is really ultimate over against what claims to be ultimate but is only preliminary, transitory, finite.

The term "ultimate concern" unites the subjective and the objective side of the act of faith—the *fides qua creditur* (the faith through which one believes) and the *fides quae creditur* (the faith which is believed). The first is the classical term for the centered act of the personality, the ultimate concern. The second is the classical term for that toward which this act is directed, the ultimate itself, expressed in symbols of the divine. This distinction is very important, but not ultimately so, for the one side cannot be without the other. There is no faith without a content toward which it is directed. There is always something meant in the act of faith. And there is no way of having the content of faith except in the act of faith. All speaking about divine matters which is not done in the state of ultimate concern is meaningless. Because that which is meant in the act of faith cannot be approached in any other way than through an act of faith.

In terms like ultimate, unconditional, infinite, absolute, the difference between subjectivity and objectivity is overcome. The ultimate of the act of faith and the ultimate that is meant in the act of faith are one and the same. This is symbolically expressed by the mystics when they say that their knowledge of God is the knowledge God has of himself; and it is expressed by Paul when he says (I Cor. 13) that he will know as he is known, namely, by God. God never can be object without being at the same time subject. Even a successful prayer is, according to Paul (Rom. 8), not possible without God as Spirit praying within us. The same experience expressed in abstract language is the disappearance of the ordinary subject-object scheme in the experience of the ultimate, the unconditional. In the act of faith that which is the source of this act is present beyond the cleavage of subject and object. It is present as both and beyond both.

This character of faith gives an additional criterion for distinguishing true and false ultimacy. The finite which claims infinity without having it (as, e.g., a nation or success) is not able to transcend the subject-object scheme. It remains an object which the believer looks at as a subject. He can approach it with ordinary knowledge and subject it to ordinary handling. There are, of course, many degrees in the endless realm of false ultimacies. The nation is nearer to true ultimacy than is success. Nationalistic ecstasy can produce a state in which the subject is almost swallowed by the object. But after a period the subject emerges again, disappointed radically and totally, and by looking at the nation in a skeptical and calculating way does injustice even to its justified claims. The more idolatrous a faith the less it is able to overcome the cleavage between subject and object. For that is the difference between true and idolatrous faith. In true faith the ultimate concern is a concern about the truly ultimate; while in idolatrous faith preliminary, finite realities are elevated to the rank of ultimacy. The inescapable consequence of idolatrous faith is "existential disappointment," a disappointment which penetrates into the very existence of man! This is the dynamics of idolatrous faith: that it is faith, and as such, the centered act of a personality; that the centering point is something which is more or less on the periphery; and that, therefore, the act of faith leads to a loss of the center and to a disruption of the personality. The ecstatic character of even an idolatrous faith can hide this consequence only for a certain time. But finally it breaks into the open.

4. FAITH AND THE DYNAMICS OF THE HOLY

He who enters the sphere of faith enters the sanctuary of life. Where there is faith there is an awareness of holiness. This seems to contradict what has just been said about idolatrous faith. But it does not contradict our analysis of idolatry. It only contradicts the popular way in which the word "holy" is used. What concerns one ultimately becomes holy. The awareness of the holy is awareness of the presence of the divine, namely of the content of our ultimate concern. This awareness is expressed in a grand way in the Old Testament from the visions of the patriarchs and Moses to the shaking experiences of the great prophets and psalmists. It is a presence which remains mysterious in spite of its appearance, and it exercises both an attractive and a repulsive function on those who encounter it. In his classical book, *The Idea of the Holy,* Rudolph Otto has described these two functions as the fascinating and the shaking character of the holy. (In Otto's terminology: *mysterium fascinans et tremendum.*) They can be found in all religions because they are the way in which man always encounters the representations of his ultimate concern. The reason for these two effects of the holy is obvious if we see the relation of the experience of the holy to the experience of ultimate concern. The human heart seeks the infinite because that is where the finite wants to rest. In the infinite it sees its own fulfillment. This is the reason for the ecstatic attraction and fascination of everything in which ultimacy is manifest. On the other hand, if ultimacy is manifest and exercises its fascinating attraction, one realizes at the same time the infinite distance of the finite from the infinite and, consequently, the negative judgment over any finite attempts to reach the infinite. The feeling of being consumed in the presence of the divine is a profound expression of man's relation to the holy. It is implied in every genuine act of faith, in every state of ultimate concern.

This original and only justified meaning of holiness must replace the currently distorted use of the word. "Holy" has become identified with moral perfection, especially in some Protestant groups. The historical causes of this distortion give a new insight into the nature of holiness and of faith. Originally, the holy has meant what is apart from the ordinary realm of things and experiences. It is separated from the world of finite relations. This is the reason why all religious cults have separated holy places and activities from all other places and activities. Entering the sanctuary means encountering the holy. Here the infinitely removed makes itself near and present, without losing its remoteness. For this reason, the holy has been called the "entirely other," namely, other than the ordinary course of things or—to refer to a former statement—other than the world which is determined by the cleavage of subject and object. The holy transcends this realm; this is its mystery and its unapproachable character. There is no conditional way of reaching the unconditional; there is no finite way of reaching the infinite.

The mysterious character of the holy produces an ambiguity in man's ways of experiencing it. The holy can appear as creative and as destructive. Its fascinating element can be both creative and destructive (referring again to the fascinating character of the nationalistic idolatry), and the terrifying and consuming element can be destructive and creative (as in the double function of Siva or Kali in Indian thought). This ambiguity, of which we still find traces in the Old Testament, is reflected in the ritual or quasi-ritual activities of religions and quasi religions (sacrifices of others or one's bodily or mental self) which are strongly ambiguous. One can call this ambiguity divine-demonic, whereby the divine is characterized by the victory of the creative over the destructive possibility of the holy, and the demonic is characterized by the victory of the destructive over the creative possibility of the holy. In this situation, which is most profoundly understood in the prophetic religion of the Old Testament, a fight has been waged against the demonic-destructive element in the holy. And this fight was so successful that the concept of the holy was changed. Holiness becomes justice and truth. It is creative and not destructive. The true sacrifice is obedience to the law. This is the line of thought which finally led to the identification of holiness with moral perfection. But when this point is reached, holiness loses its meaning as the "separated," the "transcending," the "fascinating and terrifying," the "entirely other." All this is gone, and the holy has become the morally good and the logically true. It has ceased to be the holy in the genuine sense of the word. Summing up this development, one could say that the holy originally lies below the alternative of the good and the evil; that it is both divine and demonic; that with the reduction of the demonic possibility the holy itself becomes transformed in its meaning; that it becomes rational and identical with the true and the good; and that its genuine meaning must be rediscovered.

These dynamics of the holy confirm what was said about the dynamics of faith. We have distinguished between true and idolatrous faith. The holy which is demonic, or ultimately destructive, is identical with the content of idolatrous faith. Idolatrous faith is still faith. The holy which is demonic is still holy. This is the point where the ambiguous character of religion is most visible and the dangers of faith are most obvious: the danger of faith is idolatry and the ambiguity of the holy is its demonic possibility. Our ultimate concern can destroy us as it can heal us. But we never can be without it.

5. FAITH AND DOUBT

We now return to a fuller description of faith as an act of the human personality, as its centered and total act. An act of faith is an act of a finite being who is grasped by and turned to the infinite. It is a finite act with all the limitations of a finite act, and it is an act in which the infinite participates beyond the limitations of a finite act. Faith is certain in so far as it is an experience of the holy. But faith is uncertain in so far as the infinite to which it is related is received by a finite being. This element of uncertainty in faith cannot be removed, it must be accepted. And the element in faith which accepts this is courage. Faith includes an element of immediate awareness which gives certainty and an element of uncertainty. To accept this is courage. In the courageous standing of uncertainty, faith shows most visibly its dynamic character.

If we try to describe the relation of faith and courage, we must use a larger concept of courage than that which is ordinarily used.[1] Courage as an element of faith is the daring self-affirmation of one's own being in spite of the powers of "nonbeing" which are the heritage of everything finite. Where there is daring and courage there is the possibility of failure. And in every act of faith this possibility is present. The risk must be taken. Whoever makes his nation his ultimate concern needs courage in order to maintain this concern. Only certain is the ultimacy as ultimacy, the infinite passion as infinite passion. This is a reality given to the self with his own nature. It is as immediate and as much beyond doubt as the self is to the self. It *is* the self in its self-transcending quality. But there is no certainty of this kind about the content of our ultimate concern, be it nation, success, a god, or the God of the Bible: They all are contents without immediate awareness. Their acceptance as matters of ultimate concern is a risk and therefore an act of courage. There is a risk if what was considered as a matter of ultimate concern proves to be a matter of preliminary and transitory concern— as, for example, the nation. The risk to faith in one's ultimate concern is indeed the greatest risk man can run. For if it proves to be a failure, the meaning of one's life breaks down; one surrenders oneself, including truth and justice, to something which is not worth it. One has given away one's personal center without having a chance to regain it. The reaction of despair in people who have experienced the breakdown of their national claims is an irrefutable proof of the idolatrous character of their national concern. In the long run this is the inescapable result of an ultimate concern, the subject matter of which is not ultimate. And this is the risk faith must take; this is the risk which is unavoidable if a finite being affirms itself. Ultimate concern is ultimate risk and ultimate courage. It is not risk and needs no courage with respect to ultimacy itself. But it is risk and demands courage if it affirms a concrete concern. And every

---

1. Cf. Paul Tillich, *The Courage to Be.* Yale University Press.

faith has a concrete element in itself. It is concerned about something or somebody. But this something or this somebody may prove to be not ultimate at all. Then faith is a failure in its concrete expression, although it is not a failure in the experience of the unconditional itself. A god disappears; divinity remains. Faith risks the vanishing of the concrete god in whom it believes. It may well be that with the vanishing of the god the believer breaks down without being able to re-establish his centered self by a new content of his ultimate concern. This risk cannot be taken away from any act of faith. There is only one point which is a matter not of risk but of immediate certainty and herein lies the greatness and the pain of being human; namely, one's standing between one's finitude and one's potential infinity.

All this is sharply expressed in the relation of faith and doubt. If faith is understood as belief that something is true, doubt is incompatible with the act of faith. If faith is understood as being ultimately concerned, doubt is a necessary element in it. It is a consequence of the risk of faith.

The doubt which is implicit in faith is not a doubt about facts or conclusions. It is not the same doubt which is the lifeblood of scientific research. Even the most orthodox theologian does not deny the right of methodological doubt in matters of empirical inquiry or logical deduction. A scientist who would say that a scientific theory is beyond doubt would at that moment cease to be scientific. He may believe that the theory can be trusted for all practical purposes. Without such belief no technical application of a theory would be possible. One could attribute to this kind of belief pragmatic certainty sufficient for action. Doubt in this case points to the preliminary character of the underlying theory.

There is another kind of doubt, which we could call skeptical in contrast to the scientific doubt which we could call methodological. The skeptical doubt is an attitude toward all the beliefs of man, from sense experiences to religious creeds. It is more an attitude than an assertion. For as an assertion it would conflict with itself. Even the assertion that there is no possible truth for man would be judged by the skeptical principle and could not stand as an assertion. Genuine skeptical doubt does not use the form of an assertion. It is an attitude of actually rejecting any certainty. Therefore, it can not be refuted logically. It does not transform its attitude into a proposition. Such an attitude necessarily leads either to despair or cynicism, or to both alternately. And often, if this alternative becomes intolerable, it leads to indifference and the attempt to develop an attitude of complete unconcern. But since man is that being who is essentially concerned about his being, such an escape finally breaks down. This is the dynamics of skeptical doubt. It has an awakening and liberating function, but it also can prevent the development of a centered personality. For personality is not possible without faith. The despair about truth by the skeptic shows that truth is still his infinite passion. The cynical superiority over every concrete truth shows that truth is still taken seriously and that the impact of the question of an ultimate concern is strongly felt. The skeptic, so long as he is a serious skeptic, is not without faith, even though it has no concrete content.

The doubt which is implicit in every act of faith is neither the methodological nor the skeptical doubt. It is the doubt which accompanies every risk. It is not the permanent doubt of the scientist, and it is not the transitory doubt of the skeptic, but it is the doubt of him who is ultimately concerned about a concrete content. One could call it the existential doubt, in contrast to the methodological and the skeptical doubt. It does not question whether a special proposition is true or false. It does not reject every concrete truth, but it is aware of the element of insecurity in every existential truth. At the same time, the doubt which is implied in faith accepts this insecurity and takes it into itself in an act of courage. Faith includes courage. Therefore, it can include the doubt about itself. Certainly faith and courage are not identical. Faith has other elements besides courage and courage has other functions beyond affirming faith. Nevertheless, an act in which courage accepts risk belongs to the dynamics of faith.

This dynamic concept of faith seems to give no place to that restful affirmative confidence which we find in the documents of all great religions, including Christianity. But this is not the case. The dynamic concept of faith is the result of a conceptual analysis, both of the subjective and of the objective side of faith. It is by no means the description of an always actualized state of the mind. An analysis of structure is not the description of a state of things. The confusion of these two is a source of many misunderstandings and errors in all realms of life. An example, taken from the current discussion of anxiety, is typical of this confusion. The description of anxiety as the awareness of one's finitude is sometimes criticized as untrue from the point of view of the ordinary state of the mind. Anxiety, one says, appears under special conditions but is not an ever-present implication of man's finitude. Certainly anxiety as an acute experience appears under definite conditions. But the underlying structure of finite life is the universal condition which makes the appearance of anxiety under special conditions possible. In the same way doubt is not a permanent experience within the act of faith. But it is always present as an element in the structure of faith. This is the difference between faith and immediate evidence either of perceptual or of logical character. There is no faith without an intrinsic "in spite of" and the courageous affirmation of oneself in the state of ultimate concern. This intrinsic element of doubt breaks into the open under special individual and social conditions. If doubt appears, it should not be considered as the negation of faith, but as an element which was always and will always be present in the act of faith. Existential doubt and faith are poles of the same reality, the state of ultimate concern.

The insight into this structure of faith and doubt is of tremendous practical importance. Many Christians, as well as members of other religious groups, feel anxiety, guilt and despair about what they call "loss of faith." But serious doubt is confirmation of faith. It indicates the seriousness of the concern, its unconditional character. This also refers to those who as future or present ministers of a church experience not only scientific doubt about doctrinal statements—this is as necessary and perpetual as theology is a perpetual need—but also existential doubt about the message of their church, e.g., that Jesus can be called the Christ. The criterion according to which they should judge themselves is the seriousness and ultimacy of their concern about the content of both their faith and their doubt.

From DYNAMICS OF FAITH by Paul Tillich, pp. 1–22. Reprinted by permission of the publisher, Harper & Row, Publishers, Inc. © 1957 Paul Tillich.

QUESTIONS

1. How does Tillich explain that faith is not an act of one's rational function?
2. Why, if the content of faith matters infinitely for the life of the believer, does Tillich say that it does not matter for the formal definition of faith?
3. What is the source of faith?
4. Distinguish between *fides qua creditur* and *fides quae creditur.*
5. How can faith be idolatrous? How can the holy be demonic?
6. How and why is doubt a necessary element of faith?

SUGGESTED READINGS

Küng, H. (1980). *Does God Exist?* New York: Doubleday.

McBrien, R. (1980). *Catholicism.* Vol. I, pp. 23–75. Minneapolis: Winston.

Mouroux, J. (1959). *I Believe: The Personal Structure of Faith.* New York: Sheed & Ward.

Otto, R. (1958). *The Idea of the Holy.* (2nd ed.) New York: Oxford University Press.

Avery Dulles, S.J.

3. The Meaning of Faith Considered in Relationship to Justice

Avery Dulles, S.J. is now professor of theology at the Catholic University of America and the author of many books on the church and on revelation. His selection presents a different view of faith. In other sections of this article he discusses two other approaches to faith—the intellectualist and the fiducial approaches. This section on the performative approaches to faith is chosen, as it links faith with action, and at the same time presents some of the dangers of accepting this view of faith exclusively.

By the "meaning of faith" in the title of this chapter, I have in mind something more than the dictionary definition. I am concerned with the reality of faith itself—with faith as it concretely exists, and should exist, in today's world. The world, of course, varies from place to place, and therefore faith has a legitimate variety of forms. But there are typical features of our age, and these place certain demands on the contemporary realizations of faith. Especially in the North Atlantic community, we live in what may be called a "socio-technical" civilization. Herbert Richardson, from whom I borrow the term, defines "socio-technics" as "the new knowledge whereby man exercises technical control not only over nature but also over all the specific institutions that make up society: i.e., economics, education, science, and politics."[1]

In this socio-technical era we are, and should be, keenly conscious of man's capacity to shape the physical and social environment and consequently of man's responsibility to avoid devastating the earth and visiting misery on other people. Amid growing evidence that the benefits of technical progress are going only to a small elite, and that the world proletariat (as it might

28

be called) is becoming frustrated and angry, even the wealthier nations of the "free world" are feeling the urgency of establishing a more equitable social system.

Christian faith has been accused both of failing to promote justice in the world and, even more seriously, of abetting injustice by inducing the wretched of the earth to accept their misery patiently, confident of abundant rewards in a future life. Faith has frequently meant little more than a confident belief in some higher or future world utterly beyond man's control and shaped by the power of God alone. If this conception were accurate, faith could rightly be accused of alienating man from his proper task in the present life and of inducing irresponsibility.

Conscious of this objection so often made by atheistic humanists and Marxists, Christians such as Teilhard de Chardin, in the first half of our century, tried to show that Christian faith could actually increase man's sense of responsibility for the earth.[2] Vatican II, in its *Pastoral Constitution on the Church in the Modern World,* favored the same thrust. It spoke of "the birth of a new humanism, one in which man is defined primarily in terms of his responsibility for his brothers and for history" (n. 55). It called upon Christians to give "the witness of a living and mature faith," a faith that proves itself "by penetrating the believer's entire life, including its worldly dimensions, and by activating him toward justice and love, especially regarding the needy" (n. 21). "The expectation of a new earth," it asserted, "must not weaken but rather stimulate our concern for cultivating this one" (n. 39). Faith, according to the Council, by casting a new light on everything, "directs the mind of man to solutions which are fully human" (n. 11).

In many post-conciliar documents, such as the Latin American Medellin documents of 1968, the statements of the International Synod of Bishops in 1971 and 1974, and the 1975 exhortation of Paul VI on "Evangelization in the Modern World," it is reiterated that evangelization—the propagation of the faith—cannot be a mere matter of words or concepts. The Gospel has to be proclaimed in an actual situation, with attention to its implications for the reordering of society. A failure to accept the social implications of the Gospel would be a lack of responsiveness to the Gospel itself, and hence a defect of faith.

Faith, if it is not to be merely nominal, involves a sincere adherence to the vision of the Kingdom of God that the Gospel holds forth to us—an adherence that reveals itself concretely in the believer's manner of living and of dealing with other persons and groups.

In a great deal of the theological literature of the past decade—especially perhaps in the new German political theology and in Latin American liberation theology—an effort is being made to show the positive bearing of Christian faith upon the transformation of human society not only in the private domain of thought and feeling but also in the public domain of law, government, and economics. While seeking to avoid any kind of political reductionism, Christians are increasingly conscious that faith, in the concrete, involves certain social attitudes and commitments. The surfacing of this consciousness entails a mutation in the concept of faith itself—a mutation that calls for careful theological evaluation.

As contrasted with many of the medieval and early modern theories, which attempted to define faith in terms of the spiritual faculties of intellect and will, contemporary theologians are inclined to say with Paul Tillich that faith is a free, centered act of the whole personality, having ramifications in all the dimensions of our human existence, including the cognitional, the volitional, and the emotional.[3] Drawing upon the phenomenology of religion previously developed by Rudolf Otto and others, the English philosopher, Ian T. Ramsey, contended that the language of religion rests upon disclosure experiences in which the two elements of discernment and commitment are inextricably interwoven.[4] Religious disclosures, Ramsey held, are peculiar in that they involve a discernment of total meaning and hence a call to total commitment. This all-encompassing and transcendent point of reference in religious experience gives rise to what is called "God-language." Although Ramsey did not, I believe, propose a new definition of faith, one might, on the basis of his work, define it as that combination of discernment and commitment which is concomitant with the disclosure of ultimate meaning and ultimate value.

Through a study of biblical history it would be possible to show that revelation was given through a series of disclosure

experiences, from the patriarchs, through Moses and the prophets, down to the climactic disclosure given in the passion and
exaltation of Jesus.[5] These disclosures fall into a pattern in
which there are recurrent themes. The later disclosures reinforce, enrich, and partly reinterpret the preceding disclosures.
For us who live in post-biblical times these disclosures come
alive when we see them as clues to the meaning of our own
world and hence to our own vocation. The Christian people are
called, as was Israel of old, to serve the righteousness of God in
a costly way. Christian faith may accordingly be described as a
combination of discernment and commitment in which we perceive and dedicate ourselves to the transcendent values dis-
closed by God in Jesus Christ. The discernment and the commitment are mutually interdependent aspects of the total
experience of faith.

A central and recurrent theme of the biblical disclosures is
that the ultimate power by which our lives are ruled is the personal reality of God, whose loving mercies surround and sustain
us. Faith therefore includes not only a conviction and commitment concerning the transcendent, but a trusting obedience to
God as a person who loves, who wills, who acts. So important
is this element that it deserves to be made explicit in the definition of faith itself—at least if we are talking about biblical or
Christian faith. Faith includes three elements: a firm conviction
regarding what is supremely important, dedication or commitment to that which one believes in, and trustful reliance on the
power and goodness of that to which one stands committed. The
three components of faith are thus conviction, commitment,
and trust.[5a]

In the classical tradition, the elements of conviction and
trust have been particularly emphasized, with Catholics concen-
trating more on the former, Protestants more on the latter. The
third component, commitment, is less prominent in the tradition, but is increasingly coming to the fore in the twentieth century under the pressure of some of the factors already mentioned. The recent developments would seem to have a solid
theological grounding, inasmuch as the Kingdom of God is a
reality at work within history, rather than simply a goal to which
history tends. Faith, as our present mode of participation in the

Kingdom, is neither the detached contemplation of a truth external to ourselves nor trust in a power totally external to the world in which we live. The truth and the power are actively at work within us. Without a sincere commitment to the healing and reconciliation of the broken world, we could not have either the discernment or the trust that is proper to children of God who share already, by grace, in the divine life opened up to us in Christ.

At several points in these pages allusion has already been made to what may be called the performative dimension of faith. In my observations regarding Vatican II and the Roman documents issued since the Council, I mentioned the frequent insistence that the Gospel cannot be heralded by word alone, and that authentic evangelization must release energies tending to transform the world in which we live. In my discussion of the intellectualist approach, I reiterated my conviction that discernment and commitment are inseparably united aspects of the disclosure experience, so that the illumination of faith is given only within a commitment to appropriate action. Again, in my analysis of the fiducial views, I made reference to the growing opinion that the acceptance of God's word, if it is sincere, must normally include an obedient submission to what the word demands. Obedience, therefore, would seem to be a component of faith itself.

Inspired by Barth and by several contemporary theologians of the word (post-Bultmannians such as Gerhard Ebeling), the American theologian Peter C. Hodgson in several recent works has sought to reinterpret the doctrine of faith in the light of an enriched theology of the word of God.[38] The transmission of the Gospel, he maintains, is a word-event in which the word of proclamation is echoed by a word of response. Because only a total response can be appropriate to the word of God, faith is never a matter of disembodied words; it becomes incarnate in faith and praxis. Jesus made himself the faithful one by his acceptance of God's will for himself, thus passing through crucifixion to resurrection. The crucifixion—the free action by which Jesus obediently goes to his death, and through it to newness of life—is the word-event par excellence. Christian faith is the embodied word by which others respond to the word of God previously embodied in Jesus. Faith is the power of God within us, making us whole, healing the fractures of physical and social existence, and opening us to a vital participation in God's rule as it breaks into our earthly existence. "Faith is a *liberating power*," writes Hodgson, "that 'saves' life, giving it wholeness and efficacy, in the midst of bondage, estrangement and guilt."[39]

In recent Latin American liberation theology, efforts are being made to develop a new theology of faith in conscious opposition to the intellectualism and fideism of earlier European theology. Among the Catholic contributors to this new theology of faith one must reckon the Brazilian theologians Hugo Assmann and Leonardo Boff, the Chilean Segundo Galilea, the Peruvian Gustavo Gutiérrez, the Mexican José Miranda, and the Uruguayan Juan Luis Segundo. A good sampling of their views on faith may be found in a volume entitled *The Mystical and Political Dimension of the Christian Faith.*[40]

These theologians take as their point of departure the inadequacies in the traditional understanding of faith. When the traditionally minded Catholic in Latin America commits himself to the liberation of workers and peasants, writes Segundo Galilea, "the categories of his faith . . . do not inspire or illuminate sufficiently his commitments."[41] This discrepancy produces an initial crisis of faith, which must be resolved by a rethinking of the nature of faith itself.

Gustavo Gutiérrez finds fault with the traditional concept of faith as assent. Rather than being a mere assent, he writes, it must be a warm welcome of the gift of the word. Truth is not just affirmed with the mind and lips but is also brought into being as a word incarnated in life and deed. Otherwise, he remarked, faith would become dissolved in idealism.[42]

Segundo Galilea objects that the mystical or illuminationist view of faith is untrue to the Bible and is vitiated by Hellenistic dualism. Faith, he contends, ought not to be directed to an abstract, mystical contemplation in which the believer, absorbed in God, tries to imitate the angels. This Platonic form of mysticism, in his view, began to contaminate authentic Christian contemplation as Greek thought, with its antithesis between spirit and body, gained influence in the nascent Church.[43] The biblical understanding of contemplation, which involves no such dualism, is on the way to being recovered, Galilea believes, in Latin America today.

The Protestant fiducial concept of faith likewise comes in for its share of criticism. Juan Luis Segundo blames the Lutheran separation of faith from good works for having spawned an immoral neutralism with regard to political systems. The Bible, he argues, is passionately concerned with the rebuilding of the earth by persons animated by selfless love.[44]

Having rejected the intellectualist and fiducial theories of faith, liberation theology proceeds to define faith from its own perspectives. Frequently in these authors faith is described as "the historical praxis of liberation." Somewhat less succinctly, they might describe faith as commitment to revolutionary praxis in a historical situation that concretely mediates for them the word of God. Their own situation is the oppression and dependency of the third world and especially of the poorer classes.

Three terms in the definition just given seem to call for further explanation: historicity, praxis, and liberation.

(a) The historicity of faith means, in the first place, that faith does not yet exist in final, complete form. The Truth presently abides with us only insofar as it is the "Way," i.e. as a word in the midst of history. These theologians would assert, as I did in my opening paragraph, that any given act of faith must correspond to the actual historical situation in which it is made. The word of God comes to us through the historical situation, which mediates it to the believer.

In Latin America today, say these theologians, the word of God is mediated by the cry of the poor and the oppressed. "In fact encounter with Christ necessarily occurs through the mediation of the poor brother who exists as an exploited class, as a forgotten race and as a marginalized culture"—so writes Claude Geffré in a clarification of the Latin American theology.[45]

According to Gutiérrez, "History is the scene of the revelation God makes of the mystery of his person. His word reaches us in the measure of our involvement in the evolution of history." In order to hear the word of God, he contends, I have to go out of my way and, like the Good Samaritan, draw near to the "distant" person who needs my help.[46]

Assmann goes so far as to speak of the present historical situation as the primary text for the theology of liberation.[47] Other texts, such as the Bible and the documents of the magisterium, are not primary, in his view; they do not contain truth in themselves, but they have to be read in relation to our own reality and practice. The canonical texts do not become revelation until they are read in correlation with the signs of the times in which we live.

(b) The term "praxis" is a technical term in Marxism and in the critical sociology of twentieth-century neo-Marxists. A helpful introduction may be found in Charles Davis' article, "Theology and Praxis" in *Cross Currents* for Summer 1973.[48]

For Marx, praxis referred to those human activities which are capable of transforming reality and society, and thus of making the world more human. More specifically, praxis is the action that tends to overcome the alienation by which man has become separated from the fruits of his labor. Praxis is therefore revolutionary: it is directed to changing the economic and social relationships. Convinced that the existing social order is alienating, the Marxists argue that any non-revolutionary theory will inevitably reinforce the existing alienation. A theory that interprets reality without doing anything to change it is defective even as a theory, for it is distorted by its uncritical acceptance of a repressive situation.

Marx sought to lay the groundwork for a new non-alienating kind of theory, which he called "critical theory." Critical theory in his thinking is dialectically united to revolutionary praxis. It is a new consciousness growing out of efforts to overcome the contradictions in the existing society. In the dialectical unity of critical theory and revolutionary praxis, the praxis is informed by the theory, and the theory is shaped by the praxis.

Applying these principles to faith, liberation theologians say in effect that the word of God is distorted and alienating whenever it is accepted without commitment to the praxis oriented toward the Kingdom of God. But if we are authentically committed to the Kingdom, we shall be involved in the struggle to subvert the existing social order, with its institutionalized injustice, and to establish on earth a just, fraternal society. In light of that commitment we shall be in a position to discern correctly the present reality and the emerging possibilities for the future. This discernment, to be sure, will not be perfectly clear, for until the consummated Kingdom is realized, the truth cannot exist in finished form. We can, however, have a truth proportioned to our situation on the way, and we shall thereby be equipped to move forward toward greater truth.

(c) The term "liberation" in the Latin American theologians functions somewhat as "humanization" does for the Marxists. It signifies the re-creation and total fulfillment of man, as does the biblical term "salvation." "Liberation," however, is untainted by the other-wordly connotations of the term "salvation" and calls attention to the current process by which people are extricated from their present situation of domination and dependence. In speaking of this situation, the Latin American theologians have in mind the condition of their own countries, but they point out that the concern is not merely regional, for in fact two-thirds of the human race live in a similar situation of degradation.

The term "liberation" is a substitute for "development" as used in some earlier documents.[49] After the Medellín Conference (1968), the notion of development was abandoned as being too gradualistic and optimistic; it seemed to imply that the present situation contains the seeds of the desired future. "Liberation" brings out the conflictual character of the process. On the other hand it is not tied to the rather specific political options that would be conveyed by a term such as "revolution." Unlike "development" and "revolution," "liberation" is a term that has deep roots in the Bible and in theology. It is closely connected with the biblical idea of redemption, which in some contexts signifies the manumission of a slave. Liberation connotes the "freedom with which Christ has set us free" (Gal. 5:1).

Liberation includes, but is not confined to, political and socioeconomic transformation. Gutiérrez distinguishes three levels: (i) political and social liberation of oppressed nations and social classes; (ii) liberation of humankind in the course of world history; (iii) liberation from sin and total reconciliation in communion with God through Jesus Christ.[50] In answer to the frequent charge of socio-political reductionism, liberation theologians reply that this has never been their program and is contrary to their intention. They do, however, wish to emphasize the inseparability of total redemption (or liberation) from the social, economic, and political factors, and in this way to escape the excesses of individualistic dualism.

Gutiérrez, in particular, insists that a true spiritual conversion is involved in the act of faith, as he understands it. "The encounter with Christ in the poor constitutes an authentic spiritual experience. It is to live in the Spirit, the link of the love of the Father and the Son, God and man, between men. Christians committed to an historical praxis of liberation try to live there this deep communion."[51] Elsewhere he says that commitment to liberation "gives rise to a new way of being a man and of believing, of living and thinking the faith, of being called together in an 'ecclesia.'"[52] When I make myself the neighbor of the wretched person whom I seek out in the barrios, when I take an effective option for the poor, my world changes, and I myself am transformed by my commitment to social transformation.

Liberation theology does not foster any utopian illusions about the future. We will never, of course, fully insert the Kingdom of God into historical time. But the biblical concept of the Kingdom stimulates our creative imagination so that we find ever new ways of provisionally realizing within history signs and anticipations of the promised Kingdom.[53]

In summary, then, faith as conceived by liberation theology is a transforming acceptance of the word, which comes as a free gift of God, breaking into human existence through the poor and oppressed, with whom Christ is seen to identify himself. Only in commitment to the liberation of the oppressed, and thus only in liberating praxis, can we give to the word the "warm welcome" that constitutes faith.

The dialectical interweaving of contemplation and praxis in the liberation theology of faith seems to me to be a definite advance over all the theories previously considered. The older theories, with their undialectical approach, inevitably tended to reduce man to passivity in the act of faith with the intention of giving greater glory to God. According to liberation theology the activity of God in shaping the content of faith includes, rather than excludes, the faithfulness of believers, so that their activity on behalf of justice in the world feeds back into their perception of the word of God. Faith, therefore, is not a passive waiting upon God's own decision to act, but it seizes the initiative and reshapes the world by its God-given power.

This dynamic view of faith has a more solid biblical basis than is commonly recognized. The dialectical inter-relationship between understanding and practice, between orthodoxy and orthopraxy, is suggested by certain biblical texts such as John 3:21. "Whoever does what is true comes to the light." According to this text truth is not only to be thought but also done, and the doing of truth is a condition of believing it. Further, the New Testament forbids us to look upon the Kingdom of God as exclusively future. It thus supports the contention of liberation theology that the Kingdom, in a provisional manner, is present and operative within history.[54] The Gospel, as grasped by faith, is the power of God revealing God's justice and leading to salvation (Rom. 1:16–17).[55] By keeping our eyes open to the signs of the times, we can perceive God's powerful action bringing about both judgment and salvation. Faith itself is an agent in salvation history. Paul, in Galatians 5:6, speaks of "faith working through love," thus implying that faith itself is efficaciously transforming the world according to the word of God.[56] In the struggle between faith and unfaith, the believer is assured of victory, for, as 1 John 5:4 tells us, "This is the victory that overcomes the world, our faith."[57] In view of texts such as these, it does not seem permissible to look upon faith as a merely passive virtue. Faith does not simply protect us from the world; it remakes that world.

Better than any of the theories previously considered in this chapter, the liberation theory of faith is able to cope with the problems raised by the socio-technical civilization. In the first place, the mobility of the world poses no threat to this kind of faith, for, in the view of these theologians, Christian faith is mediated by concrete historical experience. The very form of faith will bear the signature of the historical situation in which it is mediated. Actual experience of the human struggles of our own day constitutes a primary text in a sense in which not even Scripture or tradition is primary.

Second, this new theology of faith harmonizes excellently with the growing sense of the power of human initiative to shape the lives of everyone on this earth. For liberation theology, faith is not a merely passive virtue by which we accept and rely upon God's promises; it is an active engagement in the service of the Kingdom of God. Faith, according to this view, cannot exist without commitment to the implementation of the Gospel; and the experience of praxis, as we have said, helps to determine the concrete form of faith in a given time and place.

Third, the liberation theory is fully in tune with the increased sense of man's responsibility for the future of the world. Unlike the majority of intellectualist and fiducial theories, liberation theology does not place its hope of salvation solely in the action by which God will miraculously intervene in history at some future time. As I have said, liberation theology sees the Kingdom of God as presently existent and operative, and it sees faith as a force actually promoting the cause of justice and liberation.

Having sufficiently indicated my enthusiasm for the actual and potential contribution of liberation theology to a contemporary understanding of faith, I should like, before closing, to indicate certain reservations. I am not of the opinion that this theory of faith should be simply substituted for the earlier intellectualist and fiducial theories. Rather, I would say that the theories are mutually complementary and mutually corrective. Certain aspects of the complex reality of faith are better explained in other theories. The liberationist approach has limitations of its own.

Without denying the historical mediation of faith, we may continue to insist that God succeeds in making himself immediately present to the human spirit, as the transcendental theologians have so lucidly shown. If this immediacy of God were allowed to be obscured, as seems to be the case in some liberationist theologies, faith might seem to be a reaction to the historical situation rather than a response to a personal call from God.

By stressing the dialectical unity of theoria and praxis in the act of faith, the liberation theologians have recovered a very important biblical insight. But it must be kept in mind that this dialectical unity is a unity in difference. It is quite possible for a person to be a sincere believer and yet not to practice what he believes and preaches. The liberationist stress on external activity and social involvement runs the risk of minimizing the dimension of interiority in the life of faith. Luther with his advice to "sin boldly" brought out in a forceful if exaggerated way the possibility that faith may at times co-exist with actions that are inconsistent with itself. The traditional theologies of faith, in different ways, have tried to do justice to the religious significance of a personal faith that, for one reason or another, fails to achieve appropriate expression in actual conduct. In the liberation theologians I have read, there is no adequate study of the psychological complexity of the act of faith. Liberation theology has been in dialogue with sociology and economics but not to the same extent with the disciplines that seek to penetrate to the inner depths of the human spirit. As a result, some theologians of this school speak too glibly about overcoming dualism and bridging the gap between theory and action.

The effort of liberation theology to find God in the "signs of the times" is surely a commendable one, in line with a favorite theme of John XXIII and Vatican Council II. One may envy the confidence of some liberation theologians that they have succeeded in this demanding task, and have found without question where Christ is present in the history of our time. No Christian can deny that Jesus may come to us in the poor and the oppressed, but I confess that I feel a certain nervousness about the insistence of some liberation theologians that this is the way in which Christ is necessarily to be found in our society. The correspondence between the Gospel and Marxian class analysis is too neat to allay the suspicion that the Bible is being read through the eyes of those who are already convinced Marxists. They quote very selectively from the biblical passages that exalt the poor, and assert too sweepingly that God is always on the side of the poor and the oppressed. At times they even imply that the Christian ought to take sides with the poor against the rich, thus engaging to the full in the existing conflict among classes.

In this connection Richard Mouw has raised two interesting questions. He writes:

I accept the view that a central concern of the Christian community should be to identify with the poor and oppressed. But it seems to me that we must get clearer about what that concern comes to by dealing carefully and critically with at least two questions. First, who are to be properly included in the class of the "poor and oppressed" with whom we are biblically compelled to identify? Are we to include Nixon, who is presently an outcast and despised person? What about a financially well-off used car salesman who is experiencing a painful divorce? Or bored, pot-smoking students in an all-white suburban high school? Second, if we *can* clearly delineate the class of the poor and oppressed, then how shall we go about "identifying" with them? Is Mark Hatfield doing it? Will a professor who is properly aligned with the poor and oppressed inevitably oppose the construction of a new academic library? Will he or she refuse to buy works of art for personal enjoyment?[58]

Although the rich are subject to vices that we should, on all accounts, oppose, it would be a mistake to idealize the poor. They can sin as much by envy and covetousness as the rich by pride and avarice. In the preaching of Jesus no one class is made a paragon of virtue. All are admonished to examine their motives and to repent.

The category of liberation, with its echoes of the exodus and of Easter, is theologically acceptable. It helps to bring the Gospel to life, for there is at least an analogy between God's redeeming action in Christ, liberating us from spiritual and moral servitude, and the action of military or political leaders who deliver people from poverty and oppression. The rhetoric of liberation theology, however, could engender some confusion. It sometimes seems to suggest that social or political revolution, with a corresponding redistribution of wealth and power, is an essential means of bringing the poor and oppressed the salvation promised by the Gospel. This misunderstanding would demolish the rationale for the evangelization of those who are not likely to effect social change, and would deprive many destitute persons of the consolation which the Gospel can bring them amid their sufferings. Over-influenced by the Marxist critique of religion, some look with suspicion on all direct evangelization, treating it as though it were a mere cloak for oppression. With this exaggeration in mind, Paul VI felt obliged to warn, at the close of the 1974 Synod of Bishops:

> The totality of salvation is not to be confused with one or other aspect of liberation, and the Good News must preserve all of its own originality: that of a God who saves us from sin and death and brings us to divine life. Hence human advancement, social progress, etc., is not to be excessively emphasized on a temporal level to the detriment of the essential meaning which evangelization has for the Church of Christ: the announcement of the Good News.[59]

The liberation theologians are to be praised for urging all Christians to take seriously the obligation to work for a better political and social order, but in my estimation they assume too easily that some one social or economic system is endorsed by the Gospel itself. The Church does not have in its Scriptures, its traditions, and its sacramental heritage the resources it would need to make a sure choice among rival social systems. It is most difficult, or rather impossible, to deduce any specific social or political philosophy from occasional dicta of Jesus or the apostles. Christians, as individuals or in groups, will form their conscientious convictions in accordance with what seem to them to be the requirements of faith and the Gospel, but it will be most rare that the Church as such will see fit to endorse a particular system of government, political party, candidate, or platform.

Many of the conclusions of Latin American liberation theologians appear to be predicated on the assumption that capitalism is the great source of oppression in the world and Marxian socialism would bring peace, freedom, and general prosperity. On this point I personally find their statements unconvincing. Granting that laissez-faire capitalism has led to great inequities, I would think that the actual record of Marxian regimes is far from encouraging. Karl Marx may have been right when he thought that his own philosophy was entirely incompatible with Christianity.[60]

Because of the reservations I have just stated, I am ambivalent about the theory of faith proposed by the liberation theologians. My hesitations arise at just those points where it adopts the specific theses of Marxian social analysis. I am not sure whether, without these points, it would still merit the name of "liberation theology." I am confident, however, that a sound and contemporary vision of faith would accept the thesis, so brilliantly expounded by some liberation theologians, that Christian faith ineluctably involves an active concern with establishing justice on the earth.

In the letter to the Hebrews (12:2), Jesus is described as the author and finisher (or, as sometimes translated, the pioneer and perfecter) of faith. By the fidelity with which he completed the task assigned to him and carried out his own historic vocation to the end, and hence especially through the mystery of his redemptive death, he became the catalyst and paradigm of the faith that is ours. The faith of Jesus involved fidelity or faithfulness, and only in this way did it become foundational for our own faith. Our faith must be like his. As members of his body, Christians must carry out for the world of each generation the task that Jesus left unfinished. We must, so to speak, "fill up what is wanting" in Christ's faith by faithfulness in our own times (cf. Col. 1:24). By faith we accept our share in the mission of Jesus himself.

According to the Gospels, the mission of Jesus is prophetically set forth in the First Servant Song of Isaiah 42:1–4. The crucial passage reads as follows:

> Behold my servant whom I uphold,
>   my chosen, in whom my soul delights;
> I have put my Spirit upon him,
>   he will bring forth justice to the nations.
> He will not cry or lift up his voice,
>   or make it heard in the street;
> A bruised reed he will not break,
>   and a dimly burning wick he will not quench;
>   he will faithfully bring forth justice.
> He will not fail or be discouraged
>   till he has established justice in the earth;
>   and the coastlands wait for his law.

The Kingdom of peace and justice is not simply a remote ideal for which we long. In Jesus Christ the Kingdom of God

has entered into history. It is already at work, albeit only ger-
minally, transforming the world in which we live. Faith is the
Christian's mode of participation in that Kingdom. Insofar as
we have faith, the Kingdom takes hold of us and operates in us.
This means that through faith we become instruments in the
healing and reconciliation of the broken world. We become
agents of justice and bearers of the power of the Kingdom. Faith,
therefore, is more than intellectual assent, more than hope in
what God will do without us; it is also a present participation in
the work that God is doing—that is to say, in the task of bringing
forth justice to nations.

From THE FAITH THAT DOES JUSTICE, edited by John C. Haughey, S.J., pp. 10–
13, 32–46. Reprinted by permission of the publisher, Paulist Press © 1977 by The Missionary Society of St. Paul the Apostle in the State of New York.

NOTES

1. Herbert Richardson, *Toward an American Theology*
(New York: Harper and Row, 1967). p. 16.
2. P. Teilhard de Chardin, *How I Believe* (New York: Harper & Row, 1969).
3. P. Tillich, *Dynamics of Faith* (New York: Harper,
1957), p. 4.
4. I. T. Ramsey, *Religious Language* (New York: Macmillan Paperbacks, 1963).
5. Cf. A. Richardson, *History Sacred and Profane* (Philadelphia: Westminster, 1964).
5a. I have discussed these three dimensions in my paper,
"The Changing Forms of Faith," chap. 1 of *The Survival of
Dogma* (Garden City: Doubleday Image, 1973), pp. 15–30.
38. See especially his *Jesus—Word and Presence* (Philadelphia: Fortress, 1971), pp. 136–217, 270–81.
39. *New Birth of Freedom* (Philadelphia: Fortress, 1976), p.
333.
40. *Concilium,* vol. 96 (New York: Herder and Herder,
1974).
41. S. Galilea, "Liberation as an Encounter with Politics
and Contemplation," *ibid.,* p. 21.

42. G. Gutiérrez, "Liberation, Theology, and Proclamation," *ibid.,* pp. 67–70.

43. S. Galilea, *art. cit.,* p. 21.

44. J. L. Segundo, "Capitalism—Socialism: A Theological Crux," *ibid.,* p. 122.

45. C. Geffré, "Editorial: A Prophetic Theology," *ibid.,* p. 16.

46. "Faith as Freedom: Solidarity with the Alienated and Confidence in the Future," *Horizons* 2/1 (Spring 1975) 32.

47. H. Assmann, *Theology for a Nomad Church* (Maryknoll: Orbis, 1976), p. 104.

48. *Cross Currents* 23/2 (Summer 1973) 154–68.

49. G. Gutiérrez, *A Theology of Liberation* (Maryknoll: Orbis, 1973), pp. 25–37.

50. *Ibid.,* pp. 36–37, 176–78; cf. Assmann, *op. cit.,* p. 55.

51. "Faith as Freedom . . . ," p. 40.

52. "Liberation, Theology, and Proclamation," p. 58.

53. L. Boff, "Salvation in Jesus Christ and the Process of Liberation," *Concilium* 96, pp. 90–91.

54. J. Miranda, *Marx and the Bible* (Maryknoll: Orbis, 1974). pp. 201–229.

55. *Ibid.,* pp. 163, 172, 244–45.

56. *Ibid.,* p. 256.

57. *Ibid.,* p. 249.

58. Richard J. Mouw, "New Alignments and the Future of the Evangelicism," in P. L. Berger and R. J. Newhaus (eds.), *Against the World for the World* (New York: Seabury, 1976), pp. 123–24.

59. Paul VI, "Closing Address" (Oct. 26, 1974), *Synod of Bishops—1974* (Washington, D.C.: USCC, 1975), p. 12.

60. In his rather acerbic review of Miranda's *Marx and the Bible,* J. L. McKenzie comments: "The Bible was there for him (Marx) to study, had he wished to do so; he could have found for himself that ineffable harmony which Miranda hears echoing among the spheres. I think Marx was altogether right in finding religion alien to his theories. It takes more than a perception of the basic ugliness and viciousness of poverty to share a common vision of the redemption of humanity"—*Journal of Biblical Literature* 94 (1975) 280–281.

QUESTIONS

1. How do the contemporary definitions of faith differ from those of the medieval and early modern theologians?
2. How do events in biblical history show that the disclosure experiences led persons toward action in a costly way?
3. How does liberation theology define faith?
4. What is meant by the historicity of faith?
5. What does liberation theology mean by praxis? How does this concept differ from Marxist praxis?
6. What do the liberation theologians mean by "liberation"?
7. What value does Dulles see in liberation theology?
8. How does he critique liberation theology?

SUGGESTED READINGS

Bonhoeffer, D. (1963). *The Cost of Discipleship.* New York: Macmillan.

Bonhoeffer, D. (1972). *Letters and Papers from Prison.* New York: Macmillan.

Dulles, A. (1973). *The Survival of Dogma.* New York: Doubleday.

Gutierrez, G. (1973). *A Theology of Liberation.* Maryknoll: Orbis.

Segundo, J. (1976). *The Liberation of Theology.* Maryknoll: Orbis.

Part II

PSYCHOLOGY AND
RELIGION

G. Stephen Spinks

4. Psychology and Religion

G. Stephen Spinks, an Anglican clergyman, was one-time editor of the *Hubbert Journal* and Upton lecturer in the Psychology of Religion at Oxford University, England. This selection summarizes the history of the psychology of religion and presents various definitions of religion given by social scientists. His conclusion that the psychology of religion must include the study of man's response to that power which he regards as sacred is compatible with the discussion of faith by the theologians in Part I. The short section on the soul shows that psychology and religion are concerned with the same reality although with different conclusions.

The value of studies in the psychology of religion has in recent years been increased greatly by contributions from archaeology, anthropology, ethnology and sociology. But the difficulties of defining the exact boundaries of psychology, and the fact that the nature of religion is such that it eludes exhaustive definition, present us with problems of a special kind.

THE CONTEMPORARY POSITION

Recent studies in comparative religion show that all religions—despite considerable diversities of belief and practice—exhibit similarities which need to be explained by something more than processes of assimilation, conventionalization and cultural diffusion, though each of these factors plays an important part.[1] These similarities spring from such facts as the universality of human needs, spiritual no less than physical; from the same impulse towards unity and completeness; and from the

---

1. See Appendix III.

same awareness of powers that appear to operate within the world and yet are external to it. Man is a religious animal by birth, culture and inheritance, and as such his religious life can be examined psychologically without any verdict being passed upon the validity of his beliefs and their individual and corporate expression. The validity of spiritual truths is a matter upon which no psychologist *qua* psychologist can pronounce an opinion.[2] It may be true that:

> Religion is a difficult and refractory subject of study . . . It is not easy to dissect with the cold knife of logic what can only be accepted with a complete surrender of heart. It seems impossible to comprehend with reason that which encompasses mankind with love and supreme wisdom.[3]

Nonetheless the fact that religion is an active element in human life at all levels makes it imperative that we should attempt to estimate its nature and activities in terms of contemporary psychology.

As a discipline, psychology is concerned with body and soul *(psyche),* but it is not restricted to a study of their relationship. It is clear that psychology, while it cannot ignore the physiological aspects of man's nervous system, is neither a biological study nor yet an entirely objective examination of man's instinctual and emotional responses to his environment. If psychology is regarded as a study of the will, it calls not only for some consideration of the 'end' *(telos)* towards which man strives and is attracted, it also invites a philosophical assessment of the values which endow that end with something more than a purely prac-

---

2. In the *Psychopathology of Everyday Life* (1904) Freud gave an early expression of his naturalistic outlook on religion: 'I believe in fact that a great part of the mythological view of the world, which reaches far into the most modern religions, is nothing other than psychological processes projected into the outer world. The obscure apprehending of the psychical factors and relationships of the unconscious is mirrored—it is hard to put it otherwise; one has to use the analogy with paranoia—in the construction of a *super-sensible reality* which science has to retranslate into the psychology of the unconscious. One could venture in this manner to resolve the myths of Paradise, the Fall of Man, of God, of Good and Evil, of Immortality, and so on, thus transforming Metaphysics into Metapsychology.' Quoted with comment in Ernest Jones: *Sigmund Freud* (1957) Vol. III. pp. 377–8.

3. Bronislaw Malinowski: *The Foundations of Faith and Morals* (1934–1935).

tical nature. Life is never a purely practical affair, otherwise man living at primitive and dangerous levels of existence would never have thought it worth while to blow through a hollow reed in an attempt to make musical sounds which had no 'practical' purpose.

Furthermore, psychology shows that man does not always live on the same level of consciousness. There is the level of ordinary everyday awareness, but this awareness is continually subject to fluctuations of attention, to such common experiences as forgetfulness, daydreaming, fatigue and unexpected intrusions of memories and their emotional associations. But the activities of the psyche are not limited to conscious awareness. Some hours of every twenty-four are passed in sleep, and in sleep man becomes aware of another life which often makes his waking experience seem to be little more than the proscenium of a drama which, for beauty, mystery, strangeness and horror, transcends his daily life, so that he cannot but believe that he has a 'double' that is not limited to the confines of his body. By itself, anthropology cannot explain fully how man came to believe that he has a soul that is independent of his conscious awareness. But psychology, having proved empirically the subliminal activity of the psyche, is able to offer explanations of how primitive man, as a result of his experiences with dreams and the phenomena of death, came to formulate some concept of a 'double' (soul) which was connected with the differential between a body that breathes and a body that has ceased to breathe. A living example of breath thought of as soul is given by Jung from his own researches among the mountain tribesmen of the Elgonyi who, in the morning at the rising of the sun, 'hold their hands before their mouths and spit or blow into them vigorously. Then they turn their hands round and hold the palms forward to the sun.' Jung makes this comment on this particular ceremony:

> it is an offering to the sun which for these natives is *mungu*— that is *mana* or divine—only at the moment of rising. If they have spittle on their hands, this is the substance which, according to primitive belief, contains the personal *mana*,

the force that cures, conjures and sustains life. If they breathe upon their hands, breath is wind and spirit. . . . The action means 'I offer my living spirit to God'. It is a wordless, acted prayer, which could equally well be spoken: 'Lord, into thy hands, I commend my spirit.'[4]

This connexion remains to this day in Christian thought where the Holy Spirit is referred to in terms of 'the wind bloweth where it listeth and thou hearest the sound thereof . . . so is everyone that is born of the spirit'.[5]

The soul was also connected with other aspects of the body, such as blood, the heart, shadow or sometimes the 'name', but of all these tropes, blood and breath[6] were those most frequently associated with the soul. Blood, like breath, is one of the most natural symbols of life. This explains why blood plays such a prominent part in sacrifices (as we shall see later); it is one of the most significant means by which man is able to make 'a lively sacrifice'. Hence the expression 'the blood of the Lamb' who, in Christian theology, 'taketh away the sins of the world'.[7]

A study of the beliefs of primitive peoples[8] shows that in many of them, man regarded the soul not only as a 'double' but in many cases believed in a plurality of souls, each being identified with some function of the body. The Keokuk Indians, for instance, distinguished between the soul of the heart, the soul of

4. Jung: *Modern Man in Search of a Soul* (1936) pp. 172 ff.
5. John iii. 8.
6. Among the numerous terms used for *breath* there are many which are linguistically related to terms which refer to *soul* or *psyche*. For instance:

Akkadian and Assyrian:	*napištu* = breath, life, soul.
Hebrew:	*nephesh* = breath, life, soul or person.
Arabic:	*tanaffus* = to fetch a deep breath.
	nafs = breath of life.
Greek:	*psyche* = breath or soul.
Stoic:	*pneuma* = breath or spirit.
Latin:	*anima* &= from Greek, *anemos* = soul and wind.
	animus
Sanskrit:	*ātman* &= breath, wind or soul.
	prāna

7. John i. 29, and Rev. v. 6.
8. See Appendix I.

the flesh, of life, name and family; while the Melanesians believed that a man could have as many as seven souls. In the West these functional aspects of the soul were identified with the faculties of the unified psyche. But in addition to this variety of psychical functions, it is clear that in most religions and at all levels of culture, the soul (psyche) was believed to be *the* means whereby man apprehended the all-surrounding, all-pervading Mystery of life.[9]

Whatever other aspects the psychology of religion may have to deal with, for our present purpose it is the study of how the soul of man, both consciously and unconsciously, responds to the mystery of life and death, and to the impingement of an environment which in many ways appears to be even more mysteriously alive than man himself. But if this is the main concern of our study, we have yet to define what is meant by the term 'religion'.

DEFINITIONS

Religion includes not only the beliefs, customs, traditions and rites which belong to particular social groupings, it also involves individual experiences, Any definition which stresses the communal aspects of religion to the exclusion of the individual's psychic life, is defective since it is the individual's apprehension of some supreme Object, Power or Principle that constitutes one of the most important features of religion.

Religion embraces such a wide variety of data that it is not surprising that Professor C. C. J. Webb should have said: 'I do not believe that Religion *can* be defined.'[10] Other writers, how-

---

9. The ancient Hebrews were forbidden to eat flesh unless the blood (the soul) had first been drained from it. 'I will set my face against the [man] that eateth blood, and will cut him off from among his people. For the life of the flesh is in the blood; and I have given it to you upon the altar to make atonement for your souls; for it is the blood that maketh atonement by reason of the life.' Lev. xvii. 10, 11; see also: Deut. xii. 16, and 1 Sam. xiv. 32, 33.

10. See C. C. J. Webb: *Group Theories of Religion* (1916).

ever, have made noteworthy attempts at definition. Sir James
Frazer said that by religion

> I understand a propitiation or conciliation of powers supe-
> rior to man which are believed to direct and control the
> course of nature and of human life. Thus defined, religion
> consists of two elements, a theoretical and a practical,
> namely a belief in powers higher than man and an attempt
> to propitiate or please them.

To this definition, Frazer added the useful comment that 'belief
clearly comes first, since we must believe in the existence of a
divine being before we can attempt to please him. But unless the
belief leads to a corresponding practice, it is not a religion but
merely a theology.'[11] A different emphasis is to be found in Émile
Durkheim's definition, where the emphasis is on belief and practice within a social community:

> A religion is a unified system of beliefs and practices relative
> to sacred things, that is to say, things set apart and forbid-
> den—beliefs and practices which unite into one single moral
> community called a Church, all those who adhere to them.
> The second element which thus finds a place in our defini-
> tion is no less essential than the first; for by showing that the
> idea of religion is inseparable from that of the Church, it
> makes it clear that religion should be an eminently collective
> thing.[12]

To this definition, Durkheim adds, in a footnote, that in an earlier definition he had defined religious beliefs exclusively by
their obligatory character, but that he proposed to amend this
definition by showing that their obligatoriness was the result of
their being imposed by the group upon its members.

On the other hand, a definition by Professor George Galloway placed the main emphasis upon the individual and his

---

11. James Frazer: *The Golden Bough:* abridged edition (1925) p. 50.
12. E. Durkheim: *The Elementary Forms of the Religious Life* (1954) p. 47.

psychological needs. Religion is that which refers to 'Man's faith in a power beyond himself whereby he seeks to satisfy emotional needs and gain stability of life, and which he expresses in acts of worship and service'.[13] To which definition, Galloway adds that

> The cognitive side of the religious consciousness is repre-sented by faith, and faith is stimulated by emotion and posits the object which will satisfy the needs of the inner life. One of the most urgent and constant of man's needs is that which is expressed in the desire for self-conservation, or, as we have put it, for stability of life in the face of the manifold forces which threaten and limit him. The practical aspect is denoted by the acts of worship and service which belong to the nature of religion.[14]

The last sentence of this definition will occupy our attention in the second part of this book.

Two of the most useful definitions yet provided by any writers on the psychology of religion are to be found in J. Bissett Pratt's well-known *The Religious Consciousness* and in R. H. Thouless's much-quoted *Introduction to the Psychology of Religion*.

> Religion is the serious and social attitude of individuals or communities toward the power or powers which they conceive as having ultimate control over their interests and destinies. . . . This definition has . . . one or two characteristics to which I wish to call the reader's attention. First, it defines religion as an 'attitude'. . . . The word 'attitude' shall here be used to cover that *responsive* side of consciousness which is found in such things as attention, interest, expectancy, feeling, tendencies to action etc. . . . The advantages of defining religion as an attitude are sufficiently manifest. It shows that religion is not a matter of any one 'department' of psychic life but involves the whole man. It includes what there was

---

13. G. Galloway: *The Philosophy of Religion* (1914) p. 184.
14. G. Galloway: *The Philosophy of Religion* (1914) p. 184.

of truth in the historical attempts to identify religion with feeling, belief or will. And it draws attention to the fact that religion is immediately subjective, thus differing from science (which emphasizes 'content' rather than 'attitude'); and yet it points to the other fact also that religion involves and presupposes the acceptance of the objective. Religion is the attitude of a self towards an object in which the self genuinely believes.[15]

Dr. R. H. Thouless, having considered various definitions by other writers, came to the conclusion that any definition of religion to be adequate must include at least three factors:

a mode of behaviour, a system of intellectual beliefs and a system of feelings. In order to find a complete and satisfactory definition, we must further enquire what is the particular mark of the conduct, beliefs and feelings in question which characterises them as religious. . . . Our definition will then run in some such form as this: *Religion is a felt practical relationship with what is believed in as a superhuman being or beings.*[16]

To this definition, Dr. Thouless adds that

there are two terms in common use in the psychology of religion which must be explained. These are the *religious consciousness,* and *religious experience.* The religious consciousness is that part of religion which is present to the mind and is open to examination by introspection. It is the mental side of religious activity. *Religious experience* is a vaguer term used to describe the feeling element in the religious consciousness—the feelings which lead to religious belief or are the effects of religious behaviour.[17] . . . The main business of

---

15. J. B. Pratt: *The Religious Consciousness* (1930) pp. 2–3.
16. R. H. Thouless: *An Introduction to the Psychology of Religion* (1936) pp. 3–4.
17. One school of modern psychological study—the Behaviourist—adopts the wholly unsatisfactory attitude that psychology is concerned with *the study of behaviour*

the psychology of religion is to study the religious consciousness. But it is impossible to study that alone; we must inves-
tigate religious behaviour as well.[18]

These definitions together with their psychological explanations
are, however, not entirely representative of all the definitions
that have been made in the course of many years. In fact so
many attempts have been made to arrive at a satisfactory definition that Leuba was able to select forty-eight definitions, to
which he added two of his own, for inclusion in his famous *Psychological Study of Religion* (1912). An analysis of these definitions of religion, together with those written subsequently,
reveals that what is there defined is not in all cases the same
'activity', for the term 'religion' like the word 'God' is one of
those 'umbrella' words which gathers under its protection implications and meanings some of which are plainly opposed to or
corrective of others.

Leuba divided his rich collection of definitions into two
groups, those which treat religion as 'the recognition of a mystery pressing for interpretation', and those which adopt Schleier-
macher's view that religion is 'a feeling of absolute dependence
upon God'. To these two schools of thought, Leuba added yet a
third. Religion is 'the *propitiation* or *conciliation* of powers
which are believed to direct and control the course of nature and
human life'.[19] (A definition which is substantially the same as
that advanced by Pratt.) To which we must add—since no psychology of religion can possibly be written that does not quite

---

only. It repudiates all study of the mind as being a non-experimental concept. For this
reason it is not possible to accept any Behaviourist verdict on religion. Whatever religion
involves, it clearly involves a consideration of how man's mind reacts to and formulates
explanations of the content of experience and its environment. Religion includes at least
three factors, belief, feeling and behaviour (which includes things-done and things-not-
to-be-done, ritual and taboo), no single one of which can operate by itself.

18. op. cit. p. 5.

19. The fact that the Buddha in his opposition to Hindu metaphysics did not share
this belief in various deities nor that worship should be made to them, must not obscure
the fact that later forms of Buddhism, e.g. Mahāyāna Buddhism in particular, do in
actual practice show that they have restored this belief in the existence of supernatural
powers to whom worship must be offered.

early on begin to quote from William James—the comment that because there are so many definitions of religion and the fact that they are

> so different from one another is enough to prove that the word 'religion' can not stand for any single principle or essence. . . . The theorizing mind tends always to the over-simplification of its materials. . . . In the broadest and most general terms possible, one might say that religious life consists in the belief that there is an unseen order, and that our supreme good lies in harmoniously adjusting ourselves thereto. This belief and this adjustment are the religious attitude of the soul. . . . Moreover, there must be something solemn, serious and tender about any attitude which we denominate religious.[20]

It seems clear, therefore, that no one particular attitude to religion will suffice. Intellect, behaviour involving the operation both of will and feeling (as well as of other factors which we have not yet mentioned) are all involved. But what is not clear is the way in which these elements are related to and what is their specific importance in religion, since they all are involved in every discipline (sacred and secular) that engages human effort.

Leuba himself emphasized the importance of the will as the operative factor in religion viewed as behaviour, but wisely added that he did not exclude from his own concept of religion aspects which do not express themselves in overt acts, in rites of propitiation, submission or adoration. *Active* religion includes certain kinds of behaviour proceeding from the operation of the will and, as we shall see, from instinctual dispositions, while *passive* religion is that form in which the feeling-attitude is more prominent and where the psyche is acted upon by, rather than acts towards, the Object of its devotion. Archbishop Söderblom argued that the essential element in religion is neither formal belief nor organized worship but a response to the 'tabu-holy'.[21]

---

20. William James: *Varieties of Religious Experience:* 36th edn (1928) pp. 26 ff.
21. N. Söderblom: *Das Werden des Gottesglauben* (1916) p. 211.

The psychology of religion must, therefore, include the study of man's response to that power which he regards as 'sacred'.[22]

Appendix II
Psychology, Theology and the Soul

Psychology and theology are both concerned with the 'soul', but what grounds are there for believing that the 'soul' which is the concern of the theologian is the *psyche* which is the concern of the psychologist?[23] If the theologian regards the soul as that entity whose activities are in some measure observable as mental and emotional phenomena, then the psychologist cannot ignore it. And if the psychologist claims, as Jung does, to have discovered in the *psyche* 'the basic raw material of religion' then the theologian cannot disregard the *psyche* without serious results to his own study. The question is, do religion and psychology regard soul and *psyche* as synonymous terms? In Appendix I on 'The Nature of the Soul' we saw that many religions and historical periods did not restrict the activities of the soul to the 'supernatural' but in many cases associated it with such psychological activities as intelligence, will, memory and the like.

A study of the *Book of Psalms* shows clearly that for Judaism and, because of their continued use in Christian worship, for Christianity also, the word 'soul' is concerned with a wider

---

22. At bottom, the only helpful thing one can say of the sacred in general is contained in the very definition of the term: that it is the opposite of profane. As soon as one attempts to give a clear statement of the nature, the *modality* of that opposition, one strikes difficulty. No formula, however elementary, will cover the labyrinthine complexity of the facts.' Roger Caillois: *L'Homme et le sacré:* quoted by Mircea Eliade: *Patterns in Comparative Religion* (1958) p. xii. To which Professor Eliade adds that among the facts of this labyrinthine complexity he himself includes taboo, ritual, symbol, myth, demon, god—'but it would be an outrageous simplification to make such a list tell the whole story'.

23. This subject is dealt with at some length and in great detail by Fr Victor White O.P., in *Soul and Psyche* (1960) pp. 11–31, from which a number of references have been borrowed.

range of activity than that of praise and prayer. It is used to refer to emotion, dreams, nightmares and the like as well as to religious activities. A brief selection of passages quickly substantiates this statement.[24] Wherever the word 'soul' is referred to in the Greek version it is uniformly translated *psyche,* and in the Latin version it is always *anima.* If it be asked whether the New Testament uses the word soul in much the same ways as the Old Testament, the answer is that wherever the Greek New Testament uses the word *psyche,* the Latin translation uses *anima* and the English translation uses 'soul'—showing that in the mind of the translators these terms are to be regarded as synonymous. The following passages show that the word *psyche* in the New Testament refers to psychological as well as to spiritual activities.

Mark viii. 36: 'What shall it profit a man if he gain the whole world and lose his own soul *(psyche)?'*

Matt. vi. 25. Luke xii. 22: 'Is not the life *(psyche)* more than the meat?'

---

24. It will be seen that the following quotations from the *Psalms* refer to the soul *(psyche)* in contexts which emphasize emotion, sensation, personality or life-principle.

Ps. vi. 3, 4: 'My soul *(psyche)* is sore troubled: turn thee, O Lord, and deliver my soul *(psyche).'*

Ps. xvi. 11: 'Thou shalt not leave my soul *(psyche)* in hell.' *(contd overleaf.)*

Ps. xvii. 13: 'Deliver my soul *(psyche)* from the ungodly, which is a sword of thine.'

Ps. xxxiii. 18: 'To deliver their soul *(psyche)* from death and to feed them in the time of dearth.'

Ps. xxxv. 4: 'Let them be confounded and put to shame that seek after my soul *(psyche):* let them be turned back and brought to confusion, that imagine mischief against me.'

Ps. xxxv. 9: 'And, my soul *(psyche)* by joyful in the Lord: it shall rejoice in his salvation.'

Ps. xxxvii. 7: 'For they have privily laid their net to destroy me without a cause: yea even without a cause have they made a pit for my soul *(psyche).'*

Ps. xliii. 5: 'Why art thou so heavy, O my soul *(psyche):* and why art thou so disquieted within me?

Ps. cvii. 18: 'Their soul *(psyche)* abhorred all manner of meat: and they were even hard at death's door.'

This short selection of quotations could be greatly enlarged.

Rom. xiii. 1: 'Let every soul (*psyche*) be in subjection to the higher powers.'

1 Cor. xv. 46: 'The first man Adam became a living soul *(psyche)*. The last Adam became a life-giving spirit *(pneuma)*.'

A study of these and other quotations of a like nature shows that soul *(psyche)* in the Old and New Testaments refers to nothing less than life itself in its fullest range of interests and activities; man is viewed as a unity, an ensouled body rather than an embodied soul. This is no new conclusion. Tertullian in a famous passage asserts that religion is rooted in the nature of the soul; that the soul of every man is naturally Christian—*anima naturaliter Christiana*—and that if man would look into his uninstructed soul he would find there all the basic concepts of Christian belief.[25]

We have, therefore, adequate grounds for holding that soul or *psyche* is the common concern of theology and psychology, and since religion everywhere and at all stages of development treats the soul *(psyche)* as in some sense a life-principle, psychology and religion are concerned with the same field of inquiry though not necessarily with the same set of conclusions.

From PSYCHOLOGY AND RELIGION by G. Stephen Spinks, pp. 3–10, 193–195. Reprinted by permission of the publisher, Methuen & Co. Ltd., London.

QUESTIONS

1. What can psychology reveal about religion?
2. What are the limits of what psychology can reveal about the human experience of the ultimate?
3. Summarize the various definitions of religion and formulate your own.

———

25. See *The Writings of Tertullian:* Ante-Nicene Library, Vol. I. p. 37, quoted Victor White: *God and the Unconscious* (1952).

4. How does Spinks demonstrate that psychology and theology are concerned with the same field of inquiry although they may reach different conclusions?

SUGGESTED READINGS

Durkheim, E. (1954). *The Elementary Forms of the Religious Life.* Glencoe: Free Press.

Pratt, J. B. (1920/1971). *The Religious Consciousness.* (Reprint of 1920 edition.) New York: Hafner.

Thouless, R. H. (1972). *An Introduction to the Psychology of Religion* (3rd ed.). Cambridge: Cambridge University Press.

William James

5. Conclusion
from The Varieties of Religious Experience

William James founded the psychological laboratory of Harvard and then moved on to philosophy, where he is known for the development of philosophical theory of pragmatism. This selection from one of his most famous books says in psychological terms what the theologians have already said. James claims that the common nucleus of all creeds is a sense that there is something wrong with us. Tillich and Rahner use the term-awareness of our finiteness in face of the infinite or the ultimate. When James speaks of making a proper connection with the higher power, this "connection" might well be what the theologians call non-reflective awareness or the recognition of the ultimate. He is consistent with his pragmatism when he says that God is real to us because of the effects produced. Finally his concept of overbeliefs can be seen to correspond analogously to Tillich's concrete expressions of ultimacy and to Rahner's notion of institutional formulations encrusted by custom.

We must next pass beyond the point of view of merely subjective utility, and make inquiry into the intellectual content itself.

First, is there, under all the discrepancies of the creeds, a common nucleus to which they bear their testimony unanimously?

And second, ought we to consider the testimony true?

I will take up the first question first, and answer it immediately in the affirmative. The warring gods and formulas of the various religions do indeed cancel each other, but there is a certain uniform deliverance in which religions all appear to meet. It consists of two parts:—

1. An uneasiness; and
2. Its solution.

1. The uneasiness, reduced to its simplest terms, is a sense that there is *something wrong about us* as we naturally stand.

2. The solution is a sense the *we are saved from the wrongness* by making proper connection with the higher powers.

In those more developed minds which alone we are studying, the wrongness takes a moral character, and the salvation takes a mystical tinge. I think we shall keep well within the limits of what is common to all such minds if we formulate the essence of their religious experience in terms like these:—

The individual, so far as he suffers from his wrongness and criticises it, is to that extent consciously beyond it, and in at least possible touch with something higher, if anything higher exists. Along with the wrong part there is thus a better part of him, even though it may be but a most helpless germ. With which part he should identify his real being is by no means obvious at this stage; but when stage 2 (the stage of solution or salvation) arrives,[1] the man identifies his real being with the germinal higher part of himself; and does so in the following way. *He becomes conscious that this higher part is conterminous and continuous with a* MORE *of the same quality, which is operative in the universe outside of him, and which he can keep in working touch with, and in a fashion get on board of and save himself when all his lower being has gone to pieces in the wreck.*

It seems to me that all the phenomena are accurately describable in these very simple general terms.[2] They allow for the divided self and the struggle; they involve the change of personal centre and the surrender of the lower self; they express the appearance of exteriority of the helping power and yet account for our sense of union with it;[3] and they fully justify our feelings

---

1. Remember that for some men it arrives suddenly, for others gradually, whilst others again practically enjoy it all their life.

2. The practical difficulties are: 1, to 'realize the reality' of one's higher part; 2, to identify one's self with it exclusively; and 3, to identify it with all the rest of ideal being.

3. "When mystical activity is at its height, we find consciousness possessed by the sense of a being at once *excessive* and *identical* with the self: great enough to be God; interior enough to be *me*. The 'objectivity' of it ought in that case to be called *excessivity,* rather, or exceedingness." RÉCÉIAC: Essai sur les fondements de la conscience mystique, 1897, p. 46.

of security and joy. There is probably no autobiographic document, among all those which I have quoted, to which the description will not well apply. One need only add such specific details as will adapt it to various theologies and various experiences reconstructed in their individual forms.

So far, however, as this analysis goes, the experiences are only psychological phenomena. They possess, it is true, enormous biological worth. Spiritual strength really increases in the subject when he has them, a new life opens for him, and they seem to him a place of conflux where the forces of two universes meet; and yet this may be nothing but his subjective way of feeling things, a mood of his own fancy, in spite of the effects produced. I now turn to my second question: What is the objective 'truth' of their content?[4]

The part of the content concerning which the question of truth most pertinently arises is that 'MORE of the same quality' with which our own higher self appears in the experience to come into harmonious working relation. Is such a 'more' merely our own notion, or does it really exist? If so, in what shape does it exist? Does it act, as well as exist? And in what form should we conceive of that 'union' with it of which religious geniuses are so convinced?

It is in answering these questions that the various theologies perform their theoretic work, and that their divergencies most come to light. They all agree that the 'more' really exists; though some of them hold it to exist in the shape of a personal god or gods, while others are satisfied to conceive it as a stream of ideal tendency embedded in the eternal structure of the world. They all agree, moreover, that it acts as well as exists, and that something really is effected for the better when you throw your life into its hands. It is when they treat of the experience of 'union' with it that their speculative differences appear most clearly. Over this point pantheism and theism, nature and second birth, works and grace and karma, immortality and reincarnation, rationalism and mysticism, carry on inveterate disputes.

---

4. The word 'truth' is here taken to mean something additional to bare value for life, although the natural propensity of man is to believe that whatever has great value for life is thereby certified as true.

At the end of my lecture on Philosophy I held out the notion that an impartial science of religions might sift out from the midst of their discrepancies a common body of doctrine which she might also formulate in terms to which physical science need not object. This, I said, she might adopt as her own reconciling hypothesis, and recommend it for general belief. I also said that in my last lecture I should have to try my own hand at framing such an hypothesis.

The time has now come for this attempt. Who says 'hypothesis' renounces the ambition to be coercive in his arguments. The most I can do is, accordingly, to offer something that may fit the facts so easily that your scientific logic will find no plausible pretext for vetoing your impulse to welcome it as true.

The 'more' as we called it, and the meaning of our 'union' with it, form the nucleus of our inquiry. Into what definite description can these words be translated, and for what definite facts do they stand? It would never do for us to place ourselves offhand at the position of a particular theology, the Christian theology, for example, and proceed immediately to define the 'more' as Jehovah, and the 'union' as his imputation to us of the righteousness of Christ. That would be unfair to other religions, and, from our present standpoint at least, would be an over-belief.

We must begin by using less particularized terms; and, since one of the duties of the science of religions is to keep religion in connection with the rest of science, we shall do well to seek first of all a way of describing the 'more,' which psychologists may also recognize as real. The *subconscious self* is nowadays a well-accredited psychological entity; and I believe that in it we have exactly the mediating term required. Apart from all religious considerations, there is actually and literally more life in our total soul than we are at any time aware of. The exploration of the transmarginal field has hardly yet been seriously undertaken, but what Mr. Myers said in 1892 in his essay on the Subliminal Consciousness[5] is as true as when it was first written: "Each of

---

5. Proceedings of the Society for Psychical Research, vol. vii. p. 305. For a full statement of Mr. Myers's views, I may refer to his posthumous work, 'Human Personality in the Light of Recent Research,' which is already announced by Messrs. Long-

us is in reality an abiding psychical entity far more extensive than he knows—an individuality which can never express itself completely through any corporeal manifestation. The Self manifests through the organism; but there is always some part of the Self unmanifested; and always, as it seems, some power of organic expression in abeyance or reserve."[6] Much of the content of this larger background against which our conscious being stands out in relief is insignificant. Imperfect memories, silly jingles, inhibitive timidities, 'dissolutive' phenomena of various sorts as Myers calls them, enter into it for a large part. But in it many of the performances of genius seem also to have their origin; and in our study of conversion, of mystical experiences, and of prayer, we have seen how striking a part invasions from this region play in the religious life.

Let me then propose, as an hypothesis, that whatever it may be on its *farther* side, the 'more' with which in religious experience we feel ourselves connected is on its *hither* side the subconscious continuation of our conscious life. Starting thus with a recognized psychological fact as our basis, we seem to preserve a contact with 'science' which the ordinary theologian lacks. At the same time the theologian's contention that the religious man is moved by an external power is vindicated, for it is one of the peculiarities of invasions from the subconscious region to take on objective appearances, and to suggest to the Subject an external control. In the religious life the control is felt as 'higher'; but since on our hypothesis it is primarily the higher faculties of our own hidden mind which are controlling, the sense of union with the power beyond us is a sense of something, not merely apparently, but literally true.

---

mans, Green & Co. as being in press. Mr. Myers for the first time proposed as a general psychological problem the exploration of the subliminal region of consciousness throughout its whole extent, and made the first methodical steps in its topography by treating as a natural series a mass of subliminal facts hitherto considered only as curious isolated facts, and subjecting them to a systematized nomenclature. How important this exploration will prove, future work upon the path which Myers has opened can alone show. Compare my paper: 'Frederic Myers's Services to Psychology,' in the said Proceedings, part xlii., May, 1901.

6. Compare the inventory given above on pp. 483–4, and also what is said of the subconscious self on pp. 233–236, 240–242.

This doorway into the subject seems to me the best one for a science of religions, for it mediates between a number of different points of view. Yet it is only a doorway, and difficulties present themselves as soon as we step through it, and ask how far our transmarginal consciousness carries us if we follow it on its remoter side. Here the over-beliefs begin: here mysticism and the conversion-rapture and Vedantism and transcendental idealism bring in their monistic interpretations and tell us that the finite self rejoins the absolute self, for it was always one with God and identical with the soul of the world.[7] Here the prophets of all the different religions come with their visions, voices, raptures, and other openings, supposed by each to authenticate his own peculiar faith.

Those of us who are not personally favored with such specific revelations must stand outside of them altogether and, for the present at least, decide that, since they corroborate incompatible theological doctrines, they neutralize one another and leave no fixed result. If we follow any one of them, or if we follow philosophical theory and embrace monistic pantheism on

---

7. One more expression of this belief, to increase the reader's familiarity with the notion of it:

"If this room is full of darkness for thousands of years, and you come in and begin to weep and wail, 'Oh, the darkness,' will the darkness vanish? Bring the light in, strike a match, and light comes in a moment. So what good will it do you to think all your lives, 'Oh, I have done evil, I have made many mistakes'? It requires no ghost to tell us that. Bring in the light, and the evil goes in a moment. Strengthen the real nature, build up yourselves, the effulgent, the resplendent, the ever pure, call that up in every one whom you see. I wish that every one of us had come to such a state that even when we see the vilest of human beings we can see the God within, and instead of condemning, say, 'Rise, thou effulgent One, rise thou who art always pure, rise thou birthless and deathless, rise almighty, and manifest your nature.' ... This is the highest prayer that the Advaita teaches. This is the one prayer: remembering our nature." ... "Why does man go out to look for a God? ... It is your own heart beating, and you did not know, you were mistaking it for something external. He, nearest of the near, my own self, the reality of my own life, my body and my soul.—I am Thee and Thou art Me. That is your own nature. Assert it, manifest it. Not to become pure, you are pure already. You are not to be perfect, you are that already. Every good thought which you think or act upon is simply tearing the veil, as it were, and the purity, the Infinity, the God behind, manifests itself—the eternal Subject of everything, the eternal Witness in this universe, your own Self. Knowledge is, as it were, a lower step, a degradation. We are It already; how to know It?" SWAMI VIVEKANANDA: Addresses, NO. XII., Practical Vedanta part iv. pp. 172, 174, London, 1897; and Lectures, The Real and the Apparent Man, p. 24, abridged.

non-mystical grounds, we do so in the exercise of our individual freedom, and build out our religion in the way most congruous with our personal susceptibilities. Among these susceptibilities intellectual ones play a decisive part. Although the religious question is primarily a question of life, of living or not living in the higher union which opens itself to us as a gift, yet the spiritual excitement in which the gift appears a real one will often fail to be aroused in an individual until certain particular intellectual beliefs or ideas which, as we say, come home to him, are touched.[8] These ideas will thus be essential to that individual's religion;—which is as much as to say that over-beliefs in various directions are absolutely indispensable, and that we should treat them with tenderness and tolerance so long as they are not intolerant themselves. As I have elsewhere written, the most interesting and valuable things about a man are usually his overbeliefs.

Disregarding the over-beliefs, and confining ourselves to what is common and generic, we have in *the fact that the conscious person is continuous with a wider self through which saving experiences come,*[9] a positive content of religious experience which, it seems to me, *is literally and objectively true as far as it goes.* If I now proceed to state my own hypothesis about the farther limits of this extension of our personality, I shall be offering my own over-belief—though I know it will appear a sorry under-

---

8. For instance, here is a case where a person exposed from her birth to Christian ideas had to wait till they came to her clad in spiritistic formulas before the saving experience set in:—

"For myself I can say that spiritualism has saved me. It was revealed to me at a critical moment of my life, and without it I don't know what I should have done. It has taught me to detach myself from worldly things and to place my hope in things to come. Through it I have learned to see in all men, even in those most criminal, even in those from whom I have most suffered, undeveloped brothers to whom I owed assistance, love, and forgiveness. I have learned that I must lose my temper over nothing, despise no one, and pray for all. Most of all I have learned to pray! And although I have still much to learn in this domain, prayer ever brings me more strength, consolation, and comfort. I feel more than ever that I have only made a few steps on the long road of progress; but I look at its length without dismay, for I have confidence that the day will come when all my efforts shall be rewarded. So Spiritualism has a great place in my life, indeed it holds the first place there." Flournoy Collection.

9. "The influence of the Holy Spirit, exquisitely called the Comforter, is a matter of actual experience, as solid a reality as that of electro-magnetism." W. C. Brownell, Scribner's Magazine, vol. xxx. p. 112.

belief to some of you—for which I can only bespeak the same indulgence which in a converse case I should accord to yours.

The further limits of our being plunge, it seems to me, into an altogether other dimension of existence from the sensible and merely 'understandable' world. Name it the mystical region, or the supernatural region, whichever you choose. So far as our ideal impulses originate in this region (and most of them do originate in it, for we find them possessing us in a way for which we cannot articulately account), we belong to it in a more intimate sense than that in which we belong to the visible world, for we belong in the most intimate sense wherever our ideals belong. Yet the unseen region in question is not merely ideal, for it produces effects in this world. When we commune with it, work is actually done upon our finite personality, for we are turned into new men, and consequences in the way of conduct follow in the natural world upon our regenerative change.[10] But that which produces effects within another reality must be termed a reality itself, so I feel as if we had no philosophic excuse for calling the unseen or mystical world unreal.

God is the natural appellation, for us Christians at least, for the supreme reality, so I will call this higher part of the universe by the name of God.[11] We and God have business with each

---

10. That the transaction of opening ourselves, otherwise called prayer, is a perfectly definite one for certain persons, appears abundantly in the preceding lectures. I append another concrete example to reinforce the impression on the reader's mind:—

"Man can learn to transcend these limitations [of finite thought] and draw power and wisdom at will ... The divine presence is known through experience. The turning to a higher plane is a distinct act of consciousness. It is not a vague, twilight or semi-conscious experience. It is not an ecstasy; it is not a trance. It is not super-consciousness in the Vedantic sense. It is not due to self-hypnotization. It is a perfectly calm, sane, sound, rational, common-sense shifting of consciousness from the phenomena of sense-perception to the phenomena of seership, from the thought of self to a distinctively higher realm ... For example, if the lower self be nervous, anxious, tense, one can in a few moments compel it to be calm. This is not done by a word simply. Again I say, it is not hypnotism. It is by the exercise of power. One feels the spirit of peace as definitely as heat is perceived on a hot summer day. The power can be as surely used as the sun's rays can be focused and made to do work, to set fire to wood." The Higher Law, vol. iv. pp. 4, 6, Boston, August, 1901.

11. Transcendentalists are fond of the term 'Over-soul,' but as a rule they use it in an intellectualist sense, as meaning only a medium of communion. 'God' is a causal agent as well as a medium of communion, and that is the aspect which I wish to emphasize.

other; and in opening ourselves to his influence our deepest destiny is fulfilled. The universe, at those parts of it which our personal being constitutes, takes a turn genuinely for the worse or for the better in proportion as each one of us fulfills or evades God's demands. As far as this goes I probably have you with me, for I only translate into schematic language what I may call the instinctive belief of mankind: God is real since he produces real effects.

The real effects in question, so far as I have as yet admitted them, are exerted on the personal centres of energy of the various subjects, but the spontaneous faith of most of the subjects is that they embrace a wider sphere than this. Most religious men believe (or 'know,' if they be mystical) that not only they themselves, but the whole universe of beings to whom God is present, are secure in his parental hands. There is a sense, a dimension, they are sure, in which we are *all* saved, in spite of the gates of hell and all adverse terrestrial appearances. God's existence is the guarantee of an ideal order that shall be permanently preserved. This world may indeed, as science assures us, some day burn up or freeze; but if it is part of his order, the old ideals are sure to be brought elsewhere to fruition, so that where God is, tragedy is only provisional and partial, and shipwreck and dissolution are not the absolutely final things. Only when this farther step of faith concerning God is taken, and remote objective consequences are predicted, does religion, as it seems to me, get wholly free from the first immediate subjective experience, and bring a *real hypothesis* into play. A good hypothesis in science must have other properties than those of the phenomenon it is immediately invoked to explain, otherwise it is not prolific enough. God, meaning only what enters into the religious man's experience of union, falls short of being an hypothesis of this more useful order. He needs to enter into wider cosmic relations in order to justify the subject's absolute confidence and peace.

That the God with whom, starting from the hither side of our own extra-marginal self, we come at its remoter margin into commerce should be the absolute world-ruler, is of course a very considerable over-belief. Over-belief as it is, though, it is an article of almost every one's religion. Most of us pretend in some way to prop it upon our philosophy, but the philosophy itself is really propped upon this faith. What is this but to say that Religion, in her fullest exercise of function, is not a mere illumination of facts already elsewhere given, not a mere passion, like love, which views things in a rosier light. It is indeed that, as we have seen abundantly. But it is something more, namely, a postulator of new *facts* as well. The world interpreted religiously is not the materialisitc world over again, with an altered expression; it must have, over and above the altered expression, *a natural constitution* different at some point from that which a materialistic world would have. It must be such that different events can be expected in it, different conduct must be required.

This thoroughly 'pragmatic' view of religion has usually been taken as a matter of course by common men. They have interpolated divine miracles into the field of nature, they have built a heaven out beyond the grave. It is only transcendentalist metaphysicians who think that, without adding any concrete details to Nature, or subtracting any, but by simply calling it the expression of absolute spirit, you make it more divine just as it stands. I believe the pragmatic way of taking religion to be the deeper way. It gives it body as well as soul, it makes it claim, as everything real must claim, some characteristic realm of fact as its very own. What the more characteristically divine facts are, apart from the actual inflow of energy in the faith-state and the prayer-state, I know not. But the over-belief on which I am ready to make my personal venture is that they exist. The whole drift of my education goes to persuade me that the world of our present consciousness is only one out of many worlds of consciousness that exist, and that those other worlds must contain experiences which have a meaning for our life also; and that although in the main their experiences and those of this world keep discrete, yet the two become continuous at certain points, and higher energies filter in. By being faithful in my poor measure to this over-belief, I seem to myself to keep more sane and true. I *can,* of course, put myself into the sectarian scientist's attitude, and imagine vividly that the world of sensations and of scientific laws and objects may be all. But whenever I do this, I hear that inward monitor of which W. K. Clifford once wrote, whispering the word 'bosh!' Humbug is humbug, even though it bear the scientific name, and the total expression of human experience, as I view it objectively, invincibly urges me beyond the narrow 'scientific' bounds. Assuredly, the real world is of a different temperament,—more intricately built than physical science allows. So my objective and my subjective conscience both hold me to the over-belief which I express. Who knows whether the faithfulness of individuals here below to their own poor over-beliefs may not actually help God in turn to be more effectively faithful to his own greater tasks?

From THE VARIETIES OF RELIGIOUS EXPERIENCE by William James, pp. 7–15.

QUESTIONS

1. How does James demonstrate the objective truth of "the more"?
2. What are the real effects produced by God?
3. Why does James at first use the word "more" and then later on name it "God"?
4. Do you see any similarities between the way James explores human experience of the "more" and the way Rahner and Tillich describe human experience of the ultimate?

SUGGESTED READINGS

Allport, G. W. (1950). *The Individual and His Religion.* New York: Macmillan.

Bertocci, P. A. (1958). *Religion as Creative Insecurity.* New York: Association Press.

Clark, W. H. (1958). *The Psychology of Religion.* New York: Macmillan.

Sigmund Freud

6. The Future of an Illusion

The life of Sigmund Freud is well known. The founder of psychoanalysis in Vienna, his work on the interpretation of dreams and his later works on religion and civilization have greatly influenced twentieth century thought and society. Freud's view of religion is largely derived from his own personal experience of having lived as a Jew in Catholic Vienna. In this selection he refers to the questions he asked in the previous chapter: Where do religions get their inner force and to what do they owe their efficiency since they are not recognized by reason? In this chapter he indicates that the inner force and efficacy of religious doctrines lie in the powerful needs that all persons have for security and order. He concludes that, since illusions arise from wishes and religion also arises from strong wishes, religion is an illusion. It is true that, for some persons, religious ideas might be born of the need and wish for order and security. Because he transfers his psychoanalytic theory of personal neurosis to civilization as a whole, he sees the rejection of religion as a sign of maturity and psychological health. All of this has validity for some types of religious persons, but it needs to be seen in the light of the insights of Fowler and Kohlberg into faith and moral development respectively.

When civilization laid down the commandment that a man shall not kill the neighbour whom he hates or who is in his way or whose property he covets, this was clearly done in the interest of man's communal existence, which would not otherwise be practicable. For the murderer would draw down on himself the vengeance of the murdered man's kinsmen and the secret envy of others, who within themselves feel as much inclined as he does for such acts of violence. Thus he would not enjoy his revenge or his robbery for long, but would have every prospect of soon being killed himself. Even if he protected himself against his single foes by extraordinary strength and caution, he would be bound to succumb to a combination of weaker men. If a combination of this sort did not take place, the murdering would continue endlessly and the final outcome would be that men would exterminate one another. We should arrive at the same state of affairs between individuals as still persists in Corsica between families, though elsewhere only between nations. Insecurity of life, which is an equal danger for everyone, now unites men into a society which prohibits the individual from killing and reserves to itself the right to communal killing of anyone who violates the prohibition. Here, then, we have justice and punishment.

But we do not publish this rational explanation of the prohibition against murder. We assert that the prohibition has been issued by God. Thus we take it upon ourselves to guess His intentions, and we find that He, too, is unwilling for men to exterminate one another. In behaving in this way we are investing the cultural prohibition with a quite special solemnity, but at the same time we risk making its observance dependent on belief in God. If we retrace this step—if we no longer attribute to God what is our own will and if we content ourselves with giving the social reason—then, it is true, we have renounced the transfiguration of the cultural prohibition, but we have also avoided the risk to it. But we gain something else as well. Through some kind of diffusion or infection, the character of sanctity and inviolability—of belonging to another world, one might say—has spread from a few major prohibitions on to every other cultural regulation, law and ordinance. But on these the halo often looks far from becoming: not only do they invalidate one another by giving contrary decisions at different times and places, but apart from this they show every sign of human inadequacy. It is easy to recognize in them things that can only be the product of shortsighted apprehensiveness or an expression of selfishly narrow interests or a conclusion based on insufficient premisses. The criticism which we cannot fail to level at them also diminishes to an unwelcome extent our respect for other, more justifiable cultural demands. Since it is an awkward task to separate what God Himself has demanded from what can be traced to the authority of an all-powerful parliament or a high judiciary, it would be an undoubted advantage if we were to leave God out altogether and honestly admit the purely human origin of all the regulations and precepts of civilization. Along with their pretended sanctity, these commandments and laws would lose their rigidity and unchangeableness as well. People could understand that they are made, not so much to rule them as, on the contrary, to serve their interests; and they would adopt a more friendly attitude to them, and instead of aiming at their abolition, would aim only at their improvement. This would be an important advance along the road which leads to becoming reconciled to the burden of civilization.

But here our plea for ascribing purely rational reasons to the precepts of civilization—that is to say, for deriving them from social necessity—is interrupted by a sudden doubt. We have chosen as our example the origin of the prohibition against murder. But does our account of it tally with historical truth? We fear not; it appears to be nothing but a rationalistic construction. With the help of psycho-analysis, we have made a study of precisely this piece of the cultural history of mankind,[1] and, basing ourselves on it, we are bound to say that in reality things happened otherwise. Even in present-day man purely reasonable motives can effect little against passionate impulses. How much weaker then must they have been in the human animal of primaeval times! Perhaps his descendants would even now kill one another without inhibition, if it were not that among those murderous acts there was one—the killing of the primitive father—which evoked an irresistible emotional reaction with momentous consequences. From it arose the commandment: Thou shalt not kill. Under totemism this commandment was restricted to the father-substitute; but it was later extended to other people, though even to-day it is not universally obeyed.

But, as was shown by arguments which I need not repeat here, the primal father was the original image of God, the model on which later generations have shaped the figure of God. Hence the religious explanation is right. God actually played a part in the genesis of that prohibition; it was His influence, not any insight into social necessity, which created it. And the displacement of man's will on to God is fully justified. For men knew that they had disposed of their father by violence, and in their reaction to that impious deed, they determined to respect his

---

1. Cf. the fourth essay in *Totem and Taboo* (1912–13).

will thenceforward. Thus religious doctrine tells us the historical truth—though subject, it is true, to some modification and disguise—whereas our rational account disavows it.

We now observe that the store of religious ideas includes not only wish-fulfilments but important historical recollections. This concurrent influence of past and present must give religion a truly incomparable wealth of power. But perhaps with the help of an analogy yet another discovery may begin to dawn on us. Though it is not a good plan to transplant ideas far from the soil in which they grew up, yet here is a conformity which we cannot avoid pointing out. We know that a human child cannot successfully complete its development to the civilized stage without passing through a phase of neurosis sometimes of greater and sometimes of less distinctness. This is because so many instinctual demands which will later be unserviceable cannot be suppressed by the rational operation of the child's intellect but have to be tamed by acts of repression, behind which, as a rule, lies the motive of anxiety. Most of these infantile neuroses are overcome spontaneously in the course of growing up, and this is especially true of the obsessional neuroses of childhood. The remainder can be cleared up later still by psycho-analytic treatment. In just the same way, one might assume, humanity as a whole, in its development through the ages, fell into states analogous to the neuroses,[2] and for the same reasons—namely because in the times of its ignorance and intellectual weakness the instinctual renunciations indispensable for man's communal existence had only been achieved by it by means of purely affective forces. The precipitates of these processes resembling repression which took place in prehistoric times still remained attached to civilization for long periods. Religion would thus be the universal obsessional neurosis of humanity; like the obsessional neurosis of children, it arose out of the Oedipus complex, out of the relation to the father. If this view is right, it is to be supposed that a turning-away from religion is bound to occur with the fatal inevitability of a process of growth, and that we

---

2. Freud returned to this question at the end of his *Civilization and its Discontents* (1930a), p. 144, below in the last of the *New Introductory Lectures* (1933a) and in Chapter III of *Moses and Monotheism* (1939a).

find ourselves at this very juncture in the middle of that phase of development. Our behaviour should therefore be modelled on that of a sensible teacher who does not oppose an impending new development but seeks to ease its path and mitigate the violence of its irruption. Our analogy does not, to be sure, exhaust the essential nature of religion. If, on the one hand, religion brings with it obsessional restrictions, exactly as an individual obsessional neurosis does, on the other hand it comprises a system of wishful illusions together with a disavowal[3] of reality, such as we find in an isolated form nowhere else but in amentia,[4] in a state of blissful hallucinatory confusion. But these are only analogies, by the help of which we endeavour to understand a social phenomenon; the pathology of the individual does not supply us with a fully valid counterpart.

It has been repeatedly pointed out (by myself and in particular by Theodor Reik[5]) in how great detail the analogy between religion and obsessional neurosis can be followed out, and how many of the peculiarities and vicissitudes in the formation of religion can be understood in that light. And it tallies well with this that devout believers are safeguarded in a high degree against the risk of certain neurotic illnesses; their acceptance of the universal neurosis spares them the task of constructing a personal one.[6]

Our knowledge of the historical worth of certain religious doctrines increases our respect for them, but does not invalidate our proposal that they should cease to be put forward as the reasons for the precepts of civilization. On the contrary! Those historical residues have helped us to view religious teachings, as it were, as neurotic relics, and we may now argue that the time has probably come, as it does in an analytic treatment, for replacing the effects of repression by the results of the rational operation of the intellect. We may foresee, but hardly regret, that such a process of remoulding will not stop at renouncing the solemn transfiguration of cultural precepts, but that a general revision

---

3. See the paper on 'Fetishism' (1927*e*).

4. Meynert's amentia': a state of acute hallucinatory confusion. S.F. XXI—D

5. Cf. Freud, 'Obsessive Actions and Religious Practices' (1907*b*) and Reik (1927).

6. Freud had often made this point before: e.g. in a sentence added in 1919 to his study on Leonardo da Vinci (1910*c*), *Standard Ed.*, 11, 123.

of them will result in many of them being done away with. In this way our appointed task of reconciling men to civilization will to a great extent be achieved. We need not deplore the renunciation of historical truth when we put forward rational grounds for the precepts of civilization. The truths contained in religious doctrines are after all so distorted and systematically disguised that the mass of humanity cannot recognize them as truth. The case is similar to what happens when we tell a child that new-born babies are brought by the stork. Here, too, we are telling the truth in symbolic clothing, for we know what the large bird signifies. But the child does not know it. He hears only the distorted part of what we say, and feels that he has been deceived; and we know how often his distrust of the grown-ups and his refractoriness actually take their start from this impression. We have become convinced that it is better to avoid such symbolic disguisings of the truth in what we tell children and not to withhold from them a knowledge of the true state of affairs commensurate with their intellectual level.[7]

QUESTIONS

1. Do you agree with Freud when he gives the three reasons why the teachings of religion deserve to be believed? Is it forbidden to question the authenticity of religious teachings? Can you reconcile this idea with Tillich's statement that doubt is a necessary component of faith?
2. What are the two attempts that have been made to avoid the problem of the lack of credibility of religion?
3. What is an illusion, according to Freud? How does he demonstrate that religion is an illusion?
4. What according to Freud is the psychical origin of religious ideas?
5. What does Freud see as the effect of religion on civilization and on human beings?

---

7. Freud later drew a distinction between what he termed 'material' and 'historical' truth in several passages. See, in particular, Section G of Part II of Chapter III of *Moses and Monotheism* (1939a). Cf. also an Editor's footnote on the subject in Chapter XII (C) of *The Psychopathology of Everyday Life* (1901b), *Standard Ed.*, **6**, 256.

6. Why, according to Freud, is religion the universal obsessional neurosis of humanity?
7. Is Freud's view of religion true of some persons?

SUGGESTED READINGS

Batson, C. D. and Ventis, W. L. (1982). *The Religious Experience: A Social-Psychological Perspective.* New York: Oxford University Press.

Küng, H. (1979). *Freud and the Problem of God.* New Haven: Yale University Press.

Pruyser, P. W. (1968). *A Dynamic Psychology of Religion.* New York: Harper & Row.

Ricoeur, P. (1970). *Freud and Philosophy: An Essay on Interpretation.* New Haven: Yale University Press.

Carl G. Jung

7. Religion as the Counterbalance to Mass-Mindedness

Originally a follower of Freud, Jung broke with him early in the twentieth century on the issue of Freud's pansexualism. He went on to develop his own analytic psychology in Zurich which posits the drive toward self-realization as the basic human drive and includes the collective unconscious in addition to the personal unconscious of Freud. Because he was Protestant he was not subjected to the scorn accorded Jews. His view of religion denies that religion necessarily prevents growth and keeps persons in childish dependency. This is because he distinguishes between creed (expression of collective beliefs) and religion (a subjective relation to an extramundane reality). Jung goes on to show that the only way the individual can resist the pressures of the collective—whether they be the collective state or the collective Church or the crowd—is by relating to God who relativizes their power.

In order to free the fiction of the sovereign State—in other words, the whims of those who manipulate it—from every wholesome restriction, all sociopolitical movements tending in this direction invariably try to cut the ground from under the *religions*. For, in order to turn the individual into a function of the State, his dependence on anything beside the State must be taken from him. But religion means dependence on and submission to the irrational facts of experience. These do not refer directly to social and physical conditions; they concern far more the individual's psychic attitude.

But it is possible to have an attitude to the external conditions of life only when there is a point of reference outside them. The religions give, or claim to give, such a standpoint, thereby enabling the individual to exercise his judgement and his power of decision. They build up a reserve, as it were, against the obvious and inevitable force of circumstances to which everyone is exposed who lives only in the outer world and has no other ground under his feet except the pavement. If statistical reality is the only reality, then it is the sole authority. There is then only *one* condition, and since no contrary condition exists, judgment and decision are not only superfluous but impossible. Then the individual is bound to be a function of statistics and hence a function of the State or whatever the abstract principle of order may be called.

The religions, however, teach another authority opposed to that of the "world." The doctrine of the individual's dependence on God makes just as high a claim upon him as the world does. It may even happen that the absoluteness of this claim estranges him from the world in the same way he is estranged from himself when he succumbs to the collective mentality. He can forfeit his judgment and power of decision in the former case (for the sake of religious doctrine) quite as much as in the latter. This is the goal the religions openly aspire to unless they compromise with the State. When they do, I prefer to call them not "religions" but "creeds." A creed gives expression to a definite collective belief, whereas the word *religion* expresses a subjective relationship to certain metaphysical, extramundane factors. A creed is a confession of faith intended chiefly for the world at large and is thus an intramundane affair, while the meaning and purpose of religion lie in the relationship of the individual to God (Christianity, Judaism, Islam) or to the path of salvation and liberation (Buddhism). From this basic fact all ethics is derived, which without the individual's responsibility before God can be called nothing more than conventional morality.

Since they are compromises with mundane reality, the creeds have accordingly seen themselves obliged to undertake a progressive codification of their views, doctrines and customs and in so doing have externalized themselves to such an extent that the authentic religious element in them—the living relationship to and direct confrontation with their extramundane point of reference—has been thrust into the background. The denominational standpoint measures the worth and importance of the subjective religious relationship by the yardstick of traditional doctrine, and where this is not so frequent, as in Protestantism, one immediately hears talk of pietism, sectarianism, eccentricity, and so forth, as soon as anyone claims to be guided by God's will. A creed coincides with the established Church or, at any rate, forms a public institution whose members include not only true believers but vast numbers of people who can only be described as "indifferent" in matters of religion and who belong to it simply by force of habit. Here the difference between a creed and a religion becomes palpable.

To be the adherent of a creed, therefore, is not always a religious matter but more often a social one and, as such, it does nothing to give the individual any foundation. For support he has to depend exclusively on his relation to an authority which is not of this world. The criterion here is not lip service to a creed but the psychological fact that the life of the individual is not determined solely by the ego and its opinions or by social factors, but quite as much, if not more, by a transcendent authority. It is not ethical principles, however lofty, or creeds, however orthodox, that lay the foundations for the freedom and autonomy of the individual, but simply and solely the empirical awareness, the incontrovertible experience of an intensely personal, reciprocal relationship between man and extramundane authority which acts as a counterpoise to the "world" and its "reason."

This formulation will not please either the mass man or the collective believer. For the former the policy of the State is the supreme principle of thought and action. Indeed, this was the purpose for which he was enlightened, and accordingly the mass man grants the individual a right to exist only in so far as the individual is a function of the State. The believer, on the other hand, while admitting that the State has a moral and factual claim, confesses to the belief that not only man but the State that rules him is subject to the overlordship of "God" and that, in case of doubt, the supreme decision will be made by God and not by the State. Since I do not presume to any metaphysical judgments, I must leave it an open question whether the "world," i.e., the phenomenal world of man, and hence nature in general, is the "opposite" of God or not. I can only point to the fact that the psychological opposition between these two realms of experience is not only vouched for in the New Testament but is still exemplified very plainly today in the negative attitude of the dictator States to religion, and of the Church to atheism and materialism.

Just as man, as a social being, cannot in the long run exist without a tie to the community, so the individual will never find the real justification for his existence, and his own spiritual and moral autonomy, anywhere except in an extramundane principle capable of relativizing the overpowering influence of external factors. The individual who is not anchored in God can offer no resistance on his own resources to the physical and moral blandishments of the world. For this he needs the evidence of inner, transcendent experience which alone can protect him from the otherwise inevitable submersion in the mass. Merely intellectual or even moral insight into the stultification and moral irresponsibility of the mass man is a negative recognition only and amounts to not much more than a wavering on the road to the atomization of the individual. It lacks the driving force of religious conviction, since it is merely rational. The dictator State has one great advantage over bourgeois reason: along with the individual it swallows up his religious forces. The State has taken the place of God; that is why, seen from this angle, the socialist dictatorships are religions and State slavery is a form of worship. But the religious function cannot be dislocated and falsified in this way without giving rise to secret doubts, which are immediately repressed so as to avoid conflict with the prevailing trend towards mass-mindedness. The result, as always in such cases, is overcompensation in the form of *fanaticism,* which in its turn is used as a weapon for stamping out the least flicker of opposition. Free opinion is stifled and moral decision ruthlessly suppressed, on the plea that the end justifies the means, even the vilest. The policy of the State is exalted to a creed, the leader or party boss becomes a demigod beyond good and evil, and his votaries are honored as heroes, martyrs, apostles, missionaries. There is only *one* truth and beside it no other. It is sacrosanct and above criticism. Anyone who thinks differently is a heretic, who, as we know from history, is threatened with all manner of unpleasant things. Only the party boss, who holds the political power in his hands, can interpret the State doctrine authentically, and he does so just as suits him.

QUESTIONS

1. How does Jung distinguish between creed and religion?
2. Why does Jung claim that to be the adherent of a creed is sometimes a social matter more than a religious matter?
3. How does a personal relationship with an "extramundane authority" help the person avoid conformity or mass-mindedness?
4. Why do creeds tend to externalize themselves?

SUGGESTED READINGS

Jacobi, J. (1970). *C.G. Jung: Psychological Reflections: A New Anthology of His Writings 1905–1961.* Princeton: Princeton University Press.

Jung, C.G. (1938). *Psychology and Religion.* New Haven: Yale University Press.

Jung, C.G. (1957, 1958). *The Undiscovered Self.* Boston: Little Brown.

Ann Belford Ulanov

8. Psychology's Function for Religion

Ann Ulanov is professor of psychiatry and religion at Union Theological Seminary and is a Jungian psychotherapist. She develops more fully Jung's critique of an extrinsic form of religion and relates this to a loss of the symbolic sense. Like Rahner who speaks of the unthematic knowledge of God, both Ulanov and Jung stress that faith transcends the rational.

Analytical psychology, focusing on the symbolic aspects of our experience, can be a device to indicate the psychic equivalents of religious symbols. "Psychology," Jung writes, "is concerned with the act of seeing and not with the construction of new religious truths, when even the existing teachings have not yet been perceived and understood."[1] We do not yet perceive the meaning of religious symbols because " . . . far too many people are incapable of establishing a connection between the sacred figures and the psyche: . . . they cannot see to what extent the equivalent images are lying dormant in their own unconscious."[2] Analytical psychology can perform the useful function of reopening people's eyes to the psychic meaning of religious symbols. "To see," in this context, is to connect the religious symbol with its correspondent psychological experience of archetypal motifs and images.

To understand this view, we need to appreciate the context out of which it arose. Jung was a doctor who was concerned with what helped his patient. He observed that a recurrent theme in neurosis is the loss of a vital sense of life's meaning and that healing involves its rebirth. Jung has said of the patient that "he has to undergo an important change through the reintegration of hitherto split-off instinctivity, . . . the modern mind has forgotten those old truths that speak of the death of the old man and of the making of a new one, of spiritual rebirth and similar old-fashioned 'mystical absurdities.'"[3] Individual neuroses make explicit the problems embedded in modern culture and religious tradition. Modern man searches for his soul as well as for his split-off instinctuality. Piecing together Jung's various descriptions of modern man's spiritual malaise, it is fair to say, I think, that Jung has seen him as suffering from too much reliance on reasoning and on the outer forms of religion, as well as from a loss of inner connection to the reality that religious symbols represent. Analytical psychology tries to correct all this.

Too much reliance on external forms in all areas of life gradually brings about a leanness of experience. Jung thinks that the psychic life of Western man presents an uninviting picture intellectually, aesthetically, and morally. Too much of our energy has gone into building the external world around us. No doubt that world is impressive. "But," writes Jung, "it is so imposing only because we have spent upon the outside all that is imposing in our natures—and what we find when we look within must necessarily be as it is, shabby and insufficient."[4]

Christianity, too, emphasizes the outer forms of religion too much and therefore fails to perform its important educative task: "So long as religion is only faith and outward form, and the religious function is not experienced in our own souls, nothing of any importance has happened. It has yet to be understood that the *mysterium magnum* is not only an actuality but is first and foremost rooted in the human psyche."[5]

The Christ figure, for example, has come to represent an ideal that is external to our own persons. Because symbolically Christ carries our sin, that too becomes something outside ourselves. As a result, our souls are left empty: "if the supreme value (Christ) and the supreme negation (sin) are outside, then the soul is void; its highest and lowest are missing."[6] We hardly feel capable of evil or of good. Impotence and moral laxity go together. The individual "is more of a fragment than ever, since superficial understanding conveniently enables him, quite literally, 'to cast his sins upon Christ' and thus to evade his deepest responsibilities—which is contrary to the spirit of Christianity."[7] But without the soul's participation, "religious life congeals into externals and formalities."[8]

Too great a reliance on the outer forms of religion occurs when symbols turn into mere signs. Rituals and images no longer bring spiritual reality to the soul, and the soul's aspirations are no longer enacted in the ceremonies or expressed in the symbols of religion. The libido withdraws, finding no adequate channel in these symbols, and no new channel within the psyche. But the unused libido continues to make its demands, comes pouring back, and "the waters rise, and inundating catastrophes burst upon mankind."[9] The catastrophes may be individual breakdowns, collective breakdowns (such as mob violence), or a widespread indefinable sense of malaise and senseless drifting.

Psychology deals with this spiritual problem in its attention to our inner world. Jung goes so far as to say that modern spiritual impoverishment has led to the "discovery" of psychology.[10] Psychology compensates for the exaggerated insistence upon outer forms of religion by stressing the necessity for inner realizations. In contrast to the blind acceptance of religious traditions, psychology stresses the need for personal experience of the contents of those traditions. Jung, however, is not recommending that we correct excessive reliance on outer forms by an exclusive reliance on inner worlds. Jung attends to the psychic world because that is the one that is neglected and, because of the neglect, it is the one that causes trouble. In our time the psychic world is to be found deep down within us. But this has not always been the case: "the psyche is not always and everywhere to be found on the inner side. It is to be found on the *outside* in whole races or periods of history . . ."[11]

Modern man's excessive use of reason reinforces his reliance on the outer forms of religion. Jung uses "reason" to stand for the process of reasoning according to logic and the positivistic standards of truth and falsity that developed from the eighteenth-century Enlightenment. Gone is the "reason" of Plato that embraced the passion of deeply felt experience and articulated presentiments of unseen mysteries. Instead, reason has become a method of analysis subservient to the aim of establishing what is "certainly true" according to syllogistic logic, and pertaining even then only to its own statements and not to the disclosure of any larger facets of reality. Reasoning can also be used to establish the "truth" of empirical statements by measuring their correspondence to observable facts. Reason measures and orders facts and matches statements to facts, according to prescribed and severely limiting rules.

Jung contrasts "rational," which describes the logical and causal relationship of items to each other, with "nonrational," which describes that which makes its presence felt by its factitiousness or direct evidence, unmediated by any logic or sentiment. Modern man, in Jung's view, too often equates rational with "rationalistic" and develops an excessive reliance on the reasoning process as the sole source of knowledge and as the fundamental criterion in the solution of all problems. In contrast, modern man equates "nonrational" with blind, uncomprehending acceptance, as in the case of "faith." Faith is given, or not given, and is exclusive of reason. Jung may himself contribute to this misunderstanding of the nature of faith by narrowly interpreting it as an acceptance of something on the authority of tradition rather than on the authority of personal experience, or as a gift of grace in which truth is accepted but not really understood.

NOTES

1. Jung, *Psychology and Alchemy* (CW, XII, 1967), p. 13.
2. *Ibid.*
3. Jung, "Psychology and Religion," *Psychology and Religion: West and East* (CW, XI, 1958), p. 35.
4. Jung, *Modern Man in Search of a Soul,* trans. W.S. Dell and C.F. Baynes (New York: Harcourt, Brace & Co., 1933), p. 214.
5. Jung, *Psychology and Alchemy,* p. 12.
6. *Ibid.,* p. 8.
7. *Ibid.*
8. *Ibid.,* p. 10.

9. Jung, *The Integration of the Personality,* trans. Stanley Dell (New York: Farrar & Rinehart, 1939), p. 71.

10. See Jung, *Modern Man in Search of a Soul,* p. 201.

11. *Ibid.,* p. 200.

QUESTIONS

1. How and why do symbols turn into signs?
2. Is it always true that we should correct the contemporary reliance on outer forms by an exclusive reliance on inner worlds?
3. What are the various meanings of reason and rationality and faith that Ulanov discusses?

SUGGESTED READINGS

Jung, C. G. (1966). "On the Relation of Analytical Psychology to Poetry." In C. G. Jung, *The Spirit in Man, Art and Literature.* Princeton: Princeton University Press.

Ulanov, A. (1971). *The Feminine in Jungian Psychology and Christian Theology.* Evanston: Northwestern University Press.

Ulanov, A. and Ulanov, B. (1975). *Religion and the Unconscious.* Philadelphia: Westminster.

Whitmont, E. (1969). *The Symbolic Quest.* New York: C. G. Jung Foundation.

Part III

ADULT DEVELOPMENT— PSYCHOLOGICAL AND RELIGIOUS

Daniel J. Levinson

9. Conception of the Adult Life Course

Daniel Levinson is professor of psychology at Yale University. His book *The Seasons of a Man's Life* has been translated into many languages. His description of the mid-life transition points out that questions of the meaning of life and its purpose arise at this time. Thus a more mature intrinsic faith (as described in the excerpt by Fowler) could develop in mid-life.

Before describing the series of developmental periods in early and middle adulthood, I need to introduce briefly the concept of eras. Eras form the macrostructure of the life cycle; they provide a rough map of the underlying order in the life course as a whole, from birth through old age. The developmental periods provide a more detailed map of the life course; they form transitions between the eras and generate change within each era. Although the main emphasis here is on the periods, I want to emphasize that the conception of the life cycle and its component eras is an essential framework for the study of particular age levels.

The first era, *preadulthood,* extends from birth to about age twenty-two. This is the time of most rapid bio-psycho-social growth, during which the organism moves from helpless infancy through childhood, puberty, and adolescence to the beginnings of the capability for living as a relatively independent, responsible adult. It is the era that has been most fully studied, especially from a developmental perspective.

The second era, *early adulthood,* lasts from roughly age seventeen to forty-five (fig. 1). The Early Adult Transition period, from seventeen to twenty-two, is devoted both to the termination of preadulthood and to the initiation of early adulthood, and is thus part of both eras. Early adulthood is the adult era of

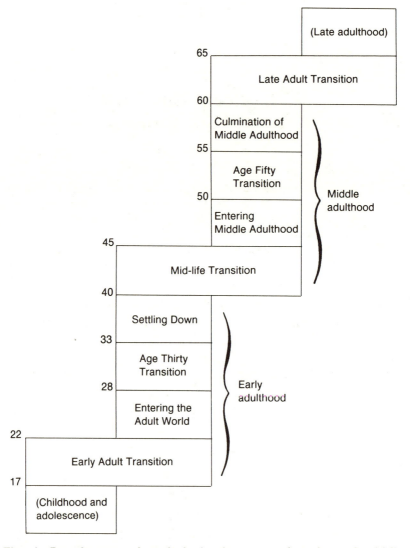

Fig. 1. Developmental periods in the eras of early and middle adulthood.

greatest energy and abundance, and of greatest contradiction and stress. Biologically, the twenties and thirties are the peak years of the life cycle. In social and psychological terms, early adulthood is the season for forming and pursuing youthful aspirations, establishing a niche in society, raising a family, and, as the era ends, reaching a more "senior" position in the adult world. This can be a time of rich satisfactions in terms of love, sexuality, family life, occupational advancement, creativity, and realization of major life goals. But there can be crushing stresses, too: undertaking the burdens of parenthood and, at the same time, of forming an occupation; incurring heavy financial obligations when one's earning power is still relatively low; having to make crucially important choices regarding marriage., family, work, and life-style before one has the maturity or life experience to choose wisely. Early adulthood is the era in which we are most buffeted by our own passions and ambitions from within, and by the demands of family, community, and society from without. Under reasonably favorable conditions, the rewards as well as the costs of living are enormous.

Before early adulthood ends, a new era, *middle adulthood,* gets underway. Middle adulthood starts at about forty. The Midlife Transition, from forty to forty-five, is a developmental period that links the two eras and is part of both. Middle adulthood lasts from about forty to sixty-five. During this era our biological capacities are below those of early adulthood, but normally still sufficient for an energetic, personally satisfying and socially valuable life. The great philosopher-historian Ortega y Gasset (1958) has suggested that people aged forty-five to sixty form the "dominant generation" in every society. In politics, industry, science, and the arts—in all social institutions— the main leadership comes from this generation. Unless our lives are hampered in some special way, most of us during our forties and fifties become "senior members" in our particular worlds, however grand or modest they may be. We are responsible not only for our own work, and perhaps the work of others, but also for the development of the current generation of young adults who will soon enter the dominant generation.

In middle adulthood, we can become more compassionate, more reflective and judicious, less tyrannized by inner conflicts and external demands, more genuinely loving of self and others. Without development of this kind, we face a middle adulthood of triviality, stagnation, and decline. The move into middle adulthood is thus a crucial phase of adult development.

Finally, the period of the Late Adult Transition, from about sixty to sixty-five, brings about both the completion of middle adulthood and the start of the next era, *late adulthood.*

We have found that each period begins and ends at a well-defined modal age, with a range of about two years above and below this average. The idea of age-linked periods in adult life goes against conventional wisdom. Nevertheless, these age findings have been so consistent in our initial research and in subsequent studies that I offer the concept of age-linked periods as a hypothesis that deserves extensive testing in various cultures.

Within early and middle adulthood, the life structure evolves through the following periods:

The Early Adult Transition (age seventeen to twenty-two) is a developmental bridge between adolescence and early adulthood. The boy-man is on the boundary between the childhood world, centered in the family, and the early-adult world with its new responsibilities, roles, and life choices. One task of the Early Adult Transition is to terminate the adolescent life structure. A young man has to modify existing relationships with important persons and institutions, and modify the self that formed during preadulthood. A second task is to make a preliminary step into the adult world: to explore its possibilities, to imagine oneself as a participant in it, to make and test some tentative choices before fully entering it.

The second period we call *Entering the Adult World* (age twenty-two to twenty-eight). Now a young man has to fashion a first life structure that provides a link between the valued self and the adult society. He must shift the center of gravity of his life from the family of origin to a new home base that is more truly his own. He has to explore the available possibilities, arrive at a crystallized (though by no means final) definition of himself as a novice adult, and live with his initial choices regarding occupation, love relationships, life-style, and values. He tries, often with limited success, to build a life structure in which he can pursue his youthful dreams and aspirations.

The Age Thirty Transition (twenty-eight to thirty-three) provides an opportunity to work on the flaws in the first adult life structure and to create a basis for the second structure that will be built in the following period. The exploratory quality of the twenties is ending and a man has a sense of greater urgency. He asks: What have I done with my life? What new directions shall I choose?

When a man of twenty-eight or twenty-nine examines his life, he usually finds a lot to be concerned about. Some men have a relatively stable, organized life, but one that excludes crucially important parts of the self. If a man recognizes this, he is likely to feel that his life is a sham, an unwanted compliance with the dictates of parents or society, and a betrayal of what he holds most dear. Or, a man with several strong interests pointing in different occupational directions may be plagued by dilemmas of choice. Or he may be married to a woman he cares for and yet have doubts about his love for her, about her feelings for him, about the durability of the relationship.

For other men, the life structure of the late twenties is relatively unstable, incomplete, and fragmented. Although a transient existence without heavy responsibilities may have suited him well for a while, the insecurity and rootlessness of this life begin to weigh on him. It is more distressing now if he does not have a wife or an occupation or a home base of his own. For most men—and for most women—the Age Thirty Transition is a time of moderate or severe crisis.

As the Age Thirty Transition ends, a man moves toward major new choices or recommits himself to past choices. A great deal hinges on the choices made at this time. If he chooses poorly and the new structure is badly flawed, his life in the next period will become increasingly painful.

The next period, *Settling Down and Becoming One's Own Man,* lasts from about thirty-three to forty. The major tasks now are to build a second adult life structure and, within this framework, to work toward the realization of one's youthful dreams. At the start of the period a man is on the bottom rung of a self-defined ladder and is entering a world in which he is a junior member. He tries to anchor his life more firmly, develop competence in a chosen craft, become a valued member of a valued world, and be affirmed in that world. The thirties is usually a time in which work, family, and other demands are at a peak.

From about thirty-six to forty there is a distinctive phase that we call Becoming One's Own Man. During this time there is a peaking of ambition: a man is eager to accomplish his goals, to become a senior member in his world, to speak more strongly with his own voice and have a greater measure of authority. The effort to become more manly in these respects may bring great rewards, but it also carries the burden of great responsibilities and pressures.

The imagery of the ladder is vivid in the late thirties. A man feels that by about forty he can no longer be a "promising young man"; it is time to achieve the goals he had set earlier and move into a senior position in the world he is just entering. By about forty-five he is already in a new world, though not necessarily the one he had sought earlier.

The next period, the *Mid-life Transition,* starts at about forty and ends around forty-five. It forms a bridge between early and middle adulthood and is part of both. For most men this is a time of great struggle within the self and with the external world. We have identified three major tasks of this period.

Perhaps the first task is to reappraise one's life, to examine critically the life structure developed during the Settling Down period. This arises in part from the person's heightened awareness of his mortality; recognizing that his remaining time is limited, he wants to use it wisely. At times he feels that the past is without value, that it provides no basis for building a future. As the life structure comes into question, a man is compelled to ask: What have I done with my life? What do I really get from and give to my wife, children, friends, work, community—and self? What is it I truly want? What are my talents and how am I using (or wasting) them? How satisfactory is my present life and how shall I change it to provide a better basis for the future? These are often painful questions to consider—but avoiding them is in the long run even more painful.

The second major task during the Mid-life Transition is to integrate the great polarities: Young/Old; Destruction/Creation; Masculine/Feminine; and Attachment/Separateness. Each of these pairs forms a polarity in the sense that the two terms represent opposing tendencies or conditions. Superficially, it would appear that a person has to be one or the other and cannot be both. In actuality, however, both sides of each polarity coexist within every person. At midlife a man feels young in many respects, but he also has a sense of being old. He feels older than the youth, but not ready to join the generation defined as "middle-aged." He feels alternately young, old, and "in-between." If he clings too strongly to the youthfulness of his twenties, he will find no place for himself in middle adulthood. If he gives up on the young, he will become dry and rigid. His developmental task is to become young-old in a new way.

The Destruction/Creation polarity presents similar problems of conflict and reintegration. The Mid-life Transition activates a man's concerns with death and destruction. He experiences more fully his own mortality and the actual or impending death of others. He becomes more aware of the many ways in which other persons, even his loved ones, have acted destructively toward him (with malice or, often, with good intentions). What is perhaps worse, he realizes that he has done irrevocably hurtful things to his parents, lovers, wife, children, friends, rivals (again, with what may have been the worst or the best of intentions). At the same time, he has a strong desire to become more creative and loving: to create products that have value for himself and others, to participate in collective enterprises that advance human welfare, to contribute more fully to the coming generations in society. In middle adulthood a man can come to know, more than ever before, that powerful forces of destructiveness and of creativity coexist in the human soul and can be integrated in many ways—though never entirely.

Likewise, every man at mid-life must come more fully to terms with the coexistence of masculine and feminine parts of the self. And finally he must integrate his powerful need for attachment to others with the antithetical but equally important need for separateness. The integration of these and other polarities is a great vision which many have sought to realize but no one can fully attain.

The third major task of the Mid-life Transition is to modify the life structure. In the midforties, as the Mid-life Transition ends, the life structure that emerges will differ in essential respects from the structure of the late thirties. Some men make decisive alterations in their lives as a result of divorce, remarriage, marked shifts in occupation, status, and life-style. Other men tend to "stay put" during the Mid-life Transition, remaining in the same marriage, job, and community. Even for these men, however, a closer look shows that important changes have occurred in the character and meaning of their relationships, work, and life goals.

At about age forty-five the Mid-life Transition is concluded. The main task of the next period, which we call *Entering Middle Adulthood,* is to build a new life structure for the launching of middle age. This structure comes into question in the *Age Fifty Transition,* which lasts from about fifty to fifty-five. For many men this transition is relatively smooth and undramatic. They use it to make minor changes in life structure, but continue on the same general path. For other men the Age Fifty Transition is a time of moderate or severe crisis. It is likely to be an especially difficult time for men who went rather smoothly through the Mid-life Transition, without examining themselves or making necessary changes in their lives. At fifty, the chickens may come home to roost.

In the *Culmination of Middle Adulthood,* the period from roughly fifty-five to sixty, the task is to build a second life structure within which one can work toward the major goals of this era. The *Late Adult Transition,* from sixty to sixty-five, brings about the completion of middle adulthood and the initiation of late adulthood.

Theoretically, the life structure forms a bridge between personality structure and social structure. It contains elements of both, but combines them in a new way and represents a separate level of analysis. I conceive of adult development as a sequence of periods in the evolution of the life structure. The idea of an orderly sequence of age-linked periods violates our usual assumptions about the adult life course. The first question it raises is: Does this sequence really exist, or is it just an artifact of a particular method or sample? When the initial positive evidence seems substantial enough to be taken seriously, a second question is raised: On what theoretical basis can this sequence be understood—what are its underlying sources or determinants? The sequence of life-structure periods cannot be derived simply from a maturationally given process of personality development in adulthood. It cannot be based on the socializing influence of any single social system such as occupation or family, nor on the interweaving of multiple systems (since the synchronization among them varies so widely). Nor does it follow directly from any known sequence of biological growth and decline. No one of the various human sciences holds the master key to the secrets of the life cycle, yet all are of major importance. The basic form of the adult life course, at this stage of human evolution, is conjointly determined by the maturational unfolding of the human psyche and the human body, and by the basic features of human society (as it has existed for, say, the last five or ten thousand years). In short, the order in the evolution of the individual life structure stems from multiple bio-psycho-social resources and not from any single source. It cannot be described or explained by an unidisciplinary approach.

I have described a series of periods in the *evolution* of the life structure. It might be argued that we should not speak of them as periods in the *development* of the life structure. The word "development" is often understood to mean personality development, and the notion of developmental stages has commonly been taken to mean the unfolding of a maturationally given sequence or the gradual realization of an inner, genetically determined potential. The life structure periods, on the other hand, represent the combined influence of development and of socialization, as these terms are generally used. Since the external world is an intrinsic component of the life structure and a major factor in its evolution, the conventional meaning of development is too narrow.

There are important reasons, nevertheless, for identifying these as developmental periods, for speaking of the development of the life structure, and for regarding this as a theory of *adult development*. The periods are developmental in the sense that they shape the fundamental sequence of the adult life course. Each period is characterized by tasks that are in principle developmental: they define essential work that people must engage in if they are to form a way of living that is appropriate to their current time of life and that provides a basis on which further development can occur in subsequent periods. Finally, the perspective of the evolution of the life structure enables us to conceive of adulthood not as a static state nor as a random flux of events but as a sequence that evolves in accord with its own developmental principles.

The periods constitute a source of order in the life cycle. This order exists at an underlying level. At the day-to-day level of concrete events and experiences, our lives are sometimes rapidly changing and fragmented, sometimes utterly stationary. At the level of personality, we change in different ways, according to different timetables. Yet, I believe that everyone lives through the same developmental periods in adulthood, just as in childhood, though people go through them in their own ways. Each individual life has its own unique character. Our theory of life structure does not specify a single, "normal" course that everyone must follow. Its function, instead, is to indicate the developmental tasks that everyone must work on in successive periods, and the infinitely varied forms that such work can take in different individuals living under different conditions. Rather than imposing a template for conformity, it increases our sense of human potentialities and of the variousness of individual lives.

The validity and usefulness of this particular theory remains to be determined. No doubt it will change considerably as a result of further research and experience. I present it as empirically grounded theory, not as demonstrated truth. The need for more and better theory is obvious. The sciences of human life are now suffering from a lack of a vital, species-encompassing conception of the adult life course that can help us understand and deal with problems that confront us today. The present volume has tried to make a contribution to the development of such a conception.

QUESTIONS

1. What are the tasks of each period of adulthood:
   a. Early adult transition?
   b. Entering the adult world?
   c. Age thirty transition?
   d. Settling down and becoming one's own person?
   e. Mid-life transition?
   f. Entering middle adulthood?
   g. Culmination of middle adulthood?
   h. Late adulthood transition?
2. Do you think that the questions faced in the mid-life transition are really religious questions?
3. Why does Levinson claim that he presents a theory of adult development? Is his theory descriptive or prescriptive?

SUGGESTED READINGS

Erikson, E. (1982). *The Life Cycle Completed: A Review.* New York: Norton.

Gould, R. (1978). *Transformations: Growth and Change in Adult Life.* New York: Simon & Schuster.

Jung, C. G. (1933). *Modern Man in Search of a Soul.* New York: Harcourt Brace.

Samuel Osherson

10. Reconstitution of Meaning in Adult Development

Dr. Osherson is currently professor of psychology in the Department of Psychiatry at Harvard Medical School. His book is a study of twenty men who at midlife left established professional careers for careers in one of the arts. Although he does not directly refer to faith, his description of the ability of the better adjusted men to range freely within inner experiences as well as their capacity to tolerate ambivalence (mystery?) may be an oblique reference to a faith or religious dimension.

WHAT IS THE VALUE OF A REFLECTIVE ATTITUDE TOWARD ONE'S EXPERIENCE?

The distinction between foreclosed and sculpted resolution of the crisis of midlife in our group hinges on the assumption that the awareness of and willingness to examine contradictory perceptions, desires, and impulses may be an important aspect of healthy development. In Chapter 4 a perspective was developed that examined the degree of awareness or acknowledgment of conflict at midlife, the degree of increased differentiation of self and others, and the quality of decision making. The underlying assumption is that individuals, to greater or lesser degree, develop means of reflecting on and integrating their experiences, so as to learn from them. The term "reflective attitude" refers to assessment and exploration of one's experience (e.g., how did I get where I am? where am I going? what is my role in having shaped events? what is it I want for the future?)

Certainly the question of what value is a reflective attitude remains an open one. Neugarten (1968) spoke of the greater "interiority" of much of her sample during midlife, and many observers of aging have spoken of a greater reassessment and sorting through one's life in the later years (Costa and Kastenbaum 1967). Vaillant touches on this theme of the value of self-examination when he comments of the Grant Study subjects during the interviews he had with them. "I learned to associate the capacity to talk of one's life frankly with mental health" (1978, p. 47).

This emphasis on a reflective or curious attitude toward one's own experience seems linked to the capacity to tolerate ambivalence. Zetzel, awhile ago (1949), wrote of the importance in personal growth of the ability to bear anxiety. This is an important point. The examination of contradictory perceptions, desires, and impulses requires a capacity to delay, to put off the premature closure of an ambiguous situation so as to better understand it. There are differences in the capacity to bear the pull of ambivalent urges, to delay foreclosing situations so as to arrive at a sculpted resolution. Since we can understand one of the major challenges of the life cycle as developing the ability to resolve experiences of loss and change, this capacity to tolerate ambivalence—the linchpin of sculpted resolutions—seems a crucial personality characteristic, and we need to delineate more carefully the precise ego functions involved in this vague capacity now called "tolerance of ambivalence" or "openness to experience." Further, there are probably developmental precursors in ego function that predispose individuals to precipitate or sculpted resolutions of grieving experiences. Certainly this is implied by Vaillant's (1978) work on the maturation of ego defenses and Loevinger and Wessler's (1970) attention to conformist vs. autonomous ego function (Hauser 1976).

A FINAL SPECULATION:
THE RECONSTITUTION OF MEANING
IN ADULT DEVELOPMENT

As a final point, note the importance of the capacity to bear ambivalence in allowing the reemergence of meaning through experiences of loss and transition. As pointed out in the discussion of Mr. Markowitz and Mr. Anderson in Chapter 4, the "reconstitution of meaning" refers to the commitment and investment in the present and future that come out of the person's free access to his individual past history. I have been impressed by the relation between the capacity to tolerate ambivalence and the person's ability to range freely within his inner experiences. This raises the question of a person's access to his past, and the role of this access in maintaining a sense of meaning and purpose in midlife. As we saw in our case discussions, more rigid (foreclosed) resolution at midlife can also be characterized as having let go of the personal past, which may also result in a more brittle, fragile sense of meaning and purpose at midlife. Again we are led to the importance of the capacity to tolerate the ambivalence of transition and change, both holding on and letting go of the past. This seems especially important in terms of a popular view of midlife and adult development that at times locates the roots of difficulty not in the personal past but solely in cultural, social, or historical factors. As Lasch (1979) has observed, some of the emphasis in the popular view of midlife—and the "second career" literature as well—is on what we might call letting go of the past; but unless one is cautioned to hold on adaptively as well, one wonders about the resulting fate of meaning and purpose.

QUESTIONS

1. Do you agree with Osherson that mid-life is a time of greater reflection on life and of the integration of one's experience?
2. Could the "tolerance of ambivalence" described by Osherson help one grow in faith?

SUGGESTED READINGS

Allman, L. R. and Jaffe, D. T. (eds.) (1977). *Readings in Adult Psychology: Contemporary Perspectives.* New York: Harper & Row.

Brewi, J. and Brennan A. (1982). *Mid-Life: Psychological and Spiritual Perspectives.* New York: Crossroad.

Giele, J. G. (ed.) (1982). *Women in the Middle Years: Current Knowledge and Directions for Research and Policy.* New York: Wiley.

Kegan, R. (1982). *The Evolving Self: Problem and Process in Human Development.* Cambridge: Harvard University Press.

Maris, P. (1975). *Loss and Change.* Garden City: Doubleday.

D. W. Winnicott

11. The Search for the Self

Dr. Winnicott was a psychiatrist in Paddington Green Children's Hospital in London until his retirement. He is well known for his theory of the development of the self and self-concept. This selection describes the search for the self on the part of one young woman. Not only does it show that this search goes on in a non-rational way but also that it needs to be reflected upon and trustworthy reflectors can help.

In this chapter I am concerned with the search for the self and the restatement of the fact that certain conditions are necessary if success is to be achieved in this search. These conditions are associated with what is usually called creativity. It is in playing and only in playing that the individual child or adult is able to be creative and to use the whole personality, and it is only in being creative that the individual discovers the self.

(Bound up with this is the fact that only in playing is communication possible; except direct communication, which belongs to psychopathology or to an extreme of immaturity.)

It is a frequent experience in clinical work to meet with persons who want help and who are searching for the self and who are trying to find themselves in the products of their creative experiences. But to help these patients we must know about creativity itself. It is as if we are looking at a baby in the early stages and jumping forward to the child who takes faeces or some substance with the texture of faeces and tries to make something out of the substance. This kind of creativity is valid and well understood, but a separate study is needed of creativity as a feature of life and total living. I am suggesting that the search for the self in terms of what can be done with waste products is a search that is doomed to be never-ending and essentially unsuccessful.

In a search for the self the person concerned may have produced something valuable in terms of art, but a successful artist may be universally acclaimed and yet have failed to find the self that he or she is looking for. The self is not really to be found in what is made out of products of body or mind, however valuable these constructs may be in terms of beauty, skill, and impact. If the artist (in whatever medium) is searching for the self, then it can be said that in all probability there is already some failure for that artist in the field of general creative living. The finished creation never heals the underlying lack of sense of self.

Before developing this idea further I must state a second theme, one that is related to the first but needs separate treatment. This second theme is that the person we are trying to help might expect to feel cured when we explain. The person might say: 'I see what you mean; I am myself when I feel creative and when I make a creative gesture, and now the search is ended.' In practice this does not seem to be a description of what happens. In this kind of work we know that even the right explanation is ineffectual. The person we are trying to help needs a new experience in a specialized setting. The experience is one of a non-purposive state, as one might say a sort of ticking over of the unintegrated personality. I referred to this as formlessness in the case description (Chapter 2).

Account has to be taken of the reliability or unreliability of the setting in which the individual is operating. We are brought up against a need for a differentiation between purposive activity and the alternative of non-purposive being. This relates to Balint's (1968) formulation of benign and malignant regression (see also Khan, 1969).

I am trying to refer to the essentials that make relaxation possible. In terms of free association this means that the patient on the couch or the child patient among the toys on the floor must be allowed to communicate a succession of ideas, thoughts, impulses, sensations that are not linked except in some way that is neurological or physiological and perhaps beyond detection. That is to say: it is where there is purpose or where there is anxiety or where there is lack of trust based on the need for defence that the analyst will be able to recognize and to point out the connection (or several connections) between the various components of free association material.

In the relaxation that belongs to trust and to acceptance of the professional reliability of the therapeutic setting (be it analytic, psychotherapeutic, social work, architectural, etc.), there is room for the idea of unrelated thought sequences which the analyst will do well to accept as such, not assuming the existence of a significant thread (cf. Milner, 1957, especially the appendix, pp. 148–163).

The contrast between these two related conditions can perhaps be illustrated if one thinks of a patient who is able to rest after work but *not able to achieve the resting state out of which a creative reaching-out can take place.* According to this theory, free association that reveals a coherent theme is already affected by anxiety, and the cohesion of ideas is a defence organization. Perhaps it is to be accepted that there are patients who at times need the therapist to note the nonsense that belongs to the mental state of the individual at rest without the need even for the patient to communicate this nonsense, that is to say, without the need for the patient to organize nonsense. Organized nonsense is already a defence, just as organized chaos is a denial of chaos. The therapist who cannot take this communication becomes engaged in a futile attempt to find some organization in the nonsense, as a result of which the patient leaves the nonsense area because of hopelessness about communicating nonsense. An opportunity for rest has been missed because of the therapist's need to find sense where nonsense is. The patient has been unable to rest because of a failure of the environmental provision, which undid the sense of trust. The therapist has, without knowing it, abandoned the professional role, and has done so by bending over backwards to be a clever analyst, and to see order in chaos.

It may be that these matters are reflected in the two kinds of sleep, sometimes denoted REM and NREM (rapid eye movements and no rapid eye movements).

In developing what I have to say I shall need the sequence:

(*a*) relaxation in conditions of trust based on experience;
(*b*) creative, physical, and mental activity manifested in play;
(*c*) the summation of these experiences forming the basis for a sense of self.

Summation or reverberation depends on there being a certain quantity of reflecting back to the individual on the part of the trusted therapist (or friend) who has taken the (indirect) communication. In these highly specialized conditions the individual can come together and exist as a unit, not as a defence against anxiety but as an expression of I AM, I am alive, I am myself (Winnicott, 1962). From this position everything is creative.

CASE IN ILLUSTRATION

I wish to use material from the record of a woman who is having treatment with me and who, as it happens, comes once a week. She had had a long treatment on a five-times-a-week basis for six years before coming to me, but found she needed a session of indefinite length, and this I could manage only once a week. We soon settled down to a session of three hours, later reduced to two hours.

If I can give a correct description of a session the reader will notice that over long periods I withhold interpretations, and often make no sound at all. This strict discipline has paid dividends. I have taken notes, because this helps me in a case seen only once a week, and I found that note-taking did not disrupt the work in this case. Also I often relieve my mind by writing down interpretations that I actually withhold. My reward for withholding interpretations comes when the patient makes the interpretation herself, perhaps an hour or two later.

My description amounts to a plea to every therapist to allow for the patient's capacity to play, that is, to be creative in the analytic work. The patient's creativity can be only too easily stolen by a therapist who knows too much. It does not really matter, of course, how much the therapist knows provided he can hide this knowledge, or refrain from advertising what he knows.

Let me try to convey the feeling of what it is like to do work with this patient. But I must ask the reader to exert patience, much as I needed to be patient when engaged in this work.

Now a change of attitude, indicating the beginning of an acceptance of my existence.

'I keep stopping you from talking!'

I said: 'You want me to talk now, but you fear I might say something good.'

She said: 'It was in my mind: "Don't make me wish to BE!"'[1] That's a line of a poem by Gerard Manley Hopkins.'

We now talked about poetry, how she makes a great deal of use of poetry that she knows by heart, and how she has lived from poem to poem (like cigarette to cigarette in chain-smoking), but without the poem's meaning being understood or felt as she now understands and feels this poem. (Her quotations are always apt, and usually she is unaware of the meaning.) I referred here to God as I AM, a useful concept when the individual cannot bear to BE.

She said: 'People use God like an analyst—someone to be there while you're playing.'

I said: 'For whom you matter'—and she said: 'I couldn't say that one, because I couldn't be sure.'

I said: 'Did it spoil things when I said this?' (I feared I had mucked up a very good session.)

But she said: 'No! It's different if you say it, because if I matter to you . . . I want to do things to please you . . . you see this is the hell of having had a religious upbringing. Blast the good girls!'

As a self-observation she said: 'That implies I have a wish *not* to get well.'

_____

1. Actual quotation, from the poem 'Carrion Comfort', would be:
'Not, I'll not . . .
. . . most weary, cry *I can no more.* I can;
Can something, hope, wish day come, not choose not to be.'

Here was an example of an interpretation made by the patient that could have been stolen from her if I had made it earlier in the session.

I pointed out that the present-day version of *good* for her is to be *well*—i.e., finish analysis, etc.

Now at last I could bring in the dream—that the girl's paintings were no better—*this negative is now positive.* The statement that the patient is not well is true; not well means not good; that she seemed better was false as her life had been false trying to be good in the sense of fitting into the family moral code.

She said: 'Yes, I'm using my eyes, ears, hands as instruments; I never 100 per cent AM. If I let my hands wander I might find a me—get into touch with a me . . . but I couldn't. I would need to wander for hours. I couldn't let myself go on.'

We discussed the way in which talking *to oneself* does not reflect back, unless this is a carry-over of such talking having been reflected back by *someone not oneself.*

She said: 'I've been trying to show you *me being alone* [the first two hours of the session]: that's the way I go on when alone, though without words at all, as I don't let myself start talking to myself' (that would be madness).

She went on to talk of her use of a lot of mirrors in her room, involving for the self a search by the mirrors for some person to reflect back. (She had been showing me, though I was there, that no person reflects back.) So now I said: *'It was yourself that was searching.'*[2]

I am doubtful about this interpretation, because it smacks of reassurance though not intended that way. I meant that she exists in the searching rather than in finding or being found.

She said: 'I'd like to stop searching and just BE. Yes, looking-for is evidence that there is a self.'

---

2. Sometimes she quotes: 'It is Margaret you mourn for' (from Hopkins's poem 'Spring and Fall').

Now at last I could refer back to the incident of being the plane, and then it crashed. As a plane she could BE, but then suicide. She accepted this easily and added: 'But I'd rather be and crash than not ever BE.'

Somewhere soon after this she was able to go away. The work of the session had been done. It will be observed that in a fifty-minute session no effective work could possibly have been done. We had had three hours to waste and to use.

If I could give the next session, it would be found that we took two hours to reach again to the position we had reached this day (which she had forgotten). Then the patient used an expression that has value in the summing up of what I am trying to convey. She had asked a question, and I said that the answer to the question could take us to a long and interesting discussion, but it was the *question* that interested me. I said: 'You had the idea to ask that question.'

After this she said the very words that I need in order to express my meaning. She said, slowly, with deep feeling: 'Yes, I see, one could postulate the existence of a ME from the question, as from the searching.'

She had now made the essential interpretation in that the question arose out of what can only be called her creativity, creativity that was a coming together after relaxation, which is the opposite of integration.

COMMENT

The searching can come only from desultory formless functioning, or perhaps from rudimentary playing, as if in a neutral zone. It is only here, in this unintegrated state of the personality, that that which we describe as creative can appear. This if reflected back, *but only if reflected back,* becomes part of the organized individual personality, and eventually this in summation makes the individual to be, to be found; and eventually enables himself or herself to postulate the existence of the self.

This gives us our indication for therapeutic procedure—to afford opportunity for formless experience, and for creative impulses, motor and sensory, which are the stuff of playing. And on the basis of playing is built the whole of man's experiential existence. No longer are we either introvert or extrovert. We experience life in the area of transitional phenomena, in the exciting interweave of subjectivity and objective observation, and in an area that is intermediate between the inner reality of the individual and the shared reality of the world that is external to individuals.

QUESTIONS

1. What, according to Winnicott, is the relationship between trusting and relaxation and between creative play and the sense of self?
2. Is there any connection between Winnicott's reference to God as "I am" and his very next question, "For whom do you matter?"
3. In the last selection in this book, Kinerk refers to spirituality as the growth of the authentic self. Is Winnicott looking at the same phenomenon?

SUGGESTED READINGS

Fairbairn, W. R. (1962). *An Object Relations Theory of Personality*. New York: Basic.

Fingarette, H. (1977). *The Self in Transformation: Psychoanalysis, Philosophy and the Life of the Spirit*. New York: Harper & Row.

Kohut, H. (1977). *The Restoration of the Self*. New York: International Universities Press.

Lee, B. and Noam, G. (eds) (1981). *The Self—Psychology, Psychoanalysis and Anthropology*. New York: Plenum.

12. Conclusions
from **Birth of the Living God**

A clinical professor of psychiatry at Tufts Medical School in Boston, Dr. Ana-Maria Rizzuto is also on the faculty of the Psychoanalytic Institute of New England. A native of Argentina, she received her medical degree from the University of Cordoba. In this selection she indicates that she uses Winnicott's notion of transitional object. It is important to note that her reference to God as "an illusory transitional object" is a description of human experience and does not refer to the essence of God as described by philosophers and theologians. Her description of the development of the God image is valuable because she shows how important early parental relationships are in its formation and how at adolescence the child is able to grasp a concept of God beyond the limits of the personal representation. Finally, she shows how changes in self-representation usually entail changes in the God representation.

This is not a book on religion. It is a book on object relations. Indeed, a book about one object relation: that of man with that special object he calls God. God, psychologically speaking, is an illusory transitional object. In chapter 5 I mentioned that the transitional space (Winnicott, 1953) is the locus where God comes to existence.

Winnicott describes the areas of human life encompassed within the transitional domain:

> Transitional objects and transitional phenomena belong to the realm of illusion which is at the basis of initiation of experience. This early stage in development is made possible by the mother's special capacity for making adaptation to the needs of her infant, thus allowing the infant the illusion that what the infant creates really exists.
> This intermediate area of experience, unchallenged in respect of its belonging to inner or external (shared) reality,

constitutes the greater part of the infant's experience, and throughout life is retained in the intense experiencing that belongs to the arts and to religion and to imaginative living, and to creative scientific work (p. 14).

A positive value of illusion can therefore be stated.[1]

The central theses of this book are as follows:

1. God is a special type of object representation created by the child in that psychic space where transitional objects—whether toys, blankets, or mental representations—are provided with their powerfully real illusory lives (see fig. 1).

2. God, like all transitional objects (Winnicott, 1953), is located *simultaneously* "outside, inside and at the border" (p. 2). God "is not a hallucination" and "in health . . . does not 'go inside' nor does the feeling about it necessarily undergo repression. It is not forgotten and it is not mourned" (p. 5).

3. God is a special transitional object because unlike teddy bears, dolls, or blankets made out of plushy fabrics, he is created from representational materials whose sources are the representations of primary objects.

4. God is also a special transitional object because he does not follow the usual course of other transitional objects. Generally, the transitional object is "gradually allowed to be decathected, so that in the course of years it becomes not so much forgotten as relegated to limbo. . . . It loses meaning . . . because the transitional phenomena have become diffused . . . over the whole cultural field" (p. 5).

God, on the other hand, is increasingly cathected during the pregenital years and reaches his most appealing moment at the peak of oedipal excitement. God, according to Freud (see chap. 2), is to become the object of sublimated libido after the resolution of the oedipal crisis. But God's representational characteristics depend heavily on the type of resolution and the compromises the child has arranged with his oedipal objects.

Instead of losing meaning, God's meaning becomes heightened by the oedipal experience and all other pregenital events that have contributed to the reelaboration of his representational characteristics. Sometimes, however, he may seem to lose meaning, paradoxically, on account of being rejected, ignored,

Erikson's Terms

	Trust versus mistrust		Autonomy vs. shame and doubt	Initiative vs. guilt	
Stage of development (Freud)	Oral		Anal	Phallic	Oedipal
Prevailing experience for sense of self	Bodily sensations	I am me if mirrored	I am me with you (self-object)	I am wonderful. I can do great things.	I am attractive. You should love me first.
Type of object	← Ministrations, play, and mirroring		You are with me.	→ You are great, powerful. You can do anything.	You are lovable and exciting.
Type of God	← Experienced through the senses	Mirroring	Self-object	→ Idealized parental imago	Aggrandized parental imago
God representation which allows belief	← I am held, fed, nurtured. I see me on your face. (You make me in your image.)		I feel you are with me.	→ You are wonderful, the Almighty.	You are love. You love me.
God representation which leads to unbelief	← I am not held, I am hungry, I feel uncared for. I cannot see me. (You are not making me.)		I cannot feel you are there for me. I despair.	→ I thought you were omnipotent. You failed.	You do not love me. I do not count.
Example of religious experience	← Schizophrenic patient while masturbating: "My penis is my God."	"I am me in the mirror."	"God is in me and I in him."	→ "God is a miracle worker."	"God is great."

Fig. 1. Formation of the God representation in the transitional space

suppressed, or found temporarily unnecessary. Nonetheless, as is true of all other objects, God cannot be fully repressed. As a transitional object representation he is always potentially available for further acceptance or further rejection. It is this characteristic of being always there for love, cold disdain, mistreatment, fear, hatred, or any other human emotion that lends the object God its psychic usefulness. This psychic usefulness is at the service of protecting the minimum amount of relatedness to primary objects and a baseline of self-respect and obscure hope through common (or, at times, paradoxical or even psychotic) maneuvers. Often, when the human objects of real life acquire profound psychic meaning, God, like a forlorn teddy bear, is left in a corner of the attic, to all appearances forgotten. A death, great pain or intense joy[2] may bring him back for an occasional hug or for further mistreatment and rejection,[3] and then he is forgotten again.

In summary, then, throughout life God remains a transitional object at the service of gaining leverage with oneself, with others, and with life itself. This is so, not because God is God, but because, like the teddy bear, he has obtained a good half of his stuffing from the primary objects the child has "found" in his life. The other half of God's stuffing comes from the child's capacity to "create" a God according to his needs.

5. The psychic process of creating and finding God—this personalized representational transitional object—never ceases in the course of human life. It is a developmental process that covers the entire life cycle from birth to death. Winnicott says:

> The task of reality-acceptance is never completed. . . . No human being is free from the strain of relating inner and outer reality, and . . . relief from this strain is provided by an intermediate area of experience which is not challenged (arts, religion, etc.) (1953, p. 13).[4]

The God representation, as an aspect of this intermediary area in the course of the life cycle, follows epigenetic and developmental laws that can be studied systematically. The process of reelaborating the God representation also follows the dynamic laws of psychic defense, adaptation, and synthesis, as well as the need for meaningful relations with oneself, others, and the world at large—relations that color all other psychic processes.

6. God is not the only mental representation used by children and adults, alike as a transitional object. Many others are available. In our culture, however, God has a special place, because he is the cultural creation offered to men for their private and public (in official religions) reelaboration of those primary ties that accompany each of us "unto the grave" (Mahler, 1972).

7. The child's and the adult's sense of self is affected by the representational traits of the individual's private God. Consciously, preconsciously, or unconsciously, God, our own creation, like a piece of art, a painting, a melody, or the imaginary woman of Louis Couperous, will, in reflecting what we have done, affect our sense of ourselves. Like the patients I describe, we may find our creation "great," hidden behind an illusory but real "door," a stubborn "enemy," or a frightening "enigma." Obviously, there are as many shapes for this creature of ours as there are human beings. And there are as many ways of dealing with it as there are vicissitudes in the course of human life. Sometimes we go about our business for long stretches of time without calling on God either to keep us company or to "interfere" with our lives. Obviously, I am talking about that private psychic space in which we, the complex and at times bewildered subject, juggle multiple experiences with people of the past, the present, or the future, trying to keep the pleasure and the mastery of the art, while still remaining who we try to be. Like jugglers we sometimes call in our God and toss him around; sometimes we discard him because he is either too colorless for our needs or too hot for us to handle. Some of us never get him out of the magician's box where we placed him in childhood; others never stop throwing him around, either for pleasure or because they cannot stop touching him in spite of their inability to keep him in their hands for long (perhaps he is too slippery, or too dangerous); others are content simply to know that he is there, if needed; others find him so fascinating that they want nothing else. Whatever the case, once created, our God, dormant or

active, remains a potentially available representation for the continuous process of psychic integration. As a transitional object representation God can be used for religion because he is beyond magic,[5] as described by Winnicott:

> The transitional object is never under magical control like the internal object, nor is it outside control as the real mother is (p. 10).

In what follows I will discuss the developmental processes that permit, condition, and influence the creating of a God representation in childhood and its transformations throughout the life cycle. I will reflect also on the implications of this study for psychoanalytic theory and technique, and specifically about problems of countertransference. I will also describe the diagnostic use of these concepts in evaluating object relations, particularly in moments of crisis. Then, leaving the psychoanalytic realm, I shall offer some suggestions for parents, educators, and pastors. Finally, I shall present a brief reflection about the implications of my study for the scientific study of religion.

It is a central thesis of this book that no child in the Western world brought up in ordinary circumstances completes the oedipal cycle without forming at least a rudimentary God representation, which he may use for belief or not. The rest of developmental life may leave that representation untouched as the individual continues to revise parent and self-representations during the life cycle. If the God representation is not revised to keep pace with changes in self-representation, it soon becomes asynchronous and is experienced as ridiculous or irrelevant or, on the contrary, threatening or dangerous.

Each epigenetic phenomenon offers a new opportunity to revise the representation or leave it unchanged. Each new life crisis or landmark—illness, death, promotions, falling in love, birth of children, catastrophes, wars, and so on—provides similar opportunities. Finally, the simple events of everyday life may bring back to memory some once highly relevant or feared aspect of the God representation. A scent, a tune, a look, a gift, a word, a threat, may awaken the forgotten God representation.

Narratives of religious revivals provide plentiful examples of the instrumentality of a trivial event in bringing about intense feelings for a suddenly manifest God.

Developmentally, after the oedipal crisis there are two new moments relevant to the history of the God representation. One is puberty, when the capacity for abstract logicomathematical conceptualization appears. For the first time the child is able to grasp a concept of God beyond the limits of his God representation. This concept follows principles of philosophical inference, and though helpful for intellectual integration of belief, it lends itself not to belief but to theorizing and to the construction of philosophical or theological arguments. Properly integrated, it adds a dimension of whatever God representation the child has at the time. Emotionally, however, it adds nothing. As mentioned in chapter 2, it was in acknowledging this component of the representation that Freud left behind his own theory of a God based on parental-object representation.

Finally, the last part of adolescence confronts the growing individual with the need to integrate a more cohesive and unified self-representation which will permit him to make major decisions about life, marriage, and profession. That developmental crisis, with its intense self-searching and reshuffling of self-images in the context of trying to find a niche in the world for oneself, brings about new encounters with both old and new God representations. They may or may not lend themselves to belief.

For the rest of the life cycle the individual will again find himself in need of critical changes in self-representation to adapt to the inexorable advance of the life cycle as well as to new encounters with peers and parental representatives. God—as a representation—may or may not be called in to undergo his share in the changes. Finally, when death arrives, the question of the existence of God returns. At that point the God representation, which may vary from a long-neglected pre-oedipal figure to a well-known life companion—or to anything in between—will return to the dying person's memory, either to obtain the grace of belief or to be thrown out for the last time.

THE CONDITIONS FOR BELIEF

In his early psychoanalytic thinking Freud devoted his attention to the psychological conditions for thought processes. The judgment of reality, belief, and doubt are some of the notions he considered.

In the "Project for a Scientific Psychology" (1895) Freud says:

> The aim and end of all thought-processes is thus to bring about a *state of identity,* the conveying of a cathexis Qἠ, emanating from outside, into a neurone cathected from the ego[18] (p. 332).

He continues:

> If after the conclusion of the act of thought the indication of reality reaches the perception, then a *judgment of reality, belief,* has been achieved and the aim of the whole activity attained (p. 333).

This conception is an antecedent to the notion of perceptual identity which Freud developed in chapter 7 of *The Interpretation of Dreams* (1900, pp. 566–67, 602–3).

In the Draft No. 5 enclosed in Letter 64 (1897) to Fliess, Freud considers belief and doubt:

> Belief (and doubt) is a phenomenon that belongs wholly to the system of the ego (the Cs) and has no counterpart in the Ucs (p. 255).

He reaffirms this notion in a more elaborate description in his book *The Unconscious* (1915):

> There are in this system no negation, no doubt, no degrees of certainty: all this is only introduced by the work of the censorship between the Ucs and the Pcs. . . . In the Ucs there are only contents, cathected with greater or lesser strength (p. 186).

For the purposes of this study there are in the unconscious and the preconscious multiple memories of objects, of oneself, and of the transitional representational object, called, at a specific moment in development, God.

I agree with Freud: belief and doubt are conscious processes in which the individual finds an identity of "perception," understood in the wider sense of identity of subjective experience.[19]

I propose that *belief in God* or its absence depends upon whether or not a *conscious "identity of experience"* can be established between the God representation of a given developmental moment and the object and self-representation needed to maintain a sense of self which provides at least a minimum of relatedness and hope.

Belief in God and absence of belief are no indicators of any type of pathology. They are indicators only of the particular private balance each individual has achieved at a given moment in his relations with primary objects and all other relevant people, whether or not he uses the mediatory services of a transitional object for this process. This transitional object appears in early childhood and must undergo transformations in the course of life if it is to keep up with the transformations of the life cycle. If it loses its meaning, however, it can be set aside without being forgotten. And it can recover its meaning at the time of a life crisis, either by a progressive new elaboration of the God representation or by regressive return to an earlier representation which once more lends itself to belief. It may also become so incompatible with psychic balance that it cannot function naturally as a transitional object; along with aspects of oneself that have become consciously unbearable, it may have to be repressed. If the God representation has been abandoned as a meaningful transitional object, it will retain the characteristics it had when it was returned to the toy box in the transitional space. Then, if the individual suddenly feels a need for it in some regressive moment—a death, a rite of passage—it may be used temporarily and then quietly returned to the box, too anachronistic to meet the daily needs of the evolved and transformed self-representation.

On the other hand, if the God representation has undergone changes so as to remain more or less satisfactory as a transitional object, a sudden change in self-representation may strain the individual's ability to reshape his God. Massive doubts, profound preoccupation and rumination, religious exercises, consultations with pastors and religious persons and texts, may produce an impressive display of religious agitation in the person's effort to wrestle with God's discordant representation. Adolescence, with its profound bodily changes, its enlarged intellectual scope, and the urgency of its need for emotional and sexual intimacy, tests the elasticity of the God representation to the extreme.

It is during these strenuous years that most people who cease to believe drop their God. Many who keep him may be loaded with an anachronistic and restrictive God, an indicator of unresolved developmental issues. Others manage to transform their God representation according to their needs, thus keeping belief compatible with development. Each new crisis of growth during the life cycle creates similar possibilities: belief ceases because it loses meaning or it remains developmentally anachronistic or it is revised. The final crisis is death, when the individual still has an opportunity to abandon his God representation, resort to it regressively or integrate it with the imminent cessation of life and its specific threat to the sense of self.

Thus God, the transitional object representation, born "between urine and feces," together with his lesser siblings, monsters, witches, ogres, imaginary companions, and others, lives his own life cycle under the alternating moods of his creative owner: sometimes he remains a lifelong companion; sometimes he takes the beating that the irritations of life provoke in his owner and is rudely told that he does not exist or that it would be a relief if he did not. Most of the time he shares the unpredictable life of the small child's teddy bear: when needed he is hurriedly pulled from his resting place, hugged or mistreated, and when the storm is over, neglectfully left wherever he may happen to be. There he remains, quietly offering the silent reassurance of an almost imperceptible presence.

Erikson (1959), speaking from another point of view, has called that silent presence basic trust, and connects it to religion:

A word must be said about one cultural and traditional institution which is deeply related to the matter of trust, namely, religion.

It is not the psychologist's job to decide whether religion should or should not be confessed and practiced in particular words and rituals. Rather the psychological observer must ask whether or not in any area under observation religion and tradition are living psychological forces creating the kind of faith and conviction which permeates a parent's personality and thus reinforces the child's basic trust in the world's trustworthiness. The psychopathologist cannot avoid observing that there are millions of people who cannot really afford to be without religion, and whose pride in not having it is that much whistling in the dark. On the other hand, there are millions who seem to derive faith from other than religious dogmas, that is, from fellowship, productive work, social action, scientific pursuit, and artistic creation. And again, there are millions who profess faith, yet in practice mistrust both life and man. With all of these in mind, it seems worth while to speculate on the fact that religion through the centuries has served to restore a sense of trust at regular intervals in the form of faith while giving tangible form to a sense of evil which it promises to ban. All religions have in common the periodical childlike surrender to a Provider or providers who dispense earthly fortune as well as spiritual health; the demonstration of one's smallness and dependence through the medium of reduced posture and humble gesture; the admission in prayer and song of misdeeds, of misthoughts, and of evil intentions; the admission of inner division and the consequent appeal for inner unification by divine guidance; the need for clearer self-delineation and self-restriction; and finally, the insight that individual trust must become a common faith, individual mistrust a commonly formulated evil, while the individual's need for restoration must become part of the ritual practice of many, and must become a sign of trustworthiness in the community.

Whosoever says he has religion must derive a faith from it which is transmitted to infants in the form of basic trust;

whosoever claims that he does not need religion must derive such basic faith from elsewhere (pp. 64–65).

He concludes his remarks by observing that

> you cannot fool children. To develop a child with a healthy personality a parent must be a genuine person in a genuine milieu (p. 99).

In an earlier chapter Erikson mentions the importance of the child's mastering reality:

> The growing child must derive a vitalized sense of reality from the awareness that his individual way of mastering experience (his ego synthesis) is a successful variant of a group identity and is in accord with its space-time and life plan (p. 22).

I propose that God as a transitional object representation is used by children to modulate the unavoidable failures of their parents, even if the modulation implies displaced rage and terror (with their painful divine enlargement) or the slightly vengeful discovery of a God who has more and better love to offer than a pedestrian oedipal parent. That God may or may not be the official God of the child's religion. But as a personal companion (sometimes being told that he does not exist) he belongs to the "ineffably private" side of human experience where we are irremediably alone. A convincing sense of being alive, connected, in communion with ourselves, others, the universe, and God himself may occur when, in the profoundest privacy of the self, "an identity of experience" takes place between vital components of our God representation, our sense of self, and some reality in the world. It may be provoked by a landscape, a newly found person (n. 2), the birth of a child, a passage in a book, a poem, a tune, or myriad other experiences. The histories of religious conversion and of mystical experience provide endless examples.

Winnicott (1965) speaks about this area of private communication as indispensable for a sense of being real, for maintaining what he calls a true self. Here is how he states his case:

> In so far as the object is subjective, *so far as it unnecessary for communication with it to be explicit.* In so far as the object is objectively perceived, communication is either explicit or else dumb. Here then appear two *new* things, the individual's use and enjoyment of modes of communication, and the individual's non-communicating self, or the personal core of the self that is a true isolate (p. 182).

Winnicott concludes:

> It is easy to see that in the cases of slighter illness, in which there is some pathology and some health, there must be expected an active noncommunication (clinical withdrawal) because of the fact that communication so easily becomes linked with some degree of false or compliant object-relating; silent or secret communication with subjective objects, carrying a sense of real, must periodically take over to restore balance.
> I am postulating that in the healthy (mature, that is, in respect of the development of object-relating) person there is a need for something that corresponds to the state of the split person in whom one part of the split communicates silently with subjective objects. There is room for the idea that significant relating and communicating is silent (p. 184).

I agree with Winnicott and propose that the private God of each man has the potential to provide "silent communication," thus increasing our sense of being real. Those who do not find their God representation subjectively meaningful need other subjective objects and transitional realities to encounter themselves.

Winnicott concludes that even the analyst has to submit to the laws which regulate this phenomenon:

> It is my opinion that the psycho-analyst has no other language in which to refer to cultural phenomena. He can talk about the mental mechanisms of the artist but not about the experience of communication in art and religion unless he is

Industry vs. inferiority	Identity vs. identity diffusion		Intimacy and generativity vs. isolation and self-absorption	Integrity vs. despair	
Latency	Early adolescence	Late adolescence	Adulthood	Senescence	Death
I am a child. I will grow up and be and do like you.	I am in a vast universe. I am me: I have an inner world.	I will make room for *me* in the world. I will find and give love.	I am / I have / I give / I take / I work / I love	I have lived. I have done well and failed. I accept both.	I am dying. I am. I was. Will I be?
You are my parent. You are big and powerful. You protect me.	You are limited. You have faults. Let me be me.	Teach me to be a man, a woman.	Now I understand you. I am an adult too.	I remember you.	We have been together— remember? Are you there, my dead ones?
		new objects			
		I found you. You, my beloved.	We are a family. We are so complex.	We were together.	
Less aggrandized parental imago	Conceptual ideation mixes with multitude of representations from other stages. Inestimable shifting.		Emotional distance from representation. Critical reassessment.	The representation is questioned. Does it represent the existing God?	Doubts: Is God what I thought he is? Is he there?
You are my God, my protector.	You are the maker of all things. You are the beloved and the loving.		You are. You let me be me.	I accept you whatever you are. Basic trust.	Whatever, whoever you are, I trust you.
You are destructive. You won't spare me.	You are unjust. You permit evil. You suffocate me.		You think I am a child. Let me be me.	You never gave me anything.	You are not there.
I do not need you. I have other protection.	I don't need you. I have myself. I found love. That is enough.		Life is all right.	Life makes sense.	I was. That is enough for me.
"God the Almighty is our heavenly Father."	"God is my creator." "I don't like that he permits evil, pain, and suffering."	"God is my beloved" (mystics).	"God is subtle but not malicious."	"The ways of the Lord are mysterious."	"Into your hands I commend my spirit." Basic trust.

Fig. 2. The individual's sense of self and the successive recreations of his transitional objects

willing to peddle in the intermediate area whose ancestor is the infant's transitional object (p. 184).

Winnicott's comment may help us to understand why imaginary companions and God are so completely absent from many analyses. While the analysis is going on, they continue to provide their services of silent communication. The analysis of their sources and the transformation of childhood imagoes and corresponding self-representations may alter the equilibrium, and as a consequence the God representation and belief may change. Whatever the changes, silent communication with transitional objects, God or others, will continue parallel to the analytic process.

To conclude, I would like to offer a graphic presentation, somewhat inspired in Erikson's (1959) notion of epigenetic principle. Like Erikson's, my diagram portrays human life as a *"gradual unfolding of the personality through phase-specific psychosocial crises,"* each stage representing a "component [that] comes to ascendance and finds its more or less lasting solution at the conclusion of 'its' stage" (p. 119). The diagram presents the relation between the unfolding sense of self and the concomitant transformations and continuous creation of the transitional object. The central thesis is that God as a transitional representation needs to be recreated in each developmental crisis if it is to be found relevant for lasting belief.

This ordering presents the transformations of the representation in a normative way, following the prevailing subjective experiences of each developmental period. It also presents a simplified version of the subjective characteristics of the God representation which condition belief or unbelief. This presentation suggests only a normative possibility. It does not imply that people *must* transform their God at any given period. Such a conclusion would contradict the essence of my findings and the very personal characteristics of each individual's God.

NOTES

1. Meissner (1978) presents a good discussion of the evolution of the concept of illusion in psychoanalysis. He concludes:

> Psychoanalysis no longer feels compelled to destroy man's illusions on the grounds that they express his inmost desires and wishes. Rather psychoanalysis has moved to the position of staking a claim for illusion as the repository of human creativity and the realm in which man's potentiality may find its greatest and most meaningful expression.

2. The nineteenth-century lyric poet Gustavo Adolfo Bécquer beautifully illustrates the relation between the joy of finding an object and temporary belief in God:

> Hoy la tierra y los cielos me sonrien;
> hoy llega al fondo de mi alma el sol;
> hoy la he visto . . . , la he visto y me ha mirado . . .
>   ¡Hoy creao en Dios!
> (Rhyme 17, p. 24)
>   [Today heaven and earth smile at me;
> today the sun lights the depth of my soul;
> today I saw her . . . , I saw her and she looked at me . . .
>   Today I believe in God!]

3. An example is the angered reactions of some individuals witnessing a natural disaster and challenging God's existence, power, or goodness.

4. Winnicott's notion of illusion and transitional space needs to be taken in all seriousness to its final implications.

In ordinary language, the language of everyday life where we all meet publicly, *illusory* and *real* are antithetical, mutually exclusive concepts.

This is not so in the private realm of transitional reality where illusory and real dimensions of experience interpenetrate each other to such an extent that they cannot be teased apart without destroying what is essential in the experience. It is impossible to separate the mother created by the child from the mother he finds.

Etymology may help. *Illusion* comes originally from the Latin verb *illudo,* which in turn is formed from the verb *ludo,* "to play." Literally, *illudo* means to play with, as well as to be the object of playing in mockery, derision, or deception.

The Oxford English Dictionary also defines *illusion* as "the action or an act, of deceiving the bodily eye by false or unreal appearances, or the mental eye by false or unreal appearances, or the mental eye by false prospects, statements, etc." In this definition, as well as in everyday language, reality and illusion are antithetical. But psychic life has a reality of its own where reality and illusion cannot be separated if the subject is to survive. Illusion, as Couperous shows, is governed by powerful and pressing psychic laws, themselves of a compelling reality: "I can only imagine," Couperous's character says, "the fatal reality of my imagination."

Reality, on the other hand, can take for the experiencing individual all the shapes that his psychic defenses need to attribute to it to make it bearable. A childish mother may appear to be a bountiful fortress to a needy Bernadine Fisher. For her the reality of her mother as seen by others is a degree of factual objectivity that she cannot afford. She needs the illusion of a strong mother capable of loving.

The risk in understanding psychic life is to apply to it the separation of subject and object indispensable in science and philosophy. Freud has shown beyond doubt that man's needs and wishes color whatever he does and whatever he sees. Man is always playing with reality, either to create himself through illusory anticipation, to sustain himself by illusory reshaping of what does not seem bearable, or simply to fool himself through illusory distortion of what he does not like. If the illusion, the playing with available reality, goes beyond immediate need, pathology and delusions ensue. Illusory transmutation of reality, however, is the indispensable and unavoidable process all of us *must* go through if we are to grow normally and acquire psychic meaning and substance.

Studies in child development, studies of narcissistic processes and of identification, prove also beyond doubt that the illusory aggrandisement of parents and of oneself beyond all reality ("I can kill a lion," says the frightened phallic boy; "My mom knows everything," brags the little girl) is not just a childish inability to test what is real but an essential psychic process of self-integration, an always available ubiquitous function to maintain self-esteem, hope, and a feeling of safety. In this sense illusory processes have a powerful psychic reality, regulated by well-structured psychic laws. Douglas O'Duffy's need to go beyond the door, however symbolic, imaginary, or illusory, is a psychic act whose impact will in fact change his present life. The nonreal, nonvisible, nonfactual, imaginary, illusory, fantasized action he has to perform in going through that door has for him the subjective quality of a compelling action as real as life itself. His predicament illustrates that a real action occurs in the representational world where he is still "punishing" his mother. The illusion of his power vis-à-vis his God and his mother has provided him with compensatory self-esteem and has spurred him to achievement, so as to show publicly what he wants to feel internally. He made a reality out of his illusion. He became a powerful athlete and a man who had power over others. Illusion and reality contributed to his self-making.

5. The well-known anthropologist Weston La Barre said in his plenary session address to the 1977 meeting of the American Psychoanalytic Association meeting in Quebec:

> Magic arrogantly *commands* impersonal external reality to obey the mana power of omnipotent wish. But religion *beseeches* person-like spirits or the ghosts of persons, parents and ancestors, omnipotently to accomplish our needs *for us.* . . . Thus, in life-history the impersonal magical commanding, or projection and incorporating, of ambiguously placed mana represents an *earlier individual phase* of adaptive ego growth than does religion, a later phase-development which knows in emotional reality the existence of persons.

18. For the reader not acquainted with the work quoted, the mysterious sign $Q\grave{\eta}$ represents the notion of intercellular quantity in Freud's early vocabulary.

19. La Barre (1977) says: "Much of religion is ineffably private. . . . Distinction between [magic and religion] must be sought elsewhere, viz. in *differing subjective stances.* Much criticized for being 'too biologistic,' Freudian body-based psychology is here peculiarly available for explaining these elusive differences, which, moreover, obtain cross-culturally in human biology."

QUESTIONS

1. What is a transitional object?
2. How and why is God a different kind of transitional object?
3. How and why do we change our image of God throughout life? What events can precipitate the change?
4. How does Rizzuto show that as the image of one's self changes, so, too, does one's image of God change?

SUGGESTED READINGS

Mahler, M. S.; Pine, F.; and Bergman, A. (1975). *The Psychological Birth of the Human Infant.* New York: Basic.

Winnicott, D. W. (1965). *Maturational Processes and the Facilitating Environment: Studies in the Theory of Emotional Development.* New York: International Universities Press.

Winnicott, D. W. (1971). *Playing and Reality.* New York: Basic.

Vergote, A., and Tamayo, A. (1980). *The Parental Figures and the Representation of God: A Psychological and Cross-Cultural Study.* Louvain: Leuven University Press.

James Fowler

13. Stages of Faith Development

James Fowler is professor of theology at Candler School of Theology in Emory University, Atlanta, Georgia. A Methodist minister, he received his doctoral degree from Harvard Divinity School and taught there and at Boston College before moving to Emory. His stages of faith development are based on the ideas of Piaget, Erikson, and Kohlberg. It is important to note that Fowler's understanding of faith is different from the understanding presented by the theologians in the first section. Because his theory is structural and developmental, he views faith as a way of making meaning of one's ultimate environment. The notion of relationship with a transcendent is not an essential component in this view of faith. Thus an atheist could be on a certain faith level in this mode. The person moves from simple non-reflective faith derived largely from one's parents to a more differentiated, reflected upon and chosen view of the ultimate environment. The chart at the end indicates the various aspects that comprise Fowler's notion of faith development.

FAITH: THE STRUCTURAL DEVELOPMENTAL APPROACH

By "faith" I mean a dynamic set of operations, more or less integrated, by which a person construes his/her ultimate environment. This construal (or construction) includes and serves the person's centering loyalties and values (conscious and unconscious), and maintains a framework of meaning and value in reference to which the person interprets, reacts and takes initiatives in life. Conceptually, in asking you to think of faith as an integrated set of operations, I am focusing upon it as a patterned process or *structure* underlying and giving form to the *contents* of believing, valuing, knowing and committing. This distinction between the *structure* and *content* of faith is important to grasp and maintain. In a sense the focus of our stages is on the "how" of faith as a dynamic but structured process, as opposed to the "what" of faith, i.e. that which is believed, known, trusted or loved in faith. (A moment's reflection will make it clear, however, that our research must focus on both, for you really have no access to the structure of a person's faith except as you 'precipitate" it out of his or her expression of its content.)

Faith, understood in this way, is not synonymous with religion or with belief. In ways that we will try to make clearer in this paper, faith, as a structured process at the center of the self's system regulating orientation and action, has a reciprocal or dialectical relationship with religion and belief as well as with language and ideology more generally. Religion and belief, symbol and ritual, ideology and ethical norms, serve as *models* in a double sense in relation to faith. On the one hand they are models for guiding the construction of a framework of meaning and value, providing vicarious experience and insight. On the other hand they provide media by which faith can express, communicate and apprehend itself. (See Geertz, Smith, and Fowler, 1974 B, Lecture I.)

Our structural-developmental approach derives in important ways from the cognitive developmental theories of Piaget and Kohlberg. In a moment we will consider how, as regards the concept "stage," and as regards the interactional epistemology underlying our theory, we are deeply under their influence. It will also become obvious that in our description of faith stages we have incorporated many insights of both these men and their followers. There is, however, one important respect in which our structural focus differs from theirs. Piaget conceptually distinguishes between *cognition* (the "structures" of knowing) and *affection* (the "energetics" or motive-force of knowing). (See Piaget, 1967, pp. 3–73; 1964; Piaget and Inhelder; and Flavell, pp. 80–82.) Kohlberg tends theoretically to follow Piaget in maintaining this distinction, but making it clear that in reality the two interpenetrate in inseparable ways. (See Beck, Crittendon and Sullivan, pp. 392 ff.) Both claim that cognitive structures tend to dominate over the affective dynamics and that only the cognitive structures can serve as the basis for describing the sequence of developmental transformations which they call *stages*. Cartesian rationalism and Kantian formalism stand behind this approach.

Our work, on the other hand, has significant indebtedness to the psychoanalytic tradition (notably through Erik Erikson's writings), which insists upon recognizing the sharp qualification of rationality by unconscious defenses, needs and strivings, and which emphasizes the role of symbolic functioning in the processes of ego development. Similarly, I am indebted to theological and philosophical traditions in which knowing and valuing are held to be inseparable, and in which *will* and *reason* are seen as serving the dominant affections or loves of persons. Faith, as we are studying it, is a structured set of operations in which cognition and affection are inextricably bound up together. As my associate Bob Kegan puts it, in faith the "rational" and the "passional" are fused.

The structural-developmental approach, represented by Piaget and Kohlberg and including our work, may best be described as *constructivist* and *interactionist* in its understanding of development. In this respect, as in many others, the structural-developmentalist epistemology fits hand-in-glove with the underlying assumptions of the religious socialization perspective. It is a fundamental Piagetian insight that the child's earliest knowing, before language and the symbolic functions have developed, derives from the child's manipulation of objects. Knowing begins with a *doing,* an *acting upon,* and *interaction with* objects and persons. Schemas, structures, or operations are, for Piaget, internalized patterns of action constructed in the child's interaction with objects and persons in order to enable him or her to organize and reliably predict their future behavior. Schemas and structures are generalizable; they become part of a set or repertoire of mental operations which the child brings to any new experience, perception or relationship. When a novelty is encountered the child tries to *assimilate* it to his or her existing schemas and structures. If it proves unassimilable the child experiments with new manipulations on it. As this is occurring new schemas are being assembled and tried. When the child finds an adaptive way of dealing with the novelty, the new schemas become part of his or her structural repertoire and, in Piagetian terms, we can say that a structural *accommodation* has occurred. Out of the interaction with a new object or person the child has developed new, generalizable structures. Development, then, in the structural-developmental approach, is understood as the *accommodatory* construction of new *schemas* or *operations* of knowing (which process is largely unconscious, formal or non-content-specific, and generalizable). In this perspective emphasis is placed on the constructive role of the knower and on the fact that knowledge is not merely an internal mental copy of something that is simply "there" in external reality, but that knowledge is the product, the "construction of reality" a person makes, using his or her available structures of knowing and interpretation. As new structures are developed the construction of reality undergoes changes.

A decisive contribution of structural-developmental theory and research is its demonstration that there are uniformities in the structural patterns persons develop in order to organize and deal with the physical, social, and ultimate environments. The uniformities are described developmentally as a sequence of *stages.* A stage, in this perspective, represents a typical set of integrated operations, a structural whole, available to and employed by a person to construct, maintain and orient him/herself in the world. Stages succeed each other by way of accommodatory structural transformations. Earlier stages are characterized by more simple, global and undifferentiated structures. Successive stages increase in complexity, inner-differentiation, flexibility and comprehensiveness. Later or more developed stages carry forward the operations of earlier stages, but integrate them into more complex and inclusive structural wholes. Each stage, therefore, builds upon previous ones, meaning that the stage sequence is *hierarchical.* Because each stage builds on the previous ones, the sequence of stages is *invariant.* A stage cannot be skipped. Similarly, unless there is organic or emotional-mental deterioration the stage sequence will be *irreversible.* Persons will employ the most adaptive and adequate structures available to them for meeting the problems or dilemmas posed by their physical, social or ultimate environments. Finally, it is the claim of structural developmentalists that stages of the kind we are describing are *universal.* Persons may move through these stages at different rates (structural stages are not strictly determined by biological maturation or chronological age) and not all persons will complete the sequence of stages. But at their rate and to their point of development, it is held, the structural stages will be descriptive of their developmental processes.

THE STAGES: A BRIEF OVERVIEW

In our effort to give a structural-developmental account of faith we have identified *six stages*—moving from simpler and undifferentiated structures to those which are more complex and differentiated. Faith manifests growing self-awareness as you move through the stages. The ages given with each of these stages represent an average *minimal* age. Many persons attain them, if at all, at later chronological ages than those indicated. Stage attainment varies from person to person and equilibrium of a stable sort may occur for different persons or groups at or in different stages.

Stage 1—Intuitive-Projective Faith
The imitative, fantasy-filled phase in which the child can be powerfully and permanently influenced by the examples, moods, actions and language of the visible faith of primal adults. (age 4)

Stage 2—Mythic-Literal Faith
The stage in which the person begins to take on for himself/herself the stories and beliefs and observances which symbolize belonging to his/her community. Attitudes are observed and adopted; beliefs are appropriated with literal interpretations, as are moral rules and attitudes. Symbols are one-dimensional and literal. Authority (parental) and example still count for more than those of peers. (6½–8)

Stage 3—Synthetic-Conventional Faith
The person's experience of the world is now extended beyond the family and primary social groups. There are a number of spheres or theaters of life: family, school or work, peers, leisure, friendship, and possibly a religious sphere. Faith must help provide a coherent and meaningful synthesis of that now more complex and diverse range of involvements. Coherence and

meaning are certified, at this stage, by either the authority of properly designated persons in each sphere, or by the authority of consensus among "those who count." The person does not yet have to take on the burden of world-synthesis for himself/herself. (12–13)

Stage 4—Individuating-Reflective Faith
The movement or break from Stage 3 to Stage 4 is particularly important for it is in this transition that the late adolescent or adult must begin to take seriously the burden of responsibility for his/her own commitments, life-style, beliefs and attitudes. Where there is genuinely a transition to Stage 4 the person must face certain universal polar tensions which Synthetic-Conventional faith allows one to evade:

individuality	v. belonging to community
subjectivity	v. objectivity
self-fulfillment	v. service to others
the relative	v. the absolute

Often Stage 4 develops under the tutelage of ideologically powerful religions, charismatic leadership, or ideologies of other kinds. It often finds it necessary to collapse these polar tensions in one direction or the other. Stage 4 both brings and requires a qualitatively new and different kind of self-awareness and responsiblity for one's choices and rejections. (18–19)

Stage 5—Paradoxical-Consolidative Faith
In Stage 4 the person is self-aware in making commitments and knows something of what is being *excluded* by the choices he/she makes. But for Stage 4, the ability to decide is grounded, in part at least, on the fact that one set of commitments is overvalued at the expense of necessarily viewing alternatives to it in a partial and limiting light.

Stage 5 represents an advance in the sense that it recognizes the integrity and truth in positions other than its own, and it affirms and lives out its own commitments and beliefs in such a way as to honor that which is true in the lives of others without denying the truth of its own. Stage 5 is ready for community of identification beyond tribal, racial, class or ideological boundaries. *To be genuine, it must know the cost of such community and be prepared to pay the cost.* A true Stage 5 requires time and testing and regard for those who are different and who oppose you which Stage 4 does not have. In a true Stage 5 *espoused values and beliefs are congruent with risk, and action taken.* (30–32)

Stage 6—Universalizing Faith
Stage 5's commitment to inclusive community remains paradoxical. To affirm others means to deny oneself. Defensiveness and egocentrism make the affirmation of others' truth difficult and threatening. One's own interests and investments in tribe, class, religion, nation, region, etc. still constitute biasing and distorting loyalties, which have to be struggled with and overcome continually.

Stage 6 Universalizing Faith *is rare.* At this stage what Christians and Jews call the Kingdom of God is a live, felt reality for the person of faith. Here one dwells *in* the world as a transforming presence, but is not *of* the world. The sense of the oneness of all persons is not a glib ideological belief but has become a permeative basis for decision and action. The paradox has gone out of being-for-others; at Stage 6, one is being more truly oneself. Stage 6's participation in the Ultimate is direct and immediate. Their community is universal in inclusiveness. Such persons are ready for fellowship with persons at any of the other stages and from any other faith tradition. They seem instinctively to know how to relate to us affirmingly, never condescendingly, yet with pricks to our pretense and with genuine bread of life. (38–40)

Appendix
Faith: The Structural-Developmental Approach
A Summary Taxonomy of Structural Competences by Stage

STAGES:	A	B	C
	FORM OF LOGIC (MODIFIED PIAGET)	FORM OF WORLD COHERENCE	ROLE TAKING (MOD. SELMAN)
1. Intuitive-Projective	Pre-operational	Episodic	Rudimentary empathy
2. Mythic-Literal	Concrete operational	Narrative-Dramatic	Simple perspective-taking
3. Synthetic-Conventional	Early Formal operations	Tacit System, symbolic mediation	Mutual role-taking, (inter-personal)
4. Individuative-Reflexive	Formal operations (Dichotomizing)	Explicit system, conceptual mediation	Mutual, with self-selected group or class
5. Paradoxical-Consolidative	Formal operations (Dialectical)	Multi-systemic, symbolic *and* conceptual mediation	Mutual, with groups, classes & traditions other than one's own
6. Universalizing	Formal operations (Synthetic)	Unitive actuality, "One beyond the many"	Mutual, with the common-wealth of being

D	E	F
BOUNDS OF SOCIAL AWARENESS	FORM OF MORAL JUDGMENT*	ROLE OF SYMBOLS
Family, primal others	Punishment-reward	Magical-Numinous
"Those like us" (in familial, ethnic, racial, class & religious terms)	Instrumental Hedonism	One-dimensional, literal
Conformity to class norms and interests	Interpersonal concord ↕ Law & Order ↕	Multi-dimensional, conventional
Self-aware adherence to chosen class norms & interests	Reflective relativism or class-biased universalism	Critical translation into ideas
Critical awareness of and transcendence of class norms & interests	Principled Higher Law (Universal-critical)	Post-critical rejoining of symbolic nuance and ideational content
Trans-class awareness and identification	Loyalty to being	Transparency of symbols

(*modified Kohlberg)

QUESTIONS

1. What does Fowler mean by faith? How does his notion differ from the descriptions of faith by the theologians Rahner, Tillich and Dulles?
2. How does Fowler adapt the structural-developmental theories of Piaget and Kohlberg to his notion of faith?
3. Do you recognize in yourself or in others any of the characteristics of a faith stage?
4. What are the implications for religious education in Fowler's description of the faith stages?

SUGGESTED READINGS

Fowler, J. (1981). *Stages of Faith: The Psychology of Human Development and the Quest for Meaning*. New York: Harper.

Fowler, J. and Lovin, R. (1980). *Trajectories in Faith: Five Life Stories*. Nashville: Abingdon.

Fowler, J. and Keen, S. (1980). *Life Maps: Conversations on the Road to Faith*. Minneapolis: Winston.

Moran, G. (1983). *Religious Education Development: Images for the Future*. Minneapolis: Winston.

William J. Bouwsma

14. Christian Adulthood

Born in Michigan, William Bouwsma is now Sather Professor of History at the University of California, Berkeley. While Fowler presents the stages of faith development, Bouwsma stresses the need for adults to continue to grow in faith. He even would say that the refusal to grow is the source of particular sins. Faith and the acceptance of one's creatureliness will and can replace anxiety and the fear of growing. Finally Christian adulthood includes close and organic community with others.

The significance of the past also points to the indelible importance of all human experience. It gives meaning to the particular temporal experiences that have shaped each individual during the whole course of his life, so that the biblical idea of time is the foundation for the conception of the worth of the individual personality.[24] But it also gives meaning to the collective experiences of mankind into which all individual experience is ultimately submerged, a conception basic to the discovery of the great historical forces that transcend individual experience.[25] Fundamental to the Christian view of man is, therefore, an insistence on a process of growth in which the past is not left behind but survives, shapes, and is absorbed into the present.[26] The unalterable past provides a stable base for the identity alike of each individual and of every society. St. Augustine's *Confessions,* with its vivid delineation of a personality changing yet continuous with its past, is a product of this conception.[27] The absence of genuine biography in the classical world has often been remarked.[28] By the same token, the great classical histories sought to reveal the changeless principles governing all change, while the biblical histories were concerned with change itself as God's work and with its shaping impact on men.

The Christian life, then, is conceived as indefinite growth, itself the product of a full engagement with temporal experience involving the whole personality. The Christian is not to evade the challenges, the struggles, the difficulties and dangers of life, but to accept, make his way through, and grow in them. He must be willing to disregard his vulnerability and to venture out, even at the risk of making mistakes, for the sake of growth.[29] This understanding of life finds expression in the figure of the Christian as wayfarer *(viator)* or pilgrim; Christian conversion is thus not, as in the mystery religions, an immediate entrance into a safe harbor but rather, though its direction has been established, the beginning of a voyage into the unknown.[30] As movement in a direction, it also implies progress, but a progress that remains incomplete in this life.[31] The "other-worldliness" of Christianity is significant, in this context, as the basis of the open-endedness of both personal and social development.

From this standpoint, just as the essential condition of Christian adulthood is the capacity for growth, the worst state of man is not so much his sinfulness (for sins can be forgiven) as the cessation of growth, arrested development, remaining fixed at any point in life. In these terms, just as adulthood requires growth, its opposite—what might be called the Christian conception of immaturity—is the refusal to grow, the inability to cope with an open and indeterminate future (that is, the future itself), in effect the rejection of life as a process.

There is, however, a close connection between the rejection of growth and the problem of sin; the refusal to grow is, in an important sense, the source of all particular sins. The story of the fall reveals the connection, and may also be taken as the biblical analysis of the causes and the consequence of human immaturity. It contrasts essential man, as God created him, with actual man, man as he appears in history, who is fearful of the future and afraid of growth. The story explains this as a result of man's faithlessness. For the fall is caused not by a breach of the moral law but by man's violation of the relationship fundamental to his existence; it belongs to religious rather than to ethical experience. Primordial man, whose goodness stems from his dependence on God, is depicted as rejecting the creatureliness basic to his perfection and claiming independent value and even divinity for himself. He seeks to become "like gods," and implicit in this pretension is the rejection of his own further development. By complacently making himself *as he is* the divine center of his universe, he rejects the possibility of change and learns to fear all experience. Thus he loses his openness to the future and his capacity for growth; in short he repudiates his capacity for adulthood.[32] The claim to divinity, therefore, paradoxically results in a pervasive anxiety. And out of this anxiety man commits a whole range of particular ethical sins, the end products of his faithlessness. Thus, too, he begins to suffer particular sensations of guilt.[33]

A further symptom of his immaturity may be seen in man's perennial tendency, implicit in his claim to divinity, to absolutize his understanding of the universe in a frantic effort to hold his anxiety in check. This, I take it, would be the Christian explanation for the relatively small influence of a biblical understanding of the human situation in Christendom itself. Man solemnly invests his culture, which is in fact always contingent on his own limited and self-centered vision and need, with ultimate meaning, thereby imprisoning himself within a man-made, rigidly bounded, and internally defined universe that further destroys the possibility for growth. He philosophizes, claims access to the real truth of things, to being-in-itself. This is the significance normative Christianity would assign to the absolute qualitative distinctions of classical culture, a man-made substitute for biblical faith. Harvey Cox has described such constructions as a "play-pen," a nice image in its implications for human development.[34] Their power to inhibit human sympathy, with its special value for personal growth, is suggested by the need of the Greek (in an impulse with which we are all quite familiar) to see the man who differed from himself as a barbarian. Without faith—what Tillich has called the courage to be, which is also the courage to become—the only escape from man's intolerable fear of chaos is the idolatry of cultural absolutism. So, without faith, man tends to bigotry, for any grasp of the universe other than his own is too dangerous for him to contemplate. It is in this light that we can understand the full implications of the pagan charge that the early Christians were enemies of culture. In a sense this was true then, and it remains true; for normative

Christianity all culture is a human artifact, and no absolute validity can be attached to its insights. Such a position is always likely to be disturbing, as every social scientist has discovered.

Yet normative Christianity does not deny the practical values of culture. It simply insists that, just as man is a creature of God, so culture is a creature of man, not his master. Secularized in this way, culture can serve many useful human purposes, and it can even become a vehicle of Christian purposes when men fully recognize their dependence on God.[35] But culture can never be ultimately serious. Indeed, there are tensions in the Scriptures that suggest that some dimensions of biblical religion itself may be understood as products of culture, or at any rate set in a larger context within which, like culture, they can be seen to possess only relative authority. Job discovered this in his confrontation with an inscrutable but infinitely holy God, and we can also sense something of this in the tension in the Old Testament between prophetic religion and the law. The law is like culture in the sense that it defines and particularizes sins, and the prophets do not deny the validity of such definition. But prophetic religion also insists, not simply that there is more to be said about man's situation before God than this, but, in addition, that definition is significant only in relation to the indefinite and open.[36]

If the Christian analysis of the evils in historical existence can be understood as a diagnosis of immaturity, the Christian conception of salvation can be similarly construed as a description of the only way to recover that capacity for growth in which true adulthood consists. The basic problem here is to replace anxiety with faith, so that man can enter an open future with confidence and grow through his experience. But here he encounters a problem he cannot solve. Faith is a function of man's dependence on God, but it is precisely this relationship that man in historical existence has repudiated. In effect he has destroyed the "true self" God made, and he must therefore be remade. And as Augustine asked, "If you could not make yourself, how could you remake yourself?"[37] Described psychologically, the predicament in which man finds himself is one of entrapment and bondage—in short, of total helplessness.[38] Furthermore, because man was created a living whole and repudiated his creatureliness as a whole, there is no area of his personality left untouched by his alienation from God and thus from his true self. This is the precise meaning of the often misunderstood doctrine of total depravity: it signifies that man has no resources by which he can save himself.

Yet exactly here, in the recognition that this is the case, lies the first step toward the resumption of growth. Once man sees himself as he is, acknowledges his limits, perceives the contingency of all his own constructions, and admits that they have their sources only in himself, he is well on the way to accepting his creaturehood and open to the possibility of faith. Faith begins, then, not in illusion but in an absolute and terrifying realism; its first impulse is paradoxically the perception that faith itself is beyond man's own control, that there is no help in him, that his only resource is the grace of a loving God. The Christian, as Barth remarked, is "moved by a grim horror of illusion." "What is pleasing to God comes into being when all human righteousness is gone, irretrievably gone, when men are uncertain and lost, when they have abandoned all ethical and religious illusions, and when they have renounced every hope in this world and in this heaven. . . . Religion is the possibility of the removal of every ground of confidence except confidence in God alone. Piety is the possibility of the removal of the last traces of a firm foundation upon which we can erect a system of thought."[39] Salvation thus begins with confession, the admission of sin and ultimately of faithlessness, which is therapeutic in the sense that it demands total honesty and is directed to the removal of every false basis for human development. Augustine's *Confessions* might be described as the Christian form of psychoanalysis, the retracing, in God's presence and with his help, of the whole course of life, which aims to recover the health of faith.[40]

By confession and repentance, themselves a response to faith, man recognizes his helplessness and thus becomes open to help. This help is revealed and made available by God himself through the saving work of Christ, in which God again demonstrates his infinite concern with history. The response to Christ in faith expresses man's full acceptance of that creatureliness which is the essential condition of his authentic existence and growth; the answer to sin is not virtue but faith. By faith man is dramatically relieved of his false maturity, his claims to a self-defined "manhood," and enabled to begin again to grow. This is why conversion can be described as a "rebirth," which resembles birth also in that it is not subject to the control of him who is reborn; baptism, the ritual of rebirth, is an initiation into true existence. Freed from the anxieties of self-sufficiency by faith, man can grow, both individually and collectively. Indeed, only now has he the strength to face directly the contingency, the inadequacy, the slavery and sinfulness of all merely human culture. He can risk seeing it clearly because, with faith, he has also received the gift of hope. From this standpoint the Gospel is the good news because it frees man for adulthood.

But this is an adulthood that involves, always, the whole man; thus its goal is symbolized not by the immortality of the soul but by the resurrection of the body as representing the total self that must be made whole. As Augustine exclaimed in old age, "I want to be healed completely, for I am a complete whole."[41] Christian maturity is manifested, therefore, not only in the understanding but more profoundly in the affective life and in the loving actions that are rooted in the feelings. Christ is above all the model of absolute love. Conformity to this loving Christ is the goal of human development; in Augustine's words, "he is our native country." But he is also the key to Christian adulthood, for "he made himself also the way to that country."[42] The Christian grows both in Christ and to Christ.

Again we encounter a set of paradoxes, the first of which is that man's full acceptance of his creatureliness, the admission of his absolute dependence on God in Christ, proves to be the essential condition of human freedom. For the only alternative to the life of faith is bondage to the self, to the anxieties and the false absolutisms embedded in human culture, by which man is otherwise imprisoned. Faith, in these terms, is the necessary condition of true autonomy, of freedom not from the constraints of experience—the Stoic ideal—but freedom to grow in and through them that is essential to adulthood. The Pauline injunction to work out one's own salvation in fear and trembling suggests this freedom, and suggests also the strains attendant on growth, but it would be impossible to fulfill without the faith that "it is God which worketh in you both to will and to do of his pleasure" (Phil. 2:13). This kind of freedom supplies the strength to challenge authority maturely, without the rebelliousness, arrogance, and destructiveness symptomatic of insecurity, or to criticize the definition of one's own life and to examine the dubious sources of one's own actions.[43]

At the same time, obedience to God paradoxically proves a far lighter burden than obedience to human ordinances or the requirements of culture, even though—another paradox—it is, in any final sense, impossible. For Christian righteousness consists not in a moral quality that must be maintained at all costs but in a relationship of favor and peace with God that is the source (rather than the consequence) of moral effort. If the Christian is in some sense virtuous, his virtue arises from love rather than duty, and if he fails, he can count on forgiveness. Thus, though he must recognize and confess his guilt as part of his more general realism, he is not to nourish or cling to it, for this would amount to the rejection of God's love. Repentance means allowing our guilt to be God's concern, and all guilt, otherwise so paralyzing for the moral life, must be swallowed up in love and gratitude. Christian adulthood is a growth away from, not toward, guilt.

By the same token it cannot be repressive, not only because no power in the human personality is entitled to excise or even to control any other (this is the happy implication of total depravity), but above all because such an effort, since it cannot touch the quality of the heart, would be superficial and in the end futile. Christian thinkers have sometimes displayed great insight into the nature of self-imposed control. Calvin's description of the process implies some acquaintance with its physiological consequences, as well as realism about the social necessity for restraint in a world in which those, too, who are growing in Christ must recognize that they are not fully and dependably adult: "the more [men] restrain themselves, the more violently they are inflamed within; they ferment, they boil, ready to break out into external acts, if they were not prevented by this dread of the law. . . . But yet this constrained and extorted righteousness is necessary to the community. . . . "[44] But the ideal of

Christian adulthood is not control but spontaneity; it is, in Augustine's words, to "love and do what you will."[45]

The spontaneity in the Christian ideal of adulthood points to still another paradox: its deliberate cultivation of, and delight in, the qualities of the child, now understood less metaphorically.[46] Childhood, after all, assumes growth, and it is in this respect fundamentally different from childishness, which rejects it; in this sense childhood is a model for adulthood. Indeed, childhood welcomes the years, unaware that they bring decay and death, and the deep and fearless interest of the child in his experience permits him to ask simple but profound questions that, later, may seem wearisome or too dangerous to be entertained. The child is not afraid to express wonder and astonishment.[47] Thus the confident trust in life of a healthy child, so different from the wariness that develops with age, has often been taken in Christian thought as a natural prototype of faith; in this sense, the adult Christian life is something like a return to childhood. As Kierkegaard remarked, it seems to reverse the natural order: "Therefore one does not begin by being a child and then becoming progressively more intimate [with God] as he grows older; no, one becomes more and more a child."[48] But there is, in this reversal, realism about the actual results of maturation, which ordinarily destroys the openness and wonder of childhood and replaces it with disguises and suspicion, with sophistication and a "knowingness" that chiefly serve to exclude a profounder knowledge. For the man, a return to the values of childhood is only possible when the inadequacies of his pretended manhood have been recognized in repentance and confession and he can take the way of faith. Then the growth of the man can again be like that of the child.[49]

This suggests a further peculiarity in the Christian view of adulthood: its lack of interest in chronological disparity. All Christians, insofar as they are growing in Christ, are equally becoming adults—or equally children.[50] Baptism is no respecter of age. An important consequence of this is to limit the authority and influence of parents, for where parent and child are both growing up in Christ,[51] the parent cannot be the only, or even the primary, pattern of maturity.[52] The Christian parent has failed unless his child achieves sufficient autonomy to establish his own direct relation to Christ. Nor is there sexual differentiation in the Christian conception: girls and boys, women and men are equally growing up in Christ.

But there is still another respect in which Christian adulthood merges with childhood: in its appreciation for play. This may be related to Paul's contrast between the wisdom of this world and the divine foolishness by which its hollowness is revealed.[53] The recurrent figure of the Christian fool, both child and saint, has sought to embody this conception. But it also has lighter, if equally serious, implications. The security of dependence on a loving God makes it unnecessary to confront life with a Stoic solemnity; the Christian can relax, even (again paradoxically) when he is most profoundly and actively confronting the sinfulness of the world. He can enjoy playfully (which also means to delight in, for itself, not to exploit instrumentally, for himself) the goodness of the creation. His culture can be an unbounded playground for free and joyous activity. He can risk the little adventures on which play depends. The loving human relationships of the Christian life can find expression in mutual play, through which we give pleasure to one another. Play is a natural expression of the joy of faith, which makes it possible to engage in life, even the hard work of life, as a game that has its own seriousness (for without their special kind of seriousness games could scarcely interest us), and that yet can be enjoyed precisely because the ultimate seriousness of existence lies elsewhere, with God.[54] But play is also related to that seriousness. Bushnell saw play as "the symbol and interpreter" of Christian liberty and pointed to its place in the eschatological vision of Zechariah 8:5: "And the streets of the city shall be full of boys and girls, playing in the streets."[55]

I have treated these various elements in the Christian conception of adulthood as aspects of an ideal for individual development, but to leave the matter at this would be to neglect an essential dimension of the Christian position. Like Judaism, Christianity has usually seen the individual in close and organic community with others. The Pauline description of growing up in Christ, though it has obvious implications for the individual, is primarily concerned with the growth of the Christian community; it is finally the church as one body, and perhaps ultimately all mankind, that must reach "mature manhood." The primary experiences through which the Christian grows are social experiences. One encounters Christ and the opportunity to serve him in others; the maturity of the individual is realized only in loving unity with others.[56] The power of growth is thus finally a function of community, and, at the same time, maturity finds expression in identification with other men; Christ, the model of human adulthood, was supremely "the man for others."[57] Through this identification of the individual with the body of Christ, the Christian conception of adulthood merges finally into history and eschatology.

NOTES

24. On this point, cf. Charles Norris Cochrane, *Christianity and Classical Culture* (New York, 1957), p. 456; Niebuhr, I, p. 69; Bultmann, p. 180; and Kierkegaard, *The Concept of Dread,* tr. Walter Lowrie (Princeton, 1957), p. 26: " ... the essential characteristic of human existence, that man is an individual and as such is at once himself and the whole race, in such wise that the whole race has part in the individual, and the individual has part in the whole race."

25. Eric Auerbach, *Mimesis,* tr. Willard Trask (Garden City, 1957), chs. 1–3, is especially perceptive on this characteristic of biblical, as opposed to classical, literature.

26. Kierkegaard's conception of the stages on life's way may perhaps be taken as a reflection of this tendency in Christian thought; Kierkegaard's three stages do not simply replace each other, but the later stages absorb the earlier.

27. Cochrane, pp. 386ff.; Peter Brown, *Augustine of Hippo: A Biography* (Berkeley, 1967), p. 173.

28. As in Bultmann, p. 130.

29. This seems to be implied in the *Divine Comedy,* in which the way to Paradise begins with the full moral experience of the Inferno.

30. Cf. Brown, p. 177, on Augustine's understanding of conversion as a beginning. As Augustine remarks in *Christian Doctrine,* p. 13, the Christian life is "a journey or voyage home." The notion of life as movement was also important for Luther: "For it is not sufficient to have done something, and now to rest . . . this present life is a kind of movement and passage, or transition . . . a pilgrimage from this world into the world to come, which is eternal rest" (quoted by Gerhard Ebeling, *Luther: An Introduction to His Thought,* tr. R. A. Wilson [Philadelphia, 1970], pp. 161–62). Calvin devoted particular attention to this theme (*Institutes,* III, vi. p. 5): "But no one . . . has sufficient strength to press on with due eagerness, and weakness so weighs down the greater number that, with wavering and limping and even creeping along the ground, they move at a feeble rate. Let each one of us, then, proceed according to the measure of his puny capacity and set out upon the journey we have begun. No one shall set out so inauspiciously as not daily to make some headway, though it be slight. Therefore, let us not cease so to act that we may make some unceasing progress in the way of the Lord. And let us not despair at the slightness of our success; for even though attainment may not correspond to desire, when today outstrips yesterday the effort is not lost. Only let us look toward our mark with sincere simplicity and aspire to our goal: not fondly flattering ourselves, nor excusing our own evil deeds, but with continuous effort striving toward this end: that we may surpass ourselves in goodness until we attain to goodness itself. It is this, indeed, which through the whole course of life we seek and follow. But we shall attain it only when we have cast off the weakness of the body, and are received into full fellowship with him" (Battles tr.). Bunyan's *Pilgrim's Progress* vividly dramatizes the conception.

31. Ricoeur, pp. 272–74, is instructive on the conception of progress implicit in Paul's understanding of the transition from the law to the grace of Christ: "the fall is turned into growth and progress; the curse of paradise lost becomes a test and a medicine." Augustine interpreted his own life as a progression in understanding: "I am the sort of man who writes because he has made progress, and who makes progress—by writing" (quoted by Brown, 353). For Thomas à Kempis; the Christian life is

marked by a concern "to conquer self, and by daily growing stronger than self, to advance in holiness" (*Imitation of Christ,* tr. Leo Sherley-Price [London, 1952], p. 31). For Luther, progress was a condition of all existence, for "progress is nothing other than constantly beginning. And to begin without progress is extinction. This is clearly the case with every movement and every act of every creature." Thus one must "constantly progress and anyone who supposes he has already apprehended does not realize that he is only beginning. For we are always travelling, and must leave behind us what we know and possess, and seek for that which we do not yet know and possess" (quoted by Ebeling, pp. 161–62).

32. Bultmann, esp. p. 184.

33. This interpretation of the fall owes a good deal to Ricoeur. For the transition from anxiety to sin, see Niebuhr, I, pp. 168, 182–86.

34. *The Secular City* (New York, 1965), p. 119.

35. For a survey of Christian attitudes to culture, see H. Richard Niebuhr, *Christ and Culture* (New York, 1951).

36. Ricoeur, pp. 58–59, 144–45, 321.

37. Quoted by Gerhart B. Ladner, *The Idea of Reform: Its Impact on Christian Thought and Action in the Age of the Fathers* (Cambridge, Mass., 1959), p. 406.

38. Ricoeur, p. 93.

39. *The Epistle to the Romans,* tr. Edwyn C. Hoskyns (London, 1933), pp. 68, 87–88.

40. Cf. Brown, p. 175.

41. Quoted by Brown, p. 366.

42. *Christian Doctrine,* p. 13.

43. Cf. Paul Tillich, *The Eternal Now* (New York, 1956), p. 158.

44. *Institutes,* II, vii, p. 10. Melanchthon was particularly subtle about human behavior that does not correspond to the impulses of the "heart"; the result is not, in fact, rationality, but, to follow Lionel Trilling's distinction, *both* insincerity *and* inauthenticity: "Therefore it can well happen that something is chosen which is entirely contrary to all affections. When this happens, insincerity takes over, as when, for example, someone treats graciously, amicably, and politely a person whom he hates

and wishes ill to from the bottom of his heart, and he does this perhaps with no definite reason" (*Loci communes theologici,* tr. Lowell J. Satre, in *Melanchthon and Bucer,* ed. Wilhelm Pauck [London, 1969], p. 28).

45. Quoted by Anders Nygren, *Agape and Eros,* tr. Philip S. Watson (New York, 1969), p. 454.

46. On the virtues of a childlike spontaneity, cf. Horace Bushnell, *Christian Nurture* (New Haven, 1916; first ed., 1888), p. 5: "A child acts out his present feelings, the feelings of the moment, without qualification or disguise."

47. Cf. Niebuhr, *Beyond Tragedy* (New York, 1937), pp. 143–48.

48. *Journals and Papers,* tr. Howard V. and Edna H. Hong (Bloomington, 1967), I, p. 122, no. 272.

49. Niebuhr, *Beyond Tragedy,* pp. 148–52. At the same time Augustine's portrayal of infancy in the *Confessions* should warn us, in its realism, that Christianity is not merely sentimental about childhood, in which it can also detect the flaws of maturity. But this is again to suggest their identity.

50. Bushnell noted, p. 136, that the apostolic church included children and observed, pp. 139–40, that "just so children are all men and women; and, if there is any law of futurition in them to justify it, may be fitly classed as believing men and women."

51. Cf. Bushnell, 10: " . . . since it is the distinction of Christian parents that they are themselves in the nurture of the Lord, since Christ and the Divine Love, communicated through him, are become the food of their life, what will they so naturally seek as to have their children partakers with them, heirs together with them, in the grace of life?"

52. Barth emphasizes this, *Church Dogmatics,* III:4, p. 248. It is a signficant feature of the Christian conception, indeed in a patriarchal society a revolutionary feature, that the Son, rather than the Father, is the model of adulthood. Lest this peculiarity seem to invite too simple an interpretation, however, the paradoxical unity of Father and Son in the Trinity must also be kept in mind.

53. Cf. Tillich, *Eternal Now,* pp. 155–57.

54. For Christianity and play, I have been stimulated by Lewis B. Smedes, "Theology and the Playful Life," in *God and the Good: Essays in Honor of Henry Stob,* ed. Clifton Orlebeke and Lewis B. Smedes (Grand Rapids, 1975), pp. 46–62. In view of common misunderstandings about the normative Christian attitude to sexuality, it is worth quoting Smedes—who certainly represents the normative position—on the playfulness of sex, p. 59: "The sexual component of our nature testifies that man was meant to find the most meaningful human communion in a playful relationship. In mutual trust and loving commitment, sexual activity is to be a playful festivity. It attests that human being is closest to fulfilling itself in a game. To be in God's image, then, includes being sexual, and sexuality is a profound call to play." Smedes also has useful comments on recent theologies of play.

55. Bushnell, pp. 290–92.

56. Cf. Augustine, *City of God,* XIX, v: "For how could the city of God . . . either take a beginning or be developed, or attain its proper destiny, if the life of the saints were not a social life?" Luther was emphatic: "We ought not to isolate ourselves but enter into companionship with our neighbor. Likewise it . . . is contrary to the life of Christ, who didn't choose solitude. Christ's life was very turbulent, for people were always moving about him. He was never alone, except when he prayed. Away with those who say, 'Be glad to be alone and your heart will be pure'" ("Table Talk," no. 1329).

57. Cf. Barth, *Church Dogmatics,* III:2, pp. 222ff.

QUESTIONS

1. Why is the Christian life conceived as one of indefinite growth?
2. How and why is the refusal to grow the source of all particular sins?
3. How does Bouwsma show that genuine faith can prevent bigotry?
4. How can one's full acceptance of one's creatureliness be the essential condition for one's freedom?

5. Are there any similarities between the notion of play and relaxation described by Winnicott (Chapter 11) and Bouwsma's description of the play of the Christian adult?

SUGGESTED READINGS

Baum, G. (ed.) (1975). *Journeys: The Impact of Personal Experience on Religious Thought.* New York: Paulist.

Kao, C. (1975). *Search for Maturity.* Philadelphia: Westminster.

Kao, C. (1981). *Psychological and Religious Development: Maturity and Motivation.* Washington, D.C.: University Press of America.

Stokes, K. (1982). *Faith Development in the Adult Life Cycle.* New York: Sadlier.

Thomas Merton

15. Final Integration

A convert to Catholicism in his twenties, Thomas Merton went on to become a Trappist monk at Gethsemani Abbey in Kentucky. He became master of novices there and wrote many books on prayer. In his effort to examine Buddhist forms of prayer, he traveled to Thailand where he died in Bangkok in a tragic electrical accident. Like the article by Bouwsma, this selection on final integration links psychological health with spiritual growth. Just as psychological health is not a mere adaptation to culture, so the notion of final integration also transcends culture. The Christian accepts all cultures and because of that is a peacemaker. He recognizes that monasticism is ideally suited to develop this kind of maturity with a universalizing vision.

Sometimes it may be very useful for us to discover new and unfamiliar ways in which the human task of maturation and self-discovery is defined. The book of a Persian psychoanalyst, Dr. Reza Arasteh, who practices and teaches in America, might prove very valuable in this respect.[1]

Dr. Arasteh has developed and deepened ideas suggested by the humanistic psychoanalysis of Erich Fromm, by existential psychotherapy and by the logotherapy of Viktor Frankl. But— and this is what is most interesting—he has also incorporated into his theories material from the mystical tradition of Persian Sufism. The *Final Integration* which is the object of his research is not just the "cure" of neurosis by adaptation to society. On the contrary, it presupposes that any psychoanalytic theory that is content merely with this is bound to be inadequate. Dr. Arasteh is interested not only in the partial and limited "health" which results from contented acceptance of a useful role in soci-

---

1. Reza Arasteh, *Final Integration in the Adult Personality,* Leiden, E. J. Brill, 1965.

ety, but in the final and complete maturing of the human psyche on a transcultural level. This requires a little clarification.

Contrary to the accepted theory and practice of most psychotherapy derived from Freud and popular in America today, Dr. Arasteh holds that adaptation to society at best helps a man "to live with his illness rather than cure it," particularly if the general atmosphere of the society is unhealthy because of its overemphasis on cerebral, competitive, acquisitive forms of ego-affirmation. Such an atmosphere may favor an apparently very active and productive mode of life but in reality it stifles true growth, leaves people lost, alienated, frustrated and bored without any way of knowing what is wrong with them. In fact, in many cases, psychoanalysis has become a technique for making people conform to a society that prevents them from growing and developing as they should. Quoting E. Knight's book *The Objective Society,* Arasteh says:

> The Western individual, while opposing the integration of the Russian and Chinese models, not only accepts the herd values of his society but he has invented psychoanalysis to prevent him from straying from them. . . . The stresses that modern life often produces in sensitive and intelligent people are no longer considered to call for a change in society; it is the individual who is wrong and he consequently becomes a neurotic, not a revolutionary. No more remarkable device than psychoanalysis has ever been devised by a society for preventing its superior citizens from giving it pain.

This interesting passage, quoted out of context, might give undue comfort to those who assume that, because they enjoy their masochism, they are superior. Nevertheless it does show to what extent psychotherapy and other techniques have been frankly drafted into the service of a massive, affluent organization that is dedicated to "freedom" and yet tolerates less and less dissent. The masochism, the anxiety, the alienation which are almost universal in such a society are forms of organized evasion. The energies that might otherwise go into productive or even revolutionary change are driven into stagnant backwaters of frustration and self-pity. People are not only made ill, but they prefer to be ill rather than face the risk of real dissent. (Note the important distinction between real and pseudo-dissent, the latter being merely a token and a symbol expressing and justifying an underlying neurosis.) We know well enough that this pattern, so familiar in "the world," is even more familiar in "the cloister."

Nevertheless there is an important distinction between mere neurotic anxiety which comes from a commitment to defeat and existential anxiety which is the healthy pain caused by the blocking of vital energies that still remain available for radical change. This is one of the main points made by Dr. Arasteh's book: the importance of existential anxiety seen not as a symptom of something wrong, but as a summons to growth and to painful development.

Carefully distinguishing existential anxiety from the petulant self-defeating sorrows of the neurotic, Dr. Arasteh shows how this anxiety is a sign of health and generates the necessary strength for psychic rebirth into a new transcultural identity. This new being is entirely personal, original, creative, unique, and it transcends the limits imposed by social convention and prejudice. Birth on this higher level is an imperative necessity for man.

The infant who lives immersed in a symbiotic relationship with the rest of nature—immersed, that is, in his own narcissism—must be "born" of this sensual self-centeredness and acquire an identity as a responsible member of society. Ordinary psychotherapy is fully aware of this. But once one has grown up, acquired an education, and assumed a useful role as a worker and provider, there is still another birth to be undergone. Dr. Arasteh studies this birth to final integration in three exceptional individuals: Rumi, the Persian mystic and poet; Goethe; and a young modern Turk who was one of Arasteh's patients.

In the past, final integration was generally a matter only for unusually gifted people. We shall return to this point later. Even today, though the need for final integration makes itself more and more widely felt, the majority not only do not try to attain it, but society, as we have seen, provides them with ways to evade the summons. Clearly, in many cases, that summons takes the form of a monastic, religious or priestly vocation.

Clearly, too, there are many who leave the monastery because they feel that the way the monastic life is structured, or the way they themselves are fitted into the structure, makes a genuine response to the summons impossible.

All of us who have had to work through vocation problems with professed monks can, on reflection, easily distinguish obvious neurotics from men whose monastic crisis has taken the form of existential anxiety: this is a crisis of authentic growth which cannot be resolved in the situation in which they find themselves, and the situation cannot be changed. (Very often, in similar situations, it is the mildly neurotic who manage to stay and make some sort of compromise adjustment, nestling fearfully in the protection of the monastery with the obscure sense that further painful growth will not be demanded!)

Since his investigation is purely psychological, not theological, the question of "sanctity" or holiness does not really arise from Dr. Arasteh. But let us make clear that ordinarily a full spiritual development and a supernatural, even charismatic, maturity, evidenced in the "saint," normally includes the idea of complete psychological integration. Doubtless many saints have been neurotics, but they have used their neurosis in the interests of growth instead of capitulating and succumbing to its dubious comforts.

Final integration is a state of transcultural maturity far beyond mere social adjustment, which always implies partiality and compromise. The man who is "fully born" has an entirely "inner experience of life." He apprehends his life fully and wholly from an inner ground that is at once more universal than the empirical ego and yet entirely his own. He is in a certain sense "cosmic" and "universal man." He has attained a deeper, fuller identity than that of his limited ego-self which is only a fragment of his being. He is in a certain sense identified with everybody: or in the familiar language of the New Testament (which Arasteh evidently has not studied) he is "all things to all men." He is able to experience their joys and sufferings as his own, without however becoming dominated by them. He has attained to a deep inner freedom—the Freedom of the Spirit we read of in the New Testament. He is guided not just by will and reason, but by "spontaneous behavior subject to dynamic insight." Now, this calls to mind the theology of St. Thomas on the Gifts of the Holy Spirit which move a man to act "in a super-human mode." Though Dr. Arasteh takes no account of specif-ically supernatural agencies, it is clear that such considerations might become relevant here. But of course they cannot be inves-tigated by experimental science.

Again, the state of insight which is final integration implies an openness, an "emptiness," a "poverty" similar to those described in such detail not only by the Rhenish mystics, by St. John of the Cross, by the early Franciscans, but also by the Sufis, the early Taoist masters and Zen Buddhists. Final integration implies the void, poverty and nonaction which leave one entirely docile to the "Spirit" and hence a potential instrument for unusual creativity.

The man who has attained final integration is no longer lim-ited by the culture in which he has grown up. "He has embraced *all of life*. . . . He has experienced qualities of every type of life": ordinary human existence, intellectual life, artistic creation, human love, religious life. He passes beyond all these limiting forms, while retaining all that is best and most universal to them, "finally giving birth to a fully comprehensive self." He accepts not only his own community, his own society, his own friends, his own culture, but all mankind. He does not remain bound to one limited set of values in such a way that he opposes them aggressively or defensively to others. He is fully "Catholic" in the best sense of the word. He has a unified vision and expe-rience of the one truth shining out in all its various manifesta-tions, some clearer than others, some more definite and more certain than others. He does not set these partial views up in opposition to each other, but unifies them in a dialectic or an insight of complementarity. With this view of life he is able to bring perspective, liberty and spontaneity into the lives of oth-ers. The finally integrated man is a peacemaker, and that is why there is such a desperate need for our leaders to become such men of insight.

It will be seen at once that this kind of maturity is exactly what the monastic life should produce. The monastic ideal is precisely this sort of freedom in the spirit, this liberation from the limits of all that is merely partial and fragmentary in a given culture. Monasticism calls for a breadth and universality of vision that sees everything in the light of the One Truth as St. Benedict beheld all creation embraced "in one ray of the sun." This too is suggested at the end of Chapter 7 of the Rule where St. Benedict speaks of the new identity, the new mode of being of the monk who no longer practices the various degrees of humility with concentrated and studied effort, but with dynamic spontaneity "in the Spirit." It is suggested also in the "Degrees of Truth" and the "Degrees of Love" in St. Bernard's tracts on humility and on the love of God.

Reprinted by permission of the publisher, Doubleday & Company, Inc., from CONTEMPLATION IN A WORLD OF ACTION, by Thomas Merton, 1965, pp. 222–226.

QUESTIONS

1. How does Merton define "final integration"?
2. Why do both Bouwsma and Merton indicate that mere adaptation to the culture or the existing society is not enough for full human growth?
3. Is the person who has reached "final integration" as described by Merton similar to a person in stage five or six as described by Fowler?

SUGGESTED READINGS

Boelen, B. (1978). *Personal Maturity.* New York: Seabury.

Groeschel, B. (1983). *Spiritual Passages: The Psychology of Spiritual Development.* New York: Crossroad.

Nouwen, H. (1981). *Thomas Merton: Contemplative Critic.* New York: Harper & Row.

Whitehead, E. and Whitehead, J. (1979). *Christian Life Patterns.* Garden City: Doubleday.

Part IV

MORAL DEVELOPMENT—
THEOLOGICAL AND
PSYCHOLOGICAL
PERSPECTIVES

Charles E. Curran

16. The Christian Conscience Today

Charles Curran is a Roman Catholic priest and professor of moral theology at The Catholic University of America in Washington, D.C. He has written several books on moral theology and with Richard McCormick, S.J. edits the series *Readings in Moral Theology*. This selection points out that a mature Christian conscience is rooted more in love than in legalism, although the various kinds of law—law of the spirit, natural law, positive law and the law of the situation—help to form conscience. As he indicates, the basis of Christian morality is not a relation to an abstract principle but to a Person—God. Above all, he points out how complex are the problems of conscience for which there are not easy solutions.

Even a superficial reflection shows the existence of moral conscience. Man experiences the joy of having done good or the remorse of having done evil. He recognizes an imperative to do this or avoid that. A more profound analysis distinguishes moral conscience from social pressure or even a religious imperative.[1]

Moral conscience has many meanings. St. Paul describes conscience as a witness or judge of past activity, a director of future action, the habitual quality of a man's Christianity, and even as the Christian ego or personality.[2] This chapter will discuss the problem of antecedent conscience; that is, conscience as pointing out to the Christian what he should do in the particular circumstances of his life.

HISTORICAL SUMMARY

Scripture reveals Christianity as a dialogue or covenant relationship between God and his people. Christian tradition frequently refers to conscience as the voice of God telling man how to respond to the divine gift of salvation. Both the reality and the concept of moral conscience have evolved in the course of salvation history. Two reasons explain the evolution. First, God speaks to primitive man in one way and to more mature man in another way. Second, only when man has acquired a certain degree of maturity can he reflect on his own subjective states.[3]

In the beginning of salvation history, conscience (the reality, not the word) appears as extrinsic, objective, and collective.[4] Theophany, however, gives way to angelophany, and finally to human prophets who speak in the name of God.[5] The prophets, the conscience of Israel, stress interior dispositions and begin to mention individual responsibility (Jer 31:29–30; Ez 14:1–8). They look forward to the day when God will plant his law in the innermost part of man (Jer 31:33–34; Ez 36:26–27; Psalm 50:12). Since the prophets insist on God as the first cause, conscience is not the voice of man but the voice of God who speaks to man.

St. Paul, with his emphasis on the internal and subjective dispositions of man, brings into Christian thought the term conscience ($\sigma \upsilon \nu \epsilon \acute{\iota} \delta \eta \sigma \iota \varsigma$), which originally appeared in Democritus and was developed by stoic philosophy.[6] Paul, while adopting the uses of the term in pagan philosophy, introduces the notion of conscience as the director of human activity—antecedent conscience.[7] Commenting on the different Pauline uses of the term conscience, the Fathers of the church explicitly make the last step in the interiorization of conscience. Conscience now becomes the voice of the human person himself and only mediately and indirectly the voice of God.[8]

Scholastic theology of the thirteenth century first considered scientifically, as opposed to the pastoral approach of the Fathers, the nature of moral conscience. Is it a faculty? A habit? An act? The Thomistic school distinguished conscience, the judgment of the practical reason about a particular act, from synteresis, the quasi-innate habit of the first principles of the moral order. St. Bonaventure placed more emphasis on the will, especially with regard to synteresis. The subjective voice of reason was open to God through the mediation of law.[9]

Unfortunately, the scholastic synthesis succumbed to the dangers of sterile intellectualism, the nominalistic tendency to extrinsicism, and the increasing influence of positive juridic sciences. The decree of the Council of Trent again legislating the necessity of annual confession of sins according to their number and species orientated moral theology (and the question of conscience) toward the judgment seat of the confessional rather than toward the living of the Christian life.[10]

In this light one can better understand the famous controversy of the seventeenth and eighteenth centuries about the question of probable conscience. When I am not certain about the existence of a law, am I obliged to follow the doubtful law? Today the vast majority of moral theologians accept some form of a mitigated probabilism, which maintains that only a law which is certain can oblige a subject.[11] As a result of the controversy, *De Conscientia* became a separate and well-developed treatise in the manuals of moral theology. Among the benefits accruing to moral theology from such a development are the balance and equilibrium finally attained, the precise terminology acquired, and the realization that conscience must consider the many problems of daily living.

However, the defects of the manualistic treatises on conscience are great. Briefly, legalism, extrinsicism, impersonalism, and an ethic of obligation characterize such considerations of conscience. Positive law and objective considerations are greatly exaggerated. Conscience becomes negative, oppressive, and sin-orientated.[12] The dire consequences are not restricted merely to the intellectual and theoretical plane. History and empirical studies show that the linking of introspection with a legalistic approach to morality provides fertile ground for the formation of the scrupulous conscience.[13] Unfortunately, in everyday Catholic life, the average Catholic equates Christian morality with Mass on Sunday, no meat on Friday, and the need to obey what the Church teaches about sex.

In the last few decades theologians have begun to react against the manualistic treatment of conscience. Under the influence of the Thomistic renewal, authors now stress the virtue of prudence and the subjective element which cannot be found in any of the books on cases of conscience.[14] In keeping with the return to the primitive sources of scripture and the Fathers, which is characterizing all theological investigation today, theologians consider conscience in the light of charity, or the responsibility of the Christian before the call of God, or as an anticipation of the eschatological judgment.[15]

Outside the pale of theology, two divergent tendencies— exaggerated interiorization and over-objectivization—have destroyed the true notion of conscience. Ever since Descartes, philosophers like Montaigne, Rousseau, and Kant have over- emphasized the subjective element. Existentialism, the last step in the tendency, makes subjective conscience the center of the whole world completely cut off from God or any other subject. At the other extreme, conscience is considered merely a function of physiological factors (Chauchard), psychological factors (Freud), or sociological factors (Durkheim).[16]

THE NATURE OF CONSCIENCE

Guided by the lessons of history, one can better understand the nature of conscience, its function, and its formation. Catholic theologians generally distinguish synteresis, moral science, and conscience. Adopting a synthetic approach, we can define synteresis as the power of conscience situated in the inmost part of the soul *(scintilla animae)*. In its rational aspect, synteresis tends to the truth so that man almost intuitively knows the fundamental principle of the moral order—good is to be done and evil is to be avoided. In its volitional aspect, synteresis tends toward the good and the expression of such a tendency in action.

Moral science is the knowledge of the less general principles of the moral law which man deduces from the primary principles. The category of moral knowledge also includes whatever man knows from revelation or authority. It pertains to the objective, the conceptual, the essential order.

Conscience is the concrete judgment of the practical reason, made under the twofold influence of synteresis, about the moral goodness of a particular act. Conscience forms its judgment discursively from the objective principles of the moral order; but at the same time, there is also a direct connatural knowing process.

The dictate of conscience is concrete, subjective, individual, and existential.

Conscience tells man what he should do. Man's "ought" follows from his "is." Man's actions must affirm his being. St. Paul makes Christian existence the foundation of Christian morality. The Christian is baptized into the death and resurrection of Christ. Consequently, he must die to self and walk in the newness of life (Rom 6). Man's existence is a loving dependence on his God and a communion with his fellow men. Human endeavor must express this twofold personal relationship.

Conscience and human freedom are not completely autonomous. In practice man rejects the complete autonomy of conscience. In the eyes of the world Adolf Eichmann and the Nazis were guilty of crimes against humanity despite the plea of a clear conscience. Conscience must act in accord with the nature and person of man. The greatest possible freedom and the greatest possible happiness for man consist in the fulfillment of his own being.

The judgment of conscience expresses with regard to a particular act the fundamental tendency of man to truth and good. The basis of Christian morality, however, is not man's relation to an abstract principle, but to a person, *the* person, God. Since he first loved us, God has freely given us his love, his friendship, our salvation. Scripture uses the words faith and love ($\pi\iota\sigma\tau\iota\varsigma$, $\alpha\gamma\alpha\pi\eta$) to express man's acceptance and response to God's gift. Like Christ himself, man's external actions must manifest this love. At the same time man's actions dispose him to enter more intimately into the mystery of divine love. The ultimate norm of Christian conduct is this: what does the love of God demand of me in these concrete circumstances? Love, as a complete giving of self and not a mere emotion, seeks always the will of the beloved.

THE FORMATION OF CONSCIENCE

God speaks to us through the very existence he has given us—creation, salvation, our talents, abilities and even weaknesses, and the existential circumstances of our situation. In other words, the will of the beloved is made known to us through his "laws"—the law of the Spirit, the natural law, positive law, and the law of the situation.[17]

The primary law of the new covenant is the internal law of the Spirit, the law of Christ, the law of love. Even Christ, however, found it necessary to express his law in external rules; but the demands are comparatively general; e.g., the beatitudes.[18]

God also speaks to man through the human nature he has given him. The natural law, as theologians call it, is primarily a dynamic, internal law. Since it is the very law of man's existence and being, it has an absolute character.[19] Christ, at least implicitly, affirmed the value of the natural law within the framework of the new covenant.[20] The law of nature is assumed into the law of Christ, for all nature was created according to the image of Christ and all nature exists for Christ.[21] From the first principle of the natural law, more objective, detailed rules of conduct are formulated.

Unfortunately, many Catholic theologians have exaggerated the natural law. It is not the primary law for the Christian. Some have succumbed to the temptation of using the natural law as a club. Others have overextended it in attempting to prove the moral certitude of mere hypotheses. Many still tend to codify completely the natural law and thus rob the natural law of its dynamic character.

Living in human society, the Christian is also the subject of human law, both civil and ecclesiastical. Such law is purely external and consequently seen as an infringement on human liberty. Since positive legislation is not absolute, it does not oblige when in conflict with the interest of the higher laws.

God has called each person by his own name. In one sense, every individual is unique; every concrete situation is unique. The Christian's answer to the divine call must correspond to his individual circumstances.

Conscience is a supernaturally elevated subjective power of man. The law of Christ and the natural law are primarily internal laws. Why then is it necessary to have detailed, particular, external expressions of these laws? Why a code? Man's love of God is not yet perfect. Fallen human nature still experiences the tendency to self and not to God. Spiritual schizophrenia is a necessary characteristic of earthly Christianity. Even the impulsive reaction of the human will of Christ was to avoid the sacrifice willed by his Father.[22] Love of God is by its nature a self-sacrificing love. Man in his present state cannot know perfectly what the demands of love of God are. Particular, external expressions of the law of love and natural law have a value only insofar as they point out the minimum and basic demands of the law of love. Code morality is not opposed to an ethic of love.[23]

External law, if considered without any relation to the internal law, can be even an occasion of sin (Gal 3:19; Rom 5:20–21; 7:5–23). The external law is static and very incomplete. It does not and cannot express the totality of man's relationship to God. The vast majority of the decisions of conscience pertains to matters where there are no determined external expressions of law. Thus far we have not been speaking of the positive human laws which are primarily external. Here, too, self-sacrificing love of God and respect for the common good move man to obey positive law despite its inherent imperfections, unless such positive law runs counter to a higher law.

The formation and training of conscience include much more than the mere knowledge of external formulas of law. Insistence on external law is the haven of the insecure (neuroticism, scrupulosity) or the shallow (legalism, Phariseeism). Christian morality is ultimately love, an "I-thou" relationship between God and man. By mediating on true values, the Christian grows in wisdom and age and grace. Likewise, the formation of conscience must take into consideration the findings of many of the positive sciences. For example, what purports to be religious obedience might in reality be the manifestation of an inferiority complex. A proper formation, joined with the virtue of prudence acquired in daily Christian experiences, prepares the conscience to hear the call of God's love.

Space permits the mention of only two important characteristics of Christian conscience: communitarian and creative. A communitarian conscience recognizes man's relationship with his fellow men in the kingdom of God. A communitarian conscience avoids excessive individualism and the opposite extreme of mass hypnosis. A creative conscience, attuned to the Spirit, throws off the shackles of stultifying legalism. A true

Christian conscience leads man to make Christianity and Christian love "the light of the world and the salt of the earth"—a positive commitment to the kingdom of God in its reality both as the city of God and the city of man.

Reality is complex. The problems of conscience are complex. Frequently, there are no easy solutions. After prayerful consideration of all values involved, the Christian chooses what he believes to be the demands of love in the present situation. The Christian can never expect to have perfect, mathematical certitude about his actions. The virtue of humility preserves him from falling into the opposed extremes of introspective anxiety and mere formalism. Neurotic anxiety has no place in Christianity. Christianity is fundamentally a religion of joy—of man's participation in the joy and triumph of the resurrection. The paradox of Christianity is that joy comes through self-sacrificing love.

For the Christian who has made a commensurate effort to form his conscience correctly, the dictate of conscience is an infallible norm of conduct. Even though the action itself is not in objective conformity with the divine will, the Christian's conduct is pleasing to God, for it stems from a pure heart.[24]

The opposition that conscience experiences between Christian law and Christian freedom, between love and code morality, stems from man's imperfect love of God and wounded human nature. In reality, there is no dichotomy. The Christian law is the law of love—"the law of the Spirit, [giving] life in Christ Jesus, has delivered me from the law of sin and death" (Rom 8:2). Conscience leads man to participate ever more deeply in Christian love and freedom until the Christian reaches his final destiny where love, joy, freedom, and conformity with God's will are one.

Reprinted from CONSCIENCE, edited by C. Ellis Nelson, published by Newman Press, pp. 132–142, © 1973 by the Missionary Society of St. Paul the Apostle in the State of New York.

NOTES

1. Jacques Leclercq, *Les grandes lignes de la philosophie morale* (Louvain, 1953), pp. 7–13.

2. C. Spicq, "La conscience dans le Nouveau Testament," *Revue Biblique* 47 (1938), pp. 55–76. Cf., C. A. Pierce, *Conscience in the New Testament* (London, 1955).

3. For the general lines of the evolution by which God brought his people in the Old Testament to both self-knowledge and a knowledge of the true God, see Marc Oraison, *Love or Constraint?* (New York, 1959), pp. 152–163.

4. The characteristics of a primitive conscience in general are aptly described by Richard Mohr, *Die Christliche Ethik im Lichte der Ethnologie* (München, 1954).

5. Theophany abounds in the first chapters of Genesis. There is some dispute among scripture scholars on the exact nature of the "Angel of Jahweh" which appears in Genesis 16:7; 22:11; Exodus 3:2; Judges 2:1. Even if the expression here refers merely to God in a visible form, such an expression indicates a "sophisticated" reluctance to speak of a pure theophany. In the Old Testament, angels exercise the same twofold function as conscience; namely, they make known the will of God and serve as guides both for individuals and the whole people of God.

6. Spicq, pp. 51–55; Pierce, pp. 13–53. Also Th. Deman, *La Prudence* (Paris, 1949), pp. 479–487.

7. Eric D'Arcy, *Conscience and its Right to Freedom* (New York, 1961), pp. 8–12; Pietro Palazzini, *La Coscienza* (Rome, 1961), pp. 63–71; Deman, pp. 488–489. Spicq maintains that the concept of an antecedent conscience was known by Paul's contemporaries, but it is certain that Paul contributed the most to its development (pp. 63–67). Among the texts cited as instances of Paul's referring to antecedent conscience are: 1 Cor 8; 10:25–33; Rom 13:5.

8. The affirmation is made by Antonio Hortelano in unpublished notes. Hortelano refers to the following citations from *Cursus Completus Patrologiae,* ed. J. P. Migne (Paris). Augustinus, "Tractatus in Joannem," *Pat. Latina* 35, col. 1382; Origines, "Commentarium in Epistolam ad Romanos," *Pat. Graeca* 14, col. 895; Basilius, "Homilia XIII," *Pat. Graeca* 31, col. 432.

9. Odon Lottin, *Morale Fondamentale* (Tournai, 1954), pp. 163–165; 221–228. The author summarizes here the conclu-

sions derived from his multi-volumed historical study. *Psychologie et Morale aux XIIe et XIIIe siècles* (Gembloux).

10. There is no complete and authentic history of moral theology. Nor can there be until more particular studies are made. For the best available study of the development of moral theology of this time, see Bernard Häring—Lois Vereecke, "La Théologie Morale de S. Thomas d'Aquin à S. Alphonse de Liguori," *Nouvelle Revue Théologique 77* (1955), pp. 673–692. Also Louis Vereecke, "Le Council de Trente et l'enseignement de la Théologie Morale," *Divinitas 5* (1961), pp. 361–374.

11. Most of the manuals of moral theology accept such a probabilism. In practice, the antiprobabilists do not differ much from those who espouse simple probabilism. Outside the manuals, there is a reaction against the legalistic mentality of probabilism which has taken different forms. Cf., Th. Deman, "Probabilisme," *Dictionnaire de Théologie Catholique 13* (Paris, 1936), col. 417–619; also Deman, *La Prudence;* Georges Leclercq, *La Conscience du Chrétien* (Paris, 1947), pp. 127–197; P. Rousselot, *Quaestiones de Conscientia* (Paris, 1947), pp. 51–80.

12. The increasing awareness of the need for a renewal of moral theology in the last few years stems from these negative characteristics present today in most manuals. For a brief review of the recent literature on the subject of renewing moral theology, see John C. Ford and Gerald Kelly, *Contemporary Moral Theology* (Westminster, Md., 1958), pp. 42–103. It is my personal belief that the authors have not paid sufficient attention to the part played by the Tübingen school of theology, nor do they seem to fully appreciate the need for a life-centered and not confessional-orientated moral theology.

13. Juan Garcia-Vicente, "Dirección pastoral de la escrupulosidad," *Revista de Espiritualidad* 19 (1960), pp. 514–529. Also *Cahiers Laënnec* 20 (June 1960) which is totally concerned with the question of scrupulosity.

14. Deman, *La Prudence,* especially pp. 496–514. Perhaps Deman overemphasizes prudence at the expense of conscience. For a very satisfying discussion of the relationship between prudence and conscience, see Domenico Capone. *Intorno alla verità morale* (Naples, 1951). A fuller bibliography on the relationship

between prudence and conscience is given by Josephus Fuchs, *Theologia Moralis Generalis* (Rome, 1960), p. 169.

15. Bernard Häring, *The Law of Christ I* (Westminster, Md., 1961), pp. 91–213; René Carpentier, "Conscience," *Dictionnaire de Spiritualité* 2 (Paris, 1953), col. 1548–1575; Gérard Gilleman, "Eros ou agapè, Comment centrer la conscience chrétienne," *Nouvelle Revue Théologique* 72 (1950), pp. 326; 113–135.

16. For a critique of such opinions based on theological principles, see Palazzini, pp. 217–275. Also, Jacques Leclercq, *Christ and the Modern Conscience* (New York, 1962), pp. 7–104.

17. The word law is not a univocal term. Unfortunately, the coercive characteristic which essentially belongs to external positive law has been illegitimately transferred to the law of the Spirit and the natural law.

18. Some of Christ's laws are materially determined and particular; e.g., with regard to divorce, adultery, or even the thought of adultery. For an explanation of the general and more formal demands of Christ as the expression of a mentality or tendency rather than a determined material command, see C. H. Dodd, *Gospel and Law* (Cambridge, 1951). pp. 73–83.

19. A good description of the natural law with regard to its internal and historical character as well as its relationship to the law of Christ is given by J. Fuchs, *Le Droit Naturel: Essai Théologique* (Tournai, 1960).

20. Matt 5:27–48; 19:3–12, 17–20; Mark 7:20–23; Luke 12:57.

21. For Christ as the exemplar of all creation and nature, see Col 1:15–20; 1 Cor 8:6; Eph 1:3–10. Theologians speak of Christ as the final cause of all creation because of the same texts as well as John 1:1–14 and 1 Cor 3:22–23.

22. Matt 26:39. Theologians, interpreting the different acts of the will of Christ in this passage, distinguish between the *voluntas ut natura* and the *voluntas ut ratio.* Christ's human will impulsively shrank from suffering. He could accept suffering only insofar as he saw it as the will of his Father.

23. For the Catholic, the magisterium or teaching function of the Church gives an authentic interpretation of Christian morality. Doctrinal and moral pronouncements constitute just

one aspect of the teaching office of the Church. The whole Church in the lives of all members must bear living witness to the truth.

24. During the probabilism controversy, anti-probabilists frequently cited the opinion of St. Bernard that a person following an erroneous conscience in good faith commits sin. Bernard's opinion stems from his mystical insistence on conscience as the voice of God. Consequently, any error or deviation can be attributed only to the bad will of man. Philippe Delhaye, *Le problème de la conscience morale chez S. Bernard* (Namur, 1957), especially pp. 44–45.

QUESTIONS

1. What are the two divergent tendencies that have destroyed the true notion of conscience outside of theology?
2. How does Curran show how the laws of God help us to know what is right?
3. Why does the formation of conscience include more than mere knowledge of the external formulas of law?

SUGGESTED READINGS

Nelson, C. E. (1973). *Conscience: Theological and Psychological Perspectives.* New York: Newman.
Kohlberg, L. (1981). *The Philosophy of Moral Development.* New York: Harper.

Ronald Duska and Mariellen Whelan

17. Kohlberg's Moral Judgment Stages

Dr. Duska is at present professor in the department of philosophy at Rosemont College. Mariellen Whelan, formerly professor in the department of education at Rosemont College, is presently in the education department of the Insurance Society of Pennsylvania. Dr. Lawrence Kohlberg is professor of psychology in Harvard's Graduate School of Education. This selection was chosen because it is a clear succinct expression of the now well-known Kohlberg model of the stages of the development of moral judgment. It also indicates, through the description of the creation of cognitive disequilibrium, how teachers can facilitate growth in moral maturity. Finally attention is drawn to the need to help persons move from egocentrism to a view of the larger society. This expansion of the bounds of social awareness which occurs in maturing moral judgment is also present in Fowler's model of faith development in Chapter 13.

Kohlberg identified six stages, two stages occurring at three distinct levels—the pre-conventional, the conventional and the post-conventional.

PRE-CONVENTIONAL LEVEL

At this level the child is responsive to cultural rules and labels of good and bad, right or wrong, but interprets these labels in terms of either the physical or the hedonistic consequences of action (punishment, reward, exchange of favors) or in terms of the physical power of those who enunciate the rules and labels. The level is divided into two stages:

Stage 1: The Punishment and Obedience Orientation. The physical consequences of action determine its goodness or bad-

ness regardless of the human meaning or value of these consequences. Avoidance of punishment and unquestioning deference to power are valued in their own right, not in terms of
respect for an underlying moral order supported by punishment
and authority (the latter being Stage 4).

Stage 2: The Instrumental Relativist Orientation. Right
action consists of that which instrumentally satisfies one's own
needs and occasionally the needs of others. Human relations are
viewed in terms like those of the marketplace. Elements of fairness, reciprocity, and equal sharing are present, but they are
always interpreted in a physical or pragmatic way. Reciprocity
is a matter of "you scratch my back and I'll scratch yours," not
of loyalty, gratitude, or justice.

CONVENTIONAL LEVEL

At this level, maintaining the expectations of the individual's family, group, or nation is perceived as valuable in its own
right, regardless of immediate and obvious consequences. The
attitude is not only one of conformity to personal expectations
and social order, but of loyalty to it, of actively maintaining,
supporting, and justifying the order and of identifying with the
persons or group involved in it. At this level, there are two
stages:

*Stage 3: The Interpersonal Concordance of "Good Boy—
Nice Girl" Orientation.* Good behavior is that which pleases or
helps others and is approved by them. There is much conformity
to stereotypical images of what is majority or "natural" behavior. Behavior is frequently judged by intention: "He means well"
becomes important for the first time. One earns approval by
being "nice."

Stage 4: The Law and Order Orientation. There is orientation toward authority, fixed rules, and the maintenance of the
social order. Right behavior consists of doing one's duty, showing respect for authority and maintaining the given social order
for its own sake.

POST-CONVENTIONAL, AUTONOMOUS, OR PRINCIPLED LEVEL

At this level, there is a clear effort to define moral values and principles which have validity and application apart from the authority of the groups or persons holding these principles and apart from the individual's own identification with these groups. This level has two stages:

Stage 5: The Social-Contract Legalistic Orientation. Generally with utilitarian overtones. Right action tends to be defined in terms of general individual rights and in terms of standards which have been critically examined and agreed upon by the whole society. There is a clear awareness of the relativism of personal values and opinions and a corresponding emphasis upon procedural rules for reaching consensus. Aside from what is constitutionally and democratically agreed upon, the right is a matter of personal values and opinion. The result is an emphasis upon the legal point of view, but with an emphasis upon the possibility of changing law in terms of rational considerations of social utility (rather than rigidly maintaining it in terms of Stage 4 law and order). Outside the legal realm, free agreement and contract is the binding element of obligation. This is the "official" morality of the American government and Constitution.

Stage 6: The Universal Ethical Principle Orientation. Right is defined by the decision of conscience in accord with self-chosen ethical principles appealing to logical comprehensiveness, universality, and consistency. These principles are abstract and ethical (the golden rule, the categorical imperative) and are not concrete moral rules like the ten commandments. At heart, these are universal principles of justice, of the reciprocity and equality of the human rights, and of respect for the dignity of human beings as individual persons.[1]

Our main task in the rest of this chapter will be to elaborate on these definitions of each stage, indicating the relationships

---

1. L. Kohlberg, "Stages of Moral Development as a Basis for Moral Education," in *Moral Education: Interdisciplinary Approaches,* pp. 86–88 (New York: Newman Press), 1971.

between them primarily by emphasizing the changes that take place in the development from one stage to another. However, before beginning such an elaboration it is necessary to mention four qualities of stage development which have been reinforced by Kohlberg's studies.

1. *Stage development is invariant.* One must progress through the stages in order, and one cannot get to a higher stage without passing through the stage immediately preceding it. Thus, one cannot get to stage four without passing through stages one, two and three respectively. This will become more apparent as we describe the transitions from one stage to another, but for now try to imagine the sort of mental adjustment which would be required for someone who looks at the good in terms of pleasure for himself, to suddenly adopt an orientation where he looks at the good in terms of an abstract system of rights and obligations. A belief that such a leap into moral maturity is possible is in sharp contrast to the facts of developmental research. Moral development is growth and, like all growth, takes place according to a pre-determined sequence. To expect someone to grow into high moral maturity overnight would be like expecting someone to walk before he crawls.

2. *In stage development, subjects cannot comprehend moral reasoning at a stage more than one stage beyond their own.* Thus a person at stage two, who discriminates good and bad on the basis of his own pleasure, cannot comprehend reasoning at stage four which appeals to fixed duties the performance of which need not offer any promise of reward or pleasure. Since stage four reasoning requires an orientation quite different from stage two reasoning, a series of cognitive readjustments must be made in order for stage four reasoning to be comprehended. If Johnny is oriented to see good almost exclusively as that which brings him satisfaction, how will he understand a concept of the good in which the good might bring him no pleasure at all, indeed might even cause him pain? The moral maxim "It is better to give than to receive" reflects a high state of moral maturity and development. But it is incomprehensible to someone at a low level of moral development. The child who honestly asks you why it is better to give than to receive does so because he does not and cannot understand such thinking. The reason is simply

that he cannot comprehend thinking more than one stage above his own. To his mind "better" means "better for him," and how can it be better for him to give than to receive?

3. *In stage development subjects are cognitively attracted to reasoning one level above their own predominant level.* A stage one person will be attracted by stage two reasoning, a stage two person by stage three reasoning, and so on. Kohlberg asserts that reasoning at higher stages is cognitively more adequate than reasoning at lower stages, since it resolves problems and dilemmas in a more satisfactory way. Since reasoning at one stage higher is intelligible and since it makes more sense and resolves more difficulties, it is more attractive. If one is operating from an orientation where he thinks that it would be good for him to get the whole piece of pie, even while his bigger and stronger brother insists on getting the whole piece of pie, some thought about sharing, which is a higher stage of reasoning, will be a more attractive solution of the dilemma than the solution which would occur if both insisted on the pie and the stronger brother got it.

4. *In stage development, movement through the stages is effected when cognitive disequilibrium is created,* that is, when a person's cognitive outlook is not adequate to cope with a given moral dilemma. The belief of developmental theory, bolstered by the evidence, is that a person will look for more and more adequate ways of resolving dilemmas. If in a given situation one's cognitive framework cannot resolve a problem, the cognitive organism adjusts to a framework which does. Yet if a person's orientation is not disturbed (there is no cognitive disequilibrium) there is no reason to expect any development. Thus, in the apple pie example, if the bigger and stronger brother wants the pie he can have it and there is no dilemma. Only if he puts himself in the younger brother's place will he be forced to examine his self-interested point of view. For the smaller brother, however, the realization that the bigger brother will get the pie unless there is some other procedure of distribution will effect a questioning of the self-interested viewpoint. A different solution of the problem will be sought. When such a disequilibrium is provoked, it causes thinking about the inadequacies of one's reasons and a search for better and more adequate reasons.

These qualities of stage development are, as we said, important to keep in mind. They have not only been verified time and again by research but they also make sense if one looks at the development of one's cognitive capacity as a kind of orderly growth. Moral development, like all other natural growth, follows a definite pattern.

Our exposition of Kohlberg's stages will attempt to keep these qualities in mind, particularly the last two, for we will attempt to describe how a person at any specific stage reaches disequilibrium, how that person finds the next higher stage cognitively more adequate in resolving a dilemma, and why that next higher stage will be more attractive.

Besides these qualities of stage development, Kohlberg also points out another important general characteristic about the process of moral development which will govern our presentation. According to Kohlberg, up through stage four each stage represents a wider and more adequate perception of the social system and an ability to think more abstractly.[2] In our account we will describe each stage, indicate its inadequacies, and show how the next higher stage compensates for these inadequacies by being a more adequate view of the social system. We will also show how such a view requires less concrete and more abstract thinking.

Turning our attention to the six stages listed in the table, we see that Kohlberg arranges them in pairs, locating each pair in one of three levels which he names respectively the "pre-conventional," "conventional" and "post-conventional" levels. The orientations characteristic of these levels reflect specific differences in the wideness of the view of the social system and differences in one's ability to think beyond one's immediate concrete situation.

Society and groups, whether we take note of it or not, are not concrete things like individual people, discernible to the senses. To appreciate the existence of a group requires an ability to think in an abstract way and, as we saw in Piaget, the ability

---

2. L. Kohlberg, "Continuities and Discontinuities in Childhood and Adult Moral Development Revisited," in Baltes and Schaie (eds.), *Life-Span Developmental Psychology: Research and Theory* (New York: Academic Press), 1975.

to shed egocentrism and to see oneself as a member of a group. Each movement from level to level results from a different perspective of groups and one's relationship to groups. Thus while reasoning at the first two stages, the pre-conventional level, involves quite concrete reasoning about individual persons and events, with little or no perception of a society, its groups or institutions, reasoning at the third and fourth stages, the conventional level, involves gradually more abstract thinking in which a perception of society, its groups and its institutions develops.

QUESTIONS

1. How can one create cognitive disequilibrium?
2. Is there any relationship between the description of the conventional level of morality and the criticism of legalism in Curran's article (Chapter 16)?

SUGGESTED READINGS

Dykstra, C. (1981). *Vision and Character: A Christian Educator's Alternative to Kohlberg.* New York: Paulist.

Hersch, R. H., Paolitto, D. and Reimer, J. (1979). *Promoting Moral Growth: From Piaget to Kohlberg.* New York: Longman.

Joy, D. M. (ed.) (1983). *Moral Development Foundations: Judeo-Christian Alternatives to Piaget/Kohlberg.* Nashville: Abingdon.

Kohlberg, L. (1981). *The Philosophy of Moral Development: Moral Stages and the Idea of Justice.* New York: Harper.

Kohlberg, L. (1983). *The Psychology of Moral Development: Moral Stages and the Life Cycle.* New York: Harper.

John A. Meacham

18. A Dialectical Approach to Moral Judgment and Self-Esteem

Dr. Meacham is associate professor of psychology at Boystown Center in The Catholic University of America, Washington, D.C. His specialty is human development and he has published many articles on the topic. Since a theme underlying all the selections in this book is the growth of one's awareness of oneself as necessary for both faith and moral development, this article was chosen for its clear expression of that relationship. While Kohlberg emphasizes awareness of moral principles as the basis of moral judgment, Meacham points out that moral behavior is also related to the desire to behave consistently with one's view of oneself as principled. He points out that if there is a synthesis of moral principles and self-concept, then self-esteem is maintained and just solutions are decided. If not, one tends to act less out of principle and more often in order to maintain self-esteem. An awareness of the continuing transformation of one's self-concept throughout life might make for a better understanding of moral development in middle and late adulthood. Since Meacham is emphasizing a dialectical process, he closes with a description of the dialectic between individual morality and a society's moral stance.

PRINCIPLED MORALITY

The course of moral development can be seen as one of increasing integration of principles of moral judgment with the concept of self. The achievement of the principled morality of stage 5 and 6 'must be considered as a matter of personal choice and as a choice of self in a sense not true of earlier moral stages' (*Kohlberg,* 1973, p. 199). The retention of concerns for conservation of the self, rather than the exchange of selfless for unselfish motives, is made clear in *Baldwin's* (1906, p. 43) analysis of the development of the ethical self, according to which the personal, habitual self and the sympathetic, accommodating self are brought into a harmony or synthesis. Thus, for the individual who has achieved principled morality, the commitment to moral principles is at the same time a commitment to one's self.

Abortion, for example, has been a moral issue because the principles which are called upon in debate are at the same time concepts which reflect the worth which people ascribe to themselves. The point here is not to decide the question of abortion, but rather to indicate that abortion has been a difficult issue precisely because the moral judgment depends upon and threatens to change people's self-esteem. Similarly, racism, sexism, and discrimination against the aged all involve relational statements constructed between young, white males and others. The decline of such attitudes will come with increased recognition that such judgments are at the same time judgments against the self, and that emancipation of such groups from their imposed roles can also free the young white male from the constraints of his own role.

ACTIONS TOWARDS OTHERS

The relationship between self-esteem and moral behaviors has not been explored, and yet self-esteem does play a role in other research which considers evaluative relationships between individuals. For example, research evidence suggests a relationship between low self-esteem and aggression in children (*Feshbach,* 1970, pp. 198, 208). Generosity towards others also depends upon self-esteem, with success experiences making generosity more likely. Failure experiences make generosity likely when the failure has been observed by another person; *Rosenhan* (1972, p. 348) interprets such generosity as an attempt by the child to restore his self-esteem. A self-concept equilibrium model to account for altruistic behaviors has also been suggested by *Krebs* (1970, p. 266). More generally, feelings of inferiority and inadequacy are associated with conformity (*Krech et al.,* 1962, p. 526), and so it can be expected that principled moral behavior ought to be more difficult to achieve for those with low self-esteem. *Podd* (1972) has found that persons undergoing identity crises engage in inconsistent moral reasoning, while those who have achieved ego identity have a more mature level of moral judgment. Moral conduct in children has also been shown to be influenced by the child's perception of his previous behavior patterns (*Lepper,* 1973).

The relationship between self-esteem and moral judgments ought to be explored more fully: is resistance to temptation or level of moral judgment dependent upon self-esteem? Is transition between stages of moral judgment associated with temporarily lowered self-esteem? What are the changes in self-esteem associated with positive or negative judgments of others? The possibility of strong interactions between self-concept, moral judgments, altruistic acts, etc. makes inadequate theories which express self-concept as a mere reflection of the responses which are directed towards the individual. Rather, a dialectical approach emphasizes the construction of the self-concept as the individual relates himself to others by evaluative actions which are then reflected onto himself. Moral behavior may be guided not by the individual's role-playing of judgments by others, but rather by his attempts to behave in a manner consistent with his own principles.

A MORALITY OF MEDIATION

Mature moral behavior thus depends upon a synthesis of principles abstracted from the course of social interactions with a self-concept which reflects the construction of evaluative relationships with other persons. Moral behavior gains its strength not only from the intrinsic vigor of advanced principles but also from the individual's attempts to behave consistently with his self-concept as a principled person. The discussion to follow emphasizes the conservation of self-esteem, not to suggest that moral behavior must be self-oriented, but rather to indicate that consideration of both moral principles and self-esteem is necessary in order to fully describe moral behavior.

Consider an individual faced with a moral dilemma involving alternative courses of action justifiable by equally valid but contradictory principles. To act without regard for one of the principles may be to risk loss of self-esteem not only as the principle is violated, but also as the evaluative action is reflected onto the individual's own self-concept. An immature solution would consistently uphold one of the principles while disregarding the other. A mature and dialectical solution would involve an equitable compromise, violating neither principle through construction of a higher-order principle, or violating each as minimally as possible.

An indication that a mature, dialectical morality of mediation has been achieved may be an increased resistance to making such difficult decisions—not, however, because of the individual's failure to recognize the alternatives of lack of strength to choose between the alternatives, but rather because he is actively constructing and evaluating compromises or awaiting new information to help construct a synthesis of the alternatives. The dialectical individual recognizes the mutually contradictory principles, acknowledges his participation as subject in his judgment of the object, and senses the implications which his judgments have for his own self-concept. Such an individual may even engage in delaying actions in order to avoid making a premature judgment—e.g., postponing the decision until next week's meeting. (In the meantime, dialectics as a method of analysis may yield the best resolution of the moral dilemma, particularly for ill-structured problems where there is disagreement as to the nature of the problem; see *Mitroff and Sagasti, 1973*, p. 124.) A morality of mediation thus involves a reflection upon the consequences of acting, a dialectical interaction of thought and action (see, e.g., *Rappoport, 1975*). What are the legitimate coping strategies which individuals may employ in order to avoid premature judgments and gain time to construct compromise solutions to moral problems? The distinction between the individual who is unable to commit himself to a moral decision and one who puts off the decision for the sake of constructing the best possible solution is obviously important and needs further clarification.

DEVELOPMENTAL CONSIDERATIONS

The view thus far presented suggests that moral behavior is dependent upon two dialectical processes, one involving subject and object, the individual and that which is judged, and the other involving a synthesis of moral principles and self-concept. Thus, for the morally mature person there is no longer a contradiction between, but rather a unity of, moral concerns and the concerns of the self. For the individual who has not achieved this synthesis, an inconsistent morality may be displayed as the person conforms to various pressures which reinforce his self-esteem. Further, attempts to boost self-esteem may include the definition of moral principles in terms of the self, rather than the self-concept being a reflection of moral principles. For example, the extension of power by the Nixon administration (Ehrlichman has said, 'The President *is* the government') may have been a compensation for the low self-esteem of the administration during the first term (*Drew,* 1974, p. 54). In a similar fashion, the Nixon administration's Vietnam policy for 4 years, the achievement of 'Peace with honor', appears to have been motivated not by the search for an equitable solution to the conflict, but rather by the search for a solution which did not involve loss of self-esteem. If a synthesis of moral principles and self-concept has been achieved, then equitable solutions are achieved as self-esteem is maintained; in the absence of such a synthesis, self-esteem plays a disproportionate role in moral decisions.

The dialectical approach to moral dilemmas is one which seeks resolution through compromise. The cognitive abilities which are required are the ability to recognize inherent contradictions and conflicts, and the ability to construct suitable resolutions of conflicting principles. Surely such abilities will vary from individual to individual, and one can ask what progressions of changes in cultural structures (*Riegel,* 1975a), child-rearing practices, educational techniques, etc. might promote a dialectical approach to problems. Social interactions with peers may be particularly important, not merely because opportunities for role-taking are provided, but because the initial equality among peers facilitates the construction of evaluative relationships and the development of an accurate self-concept without the confounding of status differences.

A complete description of moral development ought to suggest the experiences which promote a dialectical synthesis of moral principles and self-esteem, and ought to be sensitive to the continuation of development in adulthood and old age. For example, a recent newspaper account of an American pilot who has anonymously given thousands of dollars to restore paintings in Italian churches which he may have damaged thirty years ago (Courier Express, 1974) may reflect a continuing interaction involving moral judgment and self-esteem which has reorganized the perception of earlier actions.

Because of the interdependence of self-esteem and moral judgment, questioning of even the most basic moral principles can be precipitated by radical changes in self-esteem. For example, both the elderly and doctors find it necessary, because of recent advances in medicine which make it possible to prolong life in a vegetative state, to consider more often the question of euthanasia (see, e.g., *Maguire,* 1974). Further, the wisdom of old age may reflect a morality of mediation or compromise tempered by a broadening of self-concept as one grows older (for a view of successful aging as 'compromise rather than resolution' see *Clayton,* 1975).

THE INDIVIDUAL AND SOCIETY

A complete understanding of the development of moral behavior must consider not only the importance of the society and the family for moral development in the individual, but also the importance of the individual's actions for changes in the society. Clearly the structure of society, economic conditions, etc., influence values and the transmission of values (e.g., *Maccoby,* 1968, p. 263), and theoretical attention has centered on the relative roles of the society and the family in socializing the child. Insufficient attention, however, has been paid to the reciprocal influence of the individual upon the family and upon the society (*Riegel,* 1973a, p. 13; 1975a) at critical choice points in *their* development. To achieve such an understanding will require that the individual be seen within a society which can be described in terms of cultural and historical changes, while the family and the society are seen as reflecting the continually developing morality of individuals.

The attributes which were valued at various historical periods, and which are still valued in various cultures, e.g., the Soviet Union, India, and China, are a part of the individual's self-concept. As changes in self-concept come about through communication among cultures, technological advances, etc., there will necessarily be changes in the outcomes of the moral process within individuals. In the Middle Ages all things were evaluated from a moral perspective; during the Renaissance, however, 'while the moral conventions were seemingly complied with, the spirit of morality was lacerated and violations of decency and justice unceasingly abounded' (*Rosenthal,* 1971, p. 178). *Rosenthal* further suggests that the trickery of modern psychological experiments derives from the intricacy and deception of Renaissance morality. Indeed, psychologists are becoming aware that their own research methods may contribute to significant changes in the larger society involving depersonalization and distrust (*Baumrind,* 1971, p. 890).

A number of questions can be asked regarding the individuals who from time to time bring a change in the moral principles of the society in which they live: What instigates the development of principles for this individual which transcend those of the society? What determines the extension of his principles throughout the society? The influence of the individual upon the society perhaps reaches its heights in the successful martyr, for whom a complete synthesis of self and principles has been attained, such that the self is maintained by the extension of the principles through the society and throughout time. Additional consideration of the dialectical interaction of individuals and society is essential for a complete understanding of moral development and self-esteem: 'Both of these are essential to moral conduct: that there should be a social organization and that the individual should maintain himself. The method for taking into account all of those interests which make up society on the one hand and the individual on the other is the method of morality' (*Mead,* 1934, p. 389).

CONCLUSION

A number of points put forth in this paper have certainly been offered before. Indeed, there is much that can be described in dialectical terms in the theories of *Freud, Mead,* and *Piaget,* as *Hogan* (1974) has pointed out. *Hogan* (1973) has also advanced a multidimensional model of moral conduct, in which moral maturity is defined as optimal placement on each of several dimensions—this model is similar in spirit to the morality of mediation proposed in this paper.

The present paper does not suggest a theory, but merely emphasizes certain aspects of moral development which are made apparent from a dialectical perspective. In particular, the interdependence of subject and object in the process of moral judgment is seen in the reciprocal interaction of moral judgment and self-esteem, and in the developmental synthesis of moral principles and self-concept within the individual. Second, a mature, dialectical morality of mediation is one in which the individual recognizes his own participation in his moral judgments, and further recognizes contradictions between moral principles and seeks to resolve these in higher syntheses. Finally, a dialectical approach emphasizes the interaction of the individual and the cultural-historical context, with the potential for development in the moral process continuing throughout the life span.

REFERENCES

Baldwin, J. M.: Social and ethical interpretations in mental development (Macmillian, New York, 1906).

Baumrind, D.: Principles of ethical conduct in the treatment of subjects. Am. Psychol. *26:* 887–896 (1971).

Burton, R. V.: The generality of honesty reconsidered. Psychol. Rev. *70:* 481–499 (1963).

Clayton. V.: Erikson's theory of human development as it applies to the elderly. Hum. Dev. 18 (1975).

Courier-Express: Ex-flier replacing church painting destroyed in war, p. 1 (Courier Express, Buffalo, April 4, 1974).

Drew, E.: A reporter in Washington, D.C.: autumn notes-II, pp. 41–105 (The New Yorker, New York, March 18, 1974).

Feshbach, S.: Aggression; in *Mussen* Carmichael's manual of child psychology, vol. 2 (Wiley, New York 1970).

Hoffman, M. L.: Moral development; in *Mussen* Carmichael's manual of child psychology, vol. 2 (Wiley, New York 1970).

Hogan, R.: Moral conduct and moral character: a psychological perspective. Psychol. Bull. *79:* 217–232 (1973).

Hogan, R.: Dialectical aspects of moral development. Hum. Dev. *17:* 107–117a (1974).

Hooper, F. H.: Life-span analyses of Piagetian concept tasks; in *Riegel* and *Meacham* The developing individual in a changing world, vol. 1 (Mouton, The Hague 1975).

Iannotti, R. J. and Meacham, J. A.: The nature, measurement, and development of empathy. Proc. Meet. Eastern Psychological Association, Philadelphia 1974.

Kohlberg, L.: Moral development and identification; in *Stevenson* Child psychology (National Society for the Study of Education, Chicago 1963).

Kohlberg, L.: Continuities in childhood and adult moral development revisited; in *Baltes and Schaie* Life-span developmental psychology: personality and socialization (Academic Press, New York 1973).

Krebs, D. L.: Altrusim—an examination of the concept and a review of the literature. Psychol. Bull. *73:* 258–302 (1970).

Krech, D.: Crutchfield, R. S., and Ballachey, E. L.: Individual in society. (McGraw-Hill, New York 1962).

Lepper, M. R.: Dissonance, self-perception, and honesty in children. J. Personality soc. Psychol. *25:* 65–74 (1973).

Maccoby, E. E.: The development of moral values and behavior in childhood; in *Clausen* Socialization and society (Little, Brown, Boston 1968).

Maguire, D. C.: Death by chance, death by choice. Atlantic *333:* 56–65 (1974).

Mead, G. H.: Mind, self, and society (University of Chicago Press, Chicago 1934).

Mitroff, I. I. and Sagasti, F.: Epistemology as general systems theory: an approach to the design of complex decision-making experiments. Philosophy soc. Sci. *3:* 117–134 (1973).

Overton, W. F. and Reese, H. W.: Models of development: methodological implications; in *Nesselroade and Reese* Life-span developmental psychology: methodological issues (Academic Press, New York 1973).

Podd, M. H.: Ego identity status and morality. Devl. Psychol. *6:* 497–507 (1972).

Rappoport, L.: On praxis and quasirationality. Hum. Dev. *18* (1975).

Riegel, K. F.: Developmental psychology and society: some historical and ethical considerations; in *Nesselroade and Reese* Life-span developmental psychology: methodological issues (Academic Press, New York 1973a).

Riegel, K. F.: Dialectic operations: the final period of cognitive development. Hu. Dev. *16:* 346–370 (1973b).

Riegel, K. F.: Adult life crises: a dialectic interpretation of development; in *Datan and Ginsberg* Life-span developmental psychology: normative life crises (Academic Press, New York 1975a).

Riegel, K. F.: From traits and equilibrium toward developmental dialectics; in *Arnold and Cole* 1974–75 Nebraska Symp. on Motivation (Nebraska University Press, Lincoln 1975b).

Riegel, K. F.: Subject-object alienation in psychological experimentation and testing. Hum. Dev. *18* (1975c).

Rosenhan, D. L.: Prosocial behavior of children; in *Hartup* The young child: reviews of research, vol. 2 (National Association for the Education of Young Children, Washington 1972).

Rosenthal, B. G.: The images of man (Basic Books, New York 1971).

Rychlak, J. F.: A philosophy of science for personality theory (Houghton Mifflin, Boston 1968).

Wozniak, R. H.: Verbal control of motor behavior—Soviet research and non-Soviet replications. Hum. Dev. *15:* 13–57 (1972).

Wozniak, R. H.: Dialecticism and structuralism: the philosophical foundation of Soviet and Piagetian developmental theory; in *Riegel and Rosenwald* Structure and transformation: developmental and historical aspects (Wiley, New York 1975).

Reprinted by permission from HUMAN DEVELOPMENT, Vol. 18, 1975, pp. 69–74. Copyright © 1975 by S. Karger AG, Basel.

QUESTIONS

1. How does Meacham demonstrate that self-esteem is an essential component of the capacity for a mature moral judgment?
2. Do you agree with his analysis that the grasp for power of the Nixon administration in the second term was related to low self-esteem?

SUGGESTED READINGS

Burns, R. B. (1979). *The Self-Concept: Theory, Measurement, Development and Behavior*. London: Longman.
Coopersmith, S. (1967). *The Antecedents of Self-Esteem*. San Francisco: Freeman.

Sigmund Freud

19. Some Psychical Consequences of the Anatomical Distinction Between the Sexes

The life of Sigmund Freud is well known. The founder of psychoanalysis in Vienna, his work on the interpretation of dreams and his later works on religion and civilization have greatly influenced twentieth century thought and society.

This selection is well known in feminist circles. The whole argument rests on the assumption that the resolution of the Oedipus complex is essential to the development of a moral sense. However, the universality of this complex has never been empirically validated. Freud sees the Oedipus complex as central to the development of the superego because, at its resolution, boys then identify with the father and his values and moral imperatives. Since girls do not resolve their complex in the same way because they do not identify with the father but with the mother, their superego of its very nature is weak and emotional. The argument only holds if one accepts the original assumption of the centrality of the Oedipus complex.

I have now said the essence of what I had to say: I will stop, therefore, and cast an eye over our findings. We have gained some insight into the prehistory of the Oedipus complex in girls. The corresponding period in boys is more or less unknown. In girls the Oedipus complex is a secondary formation. The operations of the castration complex precede it and prepare for it. As regards the relation between the Oedipus and castration complexes there is a fundamental contrast between the two sexes. *Whereas in boys the Oedipus complex is destroyed by the castration complex,[1] in girls it is made possible and led up to by the castration complex.* This contradiction is cleared up if we reflect

---

1. [Cf. 'The Dissolution of the Oedipus Complex'.]

that the castration complex always operates in the sense implied in its subject-matter: it inhibits and limits masculinity and encourages femininity. The difference between the sexual development of males and females at the stage we have been considering is an intelligible consequence of the anatomical distinction between their genitals and of the psychical situation involved in it; it corresponds to the difference between a castration that has been carried out and one that has merely been threatened. In their essentials, therefore, our findings are self-evident and it should have been possible to foresee them.

The Oedipus complex, however, is such an important thing that the manner in which one enters and leaves it cannot be without its effects. In boys (as I have shown at length in the paper to which I have just referred [1924d] and to which all of my present remarks are closely related) the complex is not simply repressed, it is literally smashed to pieces by the shock of threatened castration. Its libidinal cathexes are abandoned, desexualized and in part sublimated; its objects are incorporated into the ego, where they form the nucleus of the super-ego and give that new structure its characteristic qualities. In normal, or, it is better to say, in ideal cases, the Oedipus complex exists no longer, even in the unconscious; the super-ego has become its heir. Since the penis (to follow Ferenczi [1924]) owes its extraordinarily high narcissistic cathexis to its organic significance for the propagation of the species, the catastrophe to the Oedipus complex (the abandonment of incest and the institution of conscience and morality) may be regarded as a victory of the race over the individual. This is an interesting point of view when one considers that neurosis is based upon a struggle of the ego against the demands of the sexual function. But to leave the standpoint of individual psychology is not of any immediate help in clarifying this complicated situation.

In girls the motive for the demolition of the Oedipus complex is lacking. Castration has already had its effect, which was to force the child into the situation of the Oedipus complex. Thus the Oedipus complex escapes the fate which it meets with in boys: it may be slowly abandoned or dealt with by repression, or its effects may persist far into women's normal mental life. I cannot evade the notion (though I hesitate to give it expression) that for women the level of what is ethically normal is different from what it is in men. Their super-ego is never so inexorable, so impersonal, so independent of its emotional origins as we require it to be in men. Character-traits which critics of every epoch have brought up against women—that they show less sense of justice than men, that they are less ready to submit to the great exigencies of life, that they are more often influenced in their judgments by feelings of affection or hostility—all these would be amply accounted for by the modification in the formation of their super-ego which we have inferred above. We must not allow ourselves to be deflected from such conclusions by the denials of the feminists, who are anxious to force us to regard the two sexes as completely equal in position and worth; but we shall, of course, willingly agree that the majority of men are also far behind the masculine ideal and that all human individuals, as a result of their bisexual disposition and of cross-inheritance, combine in themselves both masculine and feminine characteristics, so that pure masculinity and femininity remain theoretical constructions of uncertain content.

I am inclined to set some value on the considerations I have brought forward upon the psychical consequences of the anatomical distinction between the sexes. I am aware, however, that this opinion can only be maintained if my findings, which are based on a handful of cases, turn out to have general validity and to be typical. If not, they would remain no more than a contribution to our knowledge of the different paths along which sexual life develops.

In the valuable and comprehensive studies on the masculinity and castration complexes in women by Abraham (1921), Horney (1923) and Helene Deutsch (1925) there is much that touches closely on what I have written but nothing that coincides with it completely, so that here again I feel justified in publishing this paper.

QUESTIONS

1. What argument does Freud give to demonstrate that women are morally inferior?

2. Does your observation of women's moral judgments agree with Freud's description?

SUGGESTED READINGS

Chodorow, N. (1978). *The Reproduction of Mothering.* Berkeley: University of California Press.

Gilligan, C. (1982). *Adult Development and Women's Development: Arrangements for a Marriage.* In J. Giele (ed.), *Women in Middle Years: Current Knowledge and Directions for Research and Policy.* New York: Wiley.

Miller, J. B. (1976). *Toward a New Psychology of Women.* Boston: Beacon.

Carol Gilligan

20. Woman's Place in Man's Life Cycle

Carol Gilligan is professor of psychology in the Graduate School of Education of Harvard University. Over the past years she has investigated the way that women make moral judgments. This article describes the result of her research which revealed that women are more likely to base their moral judgments on the notions of care, relationships and responsibility. Men have a more negative way of basing moral judgments on non-interference and competing rights. She shows why, since the masculine model of morality prevails, women's moral judgments seem vague and inconclusive.

"It is obvious," Virginia Woolf said, "that the values of women differ very often from the values which have been made by the other sex" (1929, p. 76). Yet, she adds, it is the masculine values that prevail. As a result, women come to question the "normality" of their feelings and to alter their judgments in deference to the opinion of others. In the nineteenth-century novels written by women, Woolf sees at work "a mind slightly pulled from the straight, altering its clear vision in the anger and confusion of deference to external authority" (1929, p. 77). The same deference that Woolf identifies in nineteenth-century fiction can be seen as well in the judgments of twentieth-century women. Women's reluctance to make moral judgments, the difficulty they experience in finding or speaking publicly in their own voice, emerge repeatedly in the form of qualification and self-doubt, in intimations of a divided judgment, a public and private assessment which are fundamentally at odds (Gilligan, 1977).

Yet the deference and confusion that Woolf criticizes in women derive from the values she sees as their strength. Women's deference is rooted not only in their social circumstances but also in the substance of their moral concern. Sensitivity to the needs of others and the assumption of responsibility for taking care lead women to attend to voices other than their own and to include in their judgment other points of view. Women's moral weakness, manifest in an apparent diffusion and confusion of judgment, is thus inseparable from women's moral strength, an overriding concern with relationships and responsibilities. The reluctance to judge can itself be indicative of the same care and concern for others that infuses the psychology of women's development and is responsible for what is characteristically seen as problematic in its nature.

Thus women not only define themselves in a context of human relationship but also judge themselves in terms of their ability to care. Woman's place in man's life cycle has been that of nurturer, caretaker, and helpmate, the weaver of those networks of relationships on which she in turn relies. While women have thus taken care of men, however, men have in their theories of psychological development tended either to assume or devalue that care. The focus on individuation and individual achievement that has dominated the description of child and adolescent development has recently been extended to the depiction of adult development as well. Levinson in his study, *The Seasons of a Man's Life* (1978), elaborates a view of adult development in which relationships are portrayed as a means to an end of individual achievement and success. In the critical relationships of early adulthood, the "Mentor" and the "Special Woman" are defined by the role they play in facilitating the man's realization of his "Dream." Along similar lines Vaillant (1977), in his study of men, considers altruism a defense, characteristic of mature ego functioning and associated with successful "adaptation to life," but conceived as derivative rather than primary in contrast to Chodorow's analysis, in which empathy is considered "built-in" to the woman's primary definition of self.

The discovery now being celebrated by men in mid-life of the importance of intimacy, relationships, and care is something that women have known from the beginning. However, because that knowledge has been considered "intuitive" or "instinctive," a function of anatomy coupled with destiny, psychologists have neglected to describe its development. In my research, I have found that women's moral development centers on the elaboration of that knowledge. Women's moral development thus delineates a critical line of psychological development whose importance for both sexes becomes apparent in the intergenerational framework of a life-cycle perspective. While the subject of moral development provides the final illustration of the reiterative pattern in the observation and assessment of sex differences in the literature on human development, it also indicates more particularly why the nature and significance of women's development has for so long been obscured and considered shrouded in mystery.

The criticism that Freud (1961) makes of women's sense of justice, seeing it as compromised in its refusal of blind impartiality, reappears not only in the work of Piaget (1934) but also in that of Kohlberg (1958). While girls are an aside in Piaget's account of *The Moral Judgment of the Child* (1934), an odd curiosity to whom he devotes four brief entries in an index that omits "boys" altogether because "the child" is assumed to be male, in Kohlberg's research on moral development, females simply do not exist. Kohlberg's six stages that describe the development of moral judgment from childhood to adulthood were derived empirically from a longitudinal study of eighty-four boys from the United States. While Kohlberg (1973) claims universality for his stage sequence and considers his conception of justice as fairness to have been naturalistically derived, those groups not included in his original sample rarely reach his higher stages (Edwards, 1975; Gilligan, 1977). Prominent among those found to be deficient in moral development when measured by Kohlberg's scale are women whose judgments on his scale seemed to exemplify the third stage in his six-stage sequence. At this stage morality is conceived in terms of relationships, and goodness is equated with helping and pleasing others. This concept of goodness was considered by Kohlberg and Kramer (1969) to be functional in the lives of mature women insofar as those lives took place in the home and thus were relationally bound. Only if women were to go out of the house to enter the arena of male activity would they realize the inadequacy of their

Stage Three perspective and progress like men toward higher stages where morality is societally or universally defined in accordance with a conception of justice as fairness.

In this version of human development, however, a particular conception of maturity is assumed, based on the study of men's lives and reflecting the importance of individuation in their development. When one begins instead with women and derives developmental constructs from their lives, then a different conception of development emerges the expansion and elaboration of which can also be traced through stages that comprise a developmental sequence. In Loevinger's (1966) test for measuring ego development that was drawn from studies of females, fifteen of the thirty-six sentence stems to complete begin with the subject of human relationships (for example, "Raising a family. . . . ; If my mother. . . . ; Being with other people. . . . ; When I am with a man. . . . ; When a child won't join in group activities. . . . ") (Loevinger & Wessler, 1970, p. 141). Thus ego development is described and measured by Loevinger through conception of relationships as well as by the concept of identity that measures the progress of individuation.

Research on moral judgment has shown that when the categories of women's thinking are examined in detail (Gilligan, 1977) the outline of a moral conception different from that described in Freud, Piaget, or Kohlberg begins to emerge and to inform a different description of moral development. In this conception, the moral problem is seen to arise from conflicting responsibilities rather than from competing rights and to require for its resolution a mode of thinking that is contextual and inductive rather than formal and abstract.

This conception of morality as fundamentally concerned with the capacity for understanding and care also develops through a structural progression of increasing differentiation and integration. This progression witnesses the shift from an egocentric through a societal to the universal moral perspective that Kohlberg described in his research on men, but it does so in different terms. The shift in women's judgments from an egocentric to a conventional to a principled ethical understanding is articulated through their use of a distinct moral language, in which the terms "selfishness" and "responsibility" define the moral problem as one of care. Moral development then consists of the progressive reconstruction of this understanding toward a more adequate conception of care.

The concern with caring centers moral development around the progressive differentiation and integration that characterize the evolution of the understanding of relationships just as the conception of fairness delineates the progressive differentiation and balancing of individual rights. Within the responsibility orientation, the infliction of hurt is the center of moral concern and is considered immoral whether or not it can otherwise be construed as fair or unfair. The reiterative use of the language of selfishness and responsibility to define the moral problem as a problem of care sets women apart from the men whom Kohlberg studied and from whose thinking he derived his six stages. This different construction of the moral problem by women may be seen as the critical reason for their failure to develop within the constraints of Kohlberg's system.

Regarding all constructions of responsibility as evidence of a conventional moral understanding, Kohlberg defines the highest stages of moral development as deriving from a reflective understanding of human rights. That the morality of rights differs from the morality of responsibility in its emphasis on separation rather than attachment, in its consideration of the individual rather than the relationship as primary, is illustrated by two quotations that exemplify these different orientations. The first comes from a twenty-five-year-old man who participated in Kohlberg's longitudinal study. The quotation itself is cited by Kohlberg to illustrate the principled conception of morality that he scores as "integrated [Stage] Five judgment, possibly moving to Stage Six."

> [What does the word morality mean to you?] Nobody in the world knows the answer. I think it is recognizing the right of the individual, the rights of other individuals, not interfering with those rights. Act as fairly as you would have them treat you. I think it is basically to preserve the human being's right to existence. I think that is the most important. Secondly, the human being's right to do as he pleases, again without interfering with somebody else's rights.

[How have your views on morality changed since the last interview?] I think I am more aware of an individual's rights now. I used to be looking at it strictly from my point of view, just for me. Now I think I am more aware of what the individual has a right to. (Note 1, p. 29)

"Clearly," Kohlberg states,

these responses represent attainment of the third level of moral theory. Moving to a perspective outside of that of his society, he identifies morality with justice (fairness, rights, the Golden Rule), with recognition of the rights of others as these are defined naturally or intrinsically. The human's right to do as he pleases without interfering with somebody else's rights is a formula defining rights prior to social legislation and opinion which defines what society may expect rather than being defined by it. (Note 1, pp. 29–30)

The second quotation comes from my interview with a woman, also twenty-five years old and at the time of the interview a third-year student at Harvard Law School. She described her conception of morality as follows:

[Is there really some correct solution to moral problems or is everybody's opinion equally right?] No, I don't think everybody's opinion is equally right. I think that in some situations . . . there may be opinions that are equally valid and one could conscientiously adopt one of several courses of action. But there are other situations which I think there are right and wrong answers, that sort of inhere in the nature of existence, of all individuals here who need to live with each other to live. We need to depend on each other and hopefully it is not only a physical need but a need of fulfillment in ourselves, that a person's life is enriched by cooperating with other people and striving to live in harmony with everybody else, and to that end, there are right and wrong, there are things which promote that end and that move away from it, and in that way, it is possible to choose in certain cases among different courses of action, that obviously promote or harm that goal.

[Is there a time in the past when you would have thought about these things differently?] Oh, yah. I think that I went through a time when I thought that things were pretty relative, that I can't tell you what to do and you can't tell me what to do, because you've got your conscience and I've got mine. . . .

[When was that?] When I was in high school, I guess that it just sort of dawned on me that my own ideas changed and because my own judgments changed, I felt I couldn't judge another person's judgment . . . but now I think even when it is only the person himself who is going to be affected, I say it is wrong to the extent it doesn't cohere with what I know about human nature and what I know about you, and just from what I think is true about the operation of the universe, I could say I think you are making a mistake.

[What led you to change, do you think?] Just seeing more of life, just recognizing that there are an awful lot of things that are common among people . . . there are certain things that you come to learn promote a better life and better relationships and more personal fulfillment than other things that in general tend to do the opposite and the things that promote these things, you would call morally right.

These responses also represent a reflective reconstruction of morality following a period of relativistic questioning and doubt, but the reconstruction of moral understanding is based not on the primacy and universality of individual rights, but rather on what she herself describes as a "very strong sense of being responsible to the world." Within this construction, the moral dilemma changes from how to exercise one's rights without interfering with the rights of others to how "to lead a moral life which includes obligations to myself and my family and people in general." The problem then becomes one of limiting responsibilities without abandoning moral concern. When asked to describe herself, this woman says that she values

having other people that I am tied to and also having people that I am responsible to. I have a very strong sense of being responsible to the world, that I can't just live for my enjoyment, but just the fact of being in the world gives me an obligation to do what I can to make the world a better place to live in, no matter how small a scale that may be on.

Thus while Kohlberg's subject worries about people interfering with one another's rights, this woman worries about "the possibility of omission, of your not helping others when you could help them."

The issue this law student raises is addressed by Loevinger's fifth "autonomous" stage of ego development. The terms of its resolution lie in achieving partial autonomy from an excessive sense of responsibility by recognizing that other people have responsibility for their own destiny (Loevinger, 1968). The autonomous stage in Loevinger's account witnesses a relinquishing of moral dichotomies and their replacement with "a feeling for the complexity and multifaceted character of real people and real situations" (1970, p. 6).

Whereas the rights conception of morality that informs Kohlberg's principled level [Stages Five and Six] is geared to arriving at an objectively fair or just resolution to the moral dilemmas to which "all rational men can agree" (Kohlberg, 1976), the responsibility conception focuses instead on the limitations of any particular resolution and describes the conflicts that remain. This limitation of moral judgment and choice is described by a woman in her thirties when she says that her guiding principle in making moral decisions has to do with "responsibility and caring about yourself and others, not just a principle that once you take hold of, you settle [the moral problem]. The principle put into practice is still going to leave you with conflict."

Given the substance and orientation of these women's judgments, it becomes clear why a morality of rights and noninterference may appear to women as frightening in its potential justification of indifference and unconcern. At the same time, however, it also becomes clear why, from a male perspective, women's judgments appear inconclusive and diffuse, given their insistent contextual relativism. Women's moral judgments thus elucidate the pattern that we have observed in the differences between the sexes, but provide an alternative conception of maturity by which these differences can be developmentally considered. The psychology of women that has consistently been described as distinctive in its greater orientation toward relationships of interdependence implies a more contextual mode of judgment and a different moral understanding. Given the differences in women's conceptions of self and morality, it is not surprising that women bring to the life cycle a different point of view and that they order human experience in terms of different priorities.

NOTE

1. Kohlberg, L. *Continuities and discontinuities in childhood and adult moral development revisited.* Unpublished manuscript, Harvard University, 1973.

REFERENCES

Bettelheim, B. *The uses of enchantment.* New York: Knopf, 1976.

Blos, P. The second individuation process of adolesence. In A. Freud (Ed.), *The psychoanalytic study of the child* (Vol. 22). New York: International Universities Press, 1967.

Chekhov, A. *The cherry orchard.* (Stark Young, trans.). New York: Modern Library, 1956. (Originally published, 1904.)

Chodorow, N. Family structure and feminine personality. In M. Rosaldo & L. Lamphere (Eds.). *Women, culture and society.* Stanford, Calif.: Stanford University Press, 1974.

Chodorow, N. *The reproduction of mothering.* Berkeley: University of California Press, 1978.

Edwards, C.P. Societal complexity and moral development: A Kenyan study. *Ethos,* 1975, **3,** 505–527.

Erikson, E. *Identity: Youth and crisis.* New York: Norton, 1968.

Freud, S. Female sexuality. In J. Strachery (Ed.). *The standard edition of the complete psychological works of Sigmund Freud* (Vol. 21). London: Hogarth Press, 1961. (Originally published, 1931.)

Freud, S. Some psychical consequences of the anatomical distinction between the sexes. In J. Strachey (Ed.), *The standard edition of the complete psychological works of Sigmund Freud* (Vol. 19). London: Hogarth Press, 1961. (Originally published, 1925.)

Freud, S. Three essays on sexuality. In J. Strachey (Ed.), *The standard edition of the complete psychological works of Sigmund Freud* (Vol. 7). London: Hogarth Press, 1961. (Originally published, 1905.)

Gilligan, C. In a different voice: Women's conceptions of the self and of morality. *Harvard Educational Review,* 1977, **47,** 481–517.

The Homeric Hymn (C. Boer, trans.). Chicago: Swallow Press, 1971.

Horner, M. Toward an understanding of achievement-related conflicts in women. *Journal of Social Issues,* 1972, **28** (2), 157–174.

Inhelder, B., & Piaget, J. *The growth of logical thinking from childhood to adolescence.* New York: Basic Books, 1958.

Kingston, M. H. *The woman warrior.* New York: Vintage Books, 1977.

Kohlberg, L., & Kramer, R. Continuities and discontinuities in childhood and adult moral development. *Human Development,* 1969, **12,** 93–120.

Kohlberg, L. From is to ought: How to commit the naturalistic fallacy and get away with it in the study of moral development. In T. Mischel (Ed.), *Cognitive development and epidomology.* New York: Academic Press, 1971.

Lever, J. Sex differences in the games children play. *Social Problems,* 1976, **23,** 478–487.

Levinson, D. *The seasons of a man's life.* New York: Knopf, 1978.

Loevinger, J., & Wessler, R. *The meaning and measurement of ego development.* San Francisco: Jossey-Bass, 1970.

McClelland, D. *The achieving society.* New York: Van Nostrand, 1961.

McClelland, D. *Power: The inner experience.* New York: Irvington Publishers, 1975.

Mead, B. H. *Mind, self and society.* Chicago: University of Chicago Press, 1934.

Perry, W. *Forms of intellectual and ethical development in the college years.* New York: Holt, Rinehart & Winston, 1968.

Piaget, J. *The moral judgment of the child.* New York: Free Press, 1965. (Originally published, 1932.)

Riesman, D. *The lonely crowd.* New Haven: Yale University Press, 1961.

Sassen, G. Success-anxiety in women: A constructivist theory of its sources and its significance. *Harvard Educational Review,* forthcoming.

Strunk, W., & White, E. B. *The elements of style.* New York: Macmillan, 1959.

Sullivan, H. S. *The interpersonal theory of psychiatry.* New York: Norton, 1953.

Vaillant, G. *Adaptation to life.* Boston: Little, Brown, 1977.

Woolf, V. *A room of one's own.* New York: Harcourt, Brace & World, 1929.

QUESTIONS

1. How do the insights of Gilligan into the way that most women seem to make moral judgments differ from or add to Freud's description of women's moral sense?
2. Show how Kohlberg's model of moral judgment, seen as a judgment of non-interference, contrasts with Gilligan's model emphasizing the positive aspect of morality as being responsible and helping others.

SUGGESTED READINGS

Gilligan, C. (1982). *In a Different Voice.* Cambridge: Harvard University Press.

Brabeck, M. (1983). Moral Judgment: Theoretical Research on Differences Between Males and Females. *Development Review* 3, 274–291.

John Michael Murphy and Carol Gilligan

21. Moral Development in Late Adolescence and Adulthood: A Critique and Reconstruction of Kohlberg's Theory

John Michael Murphy was a student of Carol Gilligan's at the Graduate School of Education of Harvard when this article was written. At present he is a licensed staff psychologist at the Laboure Mental Health Center. He is also in the department of child psychiatry at Massachusetts General Hospital but his research interests are in developmental psychology, especially adult development. This selection critiques Kohlberg's moral development from a vantage point that is slightly different from the critique by Gilligan in the previous selection. The authors point out that while Kohlberg's model of respecting human rights is clear-cut, life itself brings moral issues which are not so clear cut and might well entail a conflict of rights. Adults might then make their judgments taking into consideration the specific context of the moral issue. While this might look like a relativistic solution, it might well be a judgment based on alternate formulations, based on a sense of responsibility and on commitment in relativism. Roman Catholic theologians might refer to this manner of deciding as the principle of proportionality. Curran's article in Chapter 16 also spoke of this type of decision-making.

Abstract. This article provides an alternative conception of postconventional moral development which fits existing data on late adolescent and adult moral judgment better than *Kohlberg's* higher stage descriptions. Moral judgment data from a longitudinal study of 26 undergraduates are scored by *Kohlberg's* newly revised manual and replicate his original finding that a significant percentage of subjects appear to regress from adolescence to adulthood. The persistence of relativistic regression in these data suggests the need to revise the theory. The same hypothetical moral dilemmas are also scored according to an alternative coding scheme based on the hypothesis of an adult form of cognitive development. Results indicate that the *Kohlberg* regressors are progressors when evaluated against a standard of commitment in relativism instead of absolute principles of justice. Real-life data on the same subjects suggest that this progression is related to actual experiences of moral conflict and choice which lead to the restructuring of moral judgment to a more dialectical mode. It is suggested that this alternative notion of postconventional development is necessary for understanding (and scoring) adult moral judgment.

Moral development, in structural theory, is divided into three parts: preconventional, conventional, and postconventional. While the first two are the subject of considerable agreement among developmental psychologists, the third remains a territory of both empirical and theoretical dispute. It is to this latter region, then, that we bring new evidence and a new interpretation. On this basis we offer an integration of existing theory and data that extends the sequence of moral development beyond adolescence into adulthood.

While this essay is written within the framework of *Kohlberg's* stage theory of moral development, it is critical of that framework in an attempt to make it more broadly applicable to judgments about real-life as well as hypothetical moral dilemmas and to the changes that occur in late adolescent and adult moral thought. This attempt is grounded empirically in the difficulty encountered in trying to fit the moral judgments of late adolescents and adults about both real and hypothetical dilemmas into the stage descriptions of *Kohlberg's* sequence.

Although some psychologists (*Kurtines and Grief,* 1974) have recommended the wholesale abandonment of *Kohlberg's* theory, claiming that more than a decade of empirical research has failed to provide the data necessary to confirm it, other critics have been less harsh, focusing instead on the upper half or third of the stages as problematic (*Brown and Hernstein,* 1975; *Gilligan,* 1977; *Puka,* 1976; *Reid and Yanarella,* 1977; *Sullivan,* 1977). This line of criticism has been supported both longitudinally (*Holstein,* 1976) and cross-culturally (*Edwards,* 1975; *Simpson,* 1974) by empirical work which has confirmed the sequentiality of the first three of *Kohlberg's* six stages, while at the same time presenting evidence against invariant sequence for stages 4, 5, and 6. Based on these and other studies, one of *Kohlberg's* closest associates (*Gibbs,* 1977, 1979) claims that stages 5 and 6 are best considered not as naturally occurring stages in the strict Piagetian sense, but rather as metaethical or philosophical reflections upon the normative judgments of earlier stages. While *Gibbs'* position may solve the problem of discrepant data, it fails to deal with one very important implication. Without the postconventional level, moral stage development ends in adolescence, at least for bright subjects. This position seems so contrary to fact that it warrants another hypothesis, the possibility of cognitive transformation in late adolescence or early adulthood that would provide the new structures of thought necessary to the development of a different form of moral judgment. *Kohlberg* once proposed this idea himself and explored it at some length before rejecting it (*Kohlberg and Kramer,* 1969). Work not available at the time of that paper makes the hypothesis of an adult cognitive stage more plausible now and thus provides the basis for a reexamination of *Kohlberg and Kramer's* argument and for the alternative conception of adult moral development proposed here.

In examining the implications for moral development of an adult stage of cognitive development, there are a number of different conceptions of such a stage to consider. All, however, concur in describing that stage as more dialectical and contextually relative than exclusively formal. Most recently, *Arlin* (1975) proposed a fifth cognitive stage which she called 'problem finding' to distinguish it from the 'problem solving' orientation of formal operations. Two other approaches have begun to generate bodies of research in an attempt to elucidate the structurally new form of mature thought.

In 1973, *Riegel* (1973, 1975) launched what has become a continuing argument for a dialectical psychology that would encompass the characteristics of adult thought more accurately than *Piaget's* formal operations. Other researchers have followed the leads set out by *Perry* (1968, p. 205), who suggested 'adding an advanced period to *Piaget's* outline'. In addition to seeing more in adult thought than formal operations, both groups have explored the implications of such thought for moral development. *Perry* (1968, p. 205) described the transition to maturity as a shift from 'the moral environment to the ethical, from the formal to the existential.' While *Arlin* (1975) hypothesized that the adult stage of cognitive development was one of problem finding, *Perry* is quite specific in naming the problem found as the recognition of the contextual relativism of all knowledge which leads to a revolutionary transformation in intellectual and ethical thought. There are striking similarities between *Perry's* description of the post-relativistic quality of adult ethical thought and *Meacham's* (1975, p. 162) discussion of a dialectical approach to moral judgment which 'considers the multiple aspects of behaviors and recognizes that they can be both good and bad, moral and immoral, depending upon the framework within which they are evaluated.' Another aspect of mature thought recognized by both *Perry* and the dialectical theoreticians is the 'epistemological loneliness' that can accompany the emergence of formal operations. This often involves a kind of conceptual overkill which achieves objectivity 'at the expense of conviction, commitment, mutuality, and the comfort of participating in a consensus of shared beliefs' (*Chandler,* 1975, p. 172). *Perry* seems to be talking about the same phenomenon when he notes that, 'If one comes to look on all knowing and all valuing as contingent on context, and if one is then confronted with an infinite universe of potential contexts for truth and care, one is threatened with a loss of identity. From one context to another, what one will see as true and what one will care about will be discontinuous' (*Perry,* 1968, p. 134).

In the remainder of this paper we will entertain the contrary-to-accepted-fact hypothesis of an adult cognitive transformation along the general lines suggested by *Perry* and *Riegel.* This cognitive shift would then provide the basis for a new form of moral judgment in adulthood, structurally different from that of adolescent thought. The experiential base for such a stage change would lie in the different experiences of moral choice and moral responsibility typically encountered only after adolescence. While there may be little difference between *Inhelder and*

Piaget's (1958) discussion of adult equilibrated formal operations and the post-formal cognition envisioned here or between our view and many more traditional accounts of mature reasoning (*Guindon,* 1978; *Schwab,* 1978), there is a very real difference between *Piaget's* claim that formal operational thought is characterized by a lattice structure and the hypothesis considered here that mature cognition is characterized by a structure open to context, albeit one that may employ formal operations in solving problems. It is interesting to note that this is precisely the point that *Vygotsky* (1962) raised in his early critique of *Piaget.*

Thus, although there may be little difference between what *Piaget* (1972) means when he writes about mature cognition and what is meant here, the failure to describe adequately the structural properties of mature thought and to differentiate it from adolescent thought has led to considerable confusion in the literature on one of the major applications of Piagetian theory— *Kohlberg's* theory of moral development. While *Piaget* (1965, p. 317) noted in his early work on moral judgment that the emergence of 'the feeling of equity' is 'a development of equalitarianism in the direction of relativity' that renders moral judgment more contextual and results in a more generous and refined form of justice, these relativistic and contextual properties of mature thought have never been incorporated into *Kohlberg's* higher stage definitions (or into *Piaget's* for that matter). There are, among older adolescents and adults, people who are fully formal in their logical thinking and fully principled in their moral judgments (stage 5 and 6); and yet, as this paper attempts to demonstrate, they are not fully mature in their moral understanding. Conversely, those people whose thinking becomes more relativistic in the sense of being more open to the contextual properties of moral judgments and moral dilemmas frequently fail to be scored at the highest stages of *Kohlberg's* sequence. Instead, the relativising of their thinking over time is construed as regression or moral equivocation, rather than as a developmental advance. The present paper is an attempt to deal with both of these problems.

BACKGROUND

The problem we address was first introduced into the cognitive developmental literature on moral judgment as an anomalous regression at the higher levels of moral development reported by *Kohlberg and Kramer* (1969). This regression among some of *Kohlberg's* subjects who had previously been scored as stages 4 and 5 took the form of a reassertion of moral hedonism that resembled judgments characteristic of stage 2. This was interpreted by *Kohlberg and Kramer* as a functional regression resulting from the adolescent identity crisis rather than a structural regression in moral thought. This interpretation was supported by their finding that such moral subjectivism had disappeared by age 25, having been replaced by the discovery that moral principles of equality and reciprocity provided an objective basis for resolving moral problems. However, the persistence of relativistic moral thought in other samples following the attainment of principled moral judgment (*Fishkin,* 1975; *Gilligan and Kohlberg,* 1977; *Gilligan,* 1978) led *Kohlberg* in 1973 to reconsider his earlier argument. Retracting his earlier conclusion that moral development ends in adolescence, he posited instead a kind of structural stage change in adulthood. While he had in 1969 rejected this notion, claiming that the attainment of formal operational logic in adolescence provided no basis for further structural changes in moral judgment, he argued, in 1973, that the attainment of principled moral judgment is a phenomenon of adult development and results from 'the experience of sustained responsibility for the welfare of others and the experiences of irreversible moral choice' (*Kohlberg,* 1973, p. 196).

While this major interpretive revision eliminated the problem of adolescent relativistic regression in his data by considering all relativistic judgments as preceding the attainment of principled thought, it left unchanged the definition of the higher stages. Thus, in his revised argument, *Kohlberg* never explained how the adult experiences of commitment and responsibility that followed the discovery of the moral consequences of choice could be made to fit structures of moral judgment that he had initially derived from adolescents' responses to hypothetical dilemmas. It is difficult to believe that the adult experiences could lead to exactly the same form of moral reasoning that was originally found in some of *Kohlberg's* bright high-school students. These students had articulated formal moral justifications on the basis of the logical reversibility and universalizability of such hypothetico-deductive concepts as social contract and natural rights. While the logical concepts of equality and reciprocity can support a principled morality of universal rights and respect, experiences of moral conflict and choice seem to point rather to special obligations and responsibility for consequences that can be anticipated and understood only within a more contextual frame of reference. The balancing of these two points of view appeared to us to be the key to understanding adult moral development. In our view, this would require a restructuring of moral thought which would include but supersede the principled understanding of *Kohlberg's* highest stages.

The radical revisions of his scoring manual which followed *Kohlberg's* (1973) paper have eliminated virtually all stage 5 and 6 reasoning from the empirical moral judgment data. For instance, only 1 of *Kohlberg's* 58 reported longitudinal subjects has reached an unmixed score of stage 5 by the age of 30, while 7 are consigned to the transitional stage 4/5 range (*Kohlberg,* 1979). We argue that the problems with sequence that led to the revision of the scoring manual stem from the failure to distinguish between two essentially different kinds of moral relativism which stand in different relation to postconventional or principled moral judgment. In making this distinction, we rely on the contrast described by *Perry* (1968)[1] between relativistic *multi-*

---

1. The complete description of these positions can be found in *Perry* (1968, pp. 57–200). The following highly abbreviated outline of the positions is taken from pp. 9–10 of that volume:

Position 1: The student sees the world in polar terms of we-right-good vs. other-wrong-bad. Right Answers for everything exist in the Absolute, known to Authority whose role is to mediate (teach) them. Knowledge and goodness are perceived as quantitative accretions of discrete rightnesses to be collected by hard work and obedience (paradigm: a spelling test).

Position 2: The student perceives diversity of opinion, and uncertainty, and accounts for them as unwarranted confusion in poorly qualified Authorities or as mere exercises set by Authority 'so we can learn to find The Answer for ourselves'.

Position 3: The student accepts diversity and uncertainty as legitimate but still *tem-*

plicity (position 4 in *Perry's* scheme), the position that there are many right answers to moral problems and no way of choosing among them, and *contextual relativism* (position 5), the position that while no answers may be objectively right in the sense of being context-free, some answers and some ways of thinking are better than others. *Perry's* highest four positions of mature reasoning (6–9) add forms of commitment to this basic contextual relativism.

While *Perry's* position 4 corresponds in many ways to *Kohlberg's* description of stage 4½ relativism as a form of moral equivocation that is incompatible with principled moral judgment, *Perry's* positions of contextual relativism are quite different. For *Perry*, the realization of contextual relativism superseded conventional moral understanding and ushered in a period of ethical responsibility, compatible with principled moral judgments but also indicative of a new understanding of the contexts in which principles could operate and thus of a new responsibility for moral choice.

While *Kohlberg* attempted to solve the problem of relativistic regression in moral judgment data by radically altering his criteria for principled moral judgment in order to retain his conception that principles of justice were context-free and could

---

porary in areas where Authority 'hasn't found The Answer yet'. He supposes Authority grades him in these areas on 'good expression' but remains puzzled as to standards.

Position 4: (a) The student perceives legitimate uncertainty (and therefore diversity of opinion) to be extensive and raises it to the status of an unstructured epistemological realm of its own in which 'anyone has a right to his own opinion', a realm which he sets over against Authority's realm where right-wrong still prevails, or (b) the student discovers qualitative contextual relativistic reasoning as a special case of 'what They want' within Authority's realm.

Position 5: The student perceives all knowledge and values (including Authority's) as contextual and relativistic and subordinates dualistic right-wrong functions to the status of a special case, in context.

Position 6: The student apprehends the necessity of orienting himself in a relativistic world through some form of personal Commitment (as distinct from unquestioned or unconsidered commitment to simple belief in certainty).

Position 7: The student makes an initial Commitment in some area.

Position 8: The student experiences the implications of Commitment and explores the subjective and stylistic issues of responsibility.

Position 9: The student experiences the affirmation of identity among multiple responsibilities and realizes Commitment as an ongoing, unfolding activity through which he expresses his life style.

generate an objectively right solution to moral problems, our data show that this solution still results in the problem of stage regression. In this paper, we show how our different analysis of the phenomenon of relativism in moral development leads to a further distinction between two types of postconventional moral judgment. Although it will not be discussed until much later in this paper, a brief outline of a two-category typology we have used may be helpful here. The first, which we call PCF (postconventional formal), solves the problem of relativism by constructing a formal logical system that derives solutions to all moral problems from concepts like the social contract or natural rights. The second, which we call PCC (postconventional contextual), finds the problem in that solution which now appears as only one of several potential contexts in which moral judgments can be framed. PCC reasoning derives from an understanding of the contextual relativism of moral judgment and the ineluctable uncertainty of moral choice. On that basis, it articulates an ethic of responsibility that focuses on the actual consequences of choice. In the shift from PCF to PCC, the criterion for the adequacy of moral principles changes from objective truth to 'best fit', and can only be established within the context of the dilemma itself. According to PCC reasoning, the choice of principles for solving moral problems is an example of commitment in relativism, a commitment for which one bears personal responsibility and which allows the possibility of alternate formulations that could be equally or more adequate in a given case.

Reprinted by permission from HUMAN DEVELOPMENT, Vol. 23, 1980, pp. 77–83. Copyright © 1980 by S. Karger AG, Basel.

QUESTIONS

1. How does post-conventional contextual morality as described here differ from Kohlberg's post-conventional formal morality and from his stage 4½?
2. Do you agree with the authors that many adult moral decisions cannot be easily solved by mere recourse to objective moral standards?

REFERENCES

Arlin, P. K.: Cognitive development in adulthood: a fifth stage? Devl Psychol. *11:* 602–606 (1975).

Berkowitz, M. W.; Gibbs, J. C. and Broughton, J. M.: The relation of moral judgment stage disparity to developmental effects of peer dialogues; Harvard University (1978; unpublished).

Brown, R. and Hernstein, R.J.: Psychology (Little, Brown, Boston 1975).

Chandler, M.: Relativism and the problem of epistemological loneliness. Hum. Dev. *18:* 171–180 (1975).

Edwards, C. P.: Societal complexity and moral development: a Kenyan study. Ethos *3:* 505–527 (1975).

Fishkin, J. S.: Metaethical reasoning, ideology, and political commitment: empirical applications of a proposed theory; Yale University (1975; unpublished).

Gibbs, J. C.: Kohlberg's stages of moral judgment: a constructive critique. Harv. Educ. Rev. *47:* 42–61 (1977).

Gibbs, J. C.: Kohlberg's moral stage theory: a Piagetian revision. Hum. Dev. *22:* 89–112 (1979).

Gilligan, C.: In a different voice: Women's conceptions of self and of morality. Harv. Educ. Rev. *47:* 481–517 (1977).

Gilligan, C.: Moral development in the college years; in Chickering, The future American college (Jossey-Bass, San Francisco, in press).

Gilligan, C. and Kohlberg, L.: From adolescence to adulthood: the rediscovery of reality in a postconventional world; in Appel and Preseissen, Topics in cognitive development (Plenum Press, New York 1977).

Gilligan, C. and Murphy, J. M.: The philosopher and the dilemma of the fact: evidence for continuing development from adolescence to adulthood; in Kuhn, Intellectual development beyond childhood (Jossey-Bass, San Francisco, in press).

Guindon, A.: Moral development: form, content, and self—a critique of Kohlberg's sequence; St. Paul University, Ottawa (1978; unpublished).

Holstein, C.: Development of moral judgment: a longitudinal study of males and females. Child Dev. *47:* 51–61 (1976).

Inhelder, B. and Piaget, J.: The growth of logical thinking from childhood to adolescence (Basic Books, New York 1958).

Kohlberg, L.: Stage and sequence: the cognitive-developmental approach to socialization; in Goslin, Handbook of socialization theory and research (Rand McNally, Chicago 1969).

Kohlberg, L.: Issue scoring guide; Harvard University (1972; unpublished).

Kohlberg, L.: Continuities in childhood and adult moral development revisited; in Baltes and Schaie, Life-span developmental psychology; 2nd ed. (Academic Press, New York 1973).

Kohlberg, L.: Moral stages and moralization: the cognitive-developmental approach; in Lickona, Moral development and behavior (Holt, Rinehart & Winston, New York 1976).

Kohlberg, L.: The meaning and measurement of moral development. Heinz Werner lecture, Clark University, Worcester, Mass., April 1979.

Kohlberg, L.; Colby, A.; Gibbs, J.; Speecher-Dubin, B., and Power, C.: Assessing moral states: a manual; Harvard University (1978; unpublished).

Kohlberg, L. and Gilligan, C.: The adolescent as a philosopher: the discovery of the self in a post conventional world. Daedalus *100:* 1051–1086 (1971).

Kohlberg, L. and Kramer, R.: Continuities and discontinuities in childhood and adult moral development. Hum. Dev. *12:* 93–120 (1969).

Kurtines, W. and Grief, E.: The development of moral thought: review and evaluation of Kohlberg's approach. Psychol. Bull. *81:* 453–470 (1974).

Meacham, J. A.: A dialectical approach to moral judgment and self-esteem. Hum. Dev. *18:* 159–170 (1975).

Murphy, J. M.: Moral judgment coding based on Perry; Harvard University (1978; unpublished).

Perry, W. B.: Forms of intellectual and ethical development in the college years: a scheme (Holt, Rinehart & Winston, New York 1968).

Piaget, J.: The moral judgment of the child (Free Press, New York 1965; 1st ed. 1932).

Piaget, J.: Intellectual evolution from adolescence to adulthood. Hum. Dev. *15:* 1–12 (1972).

Puka, B.: Moral education and its cure; in Meyer, Reflections on values education (Wilfred Laurier University Press, Waterloo, Ont. 1976).

Reid, H. and Yanarella, E. J.: Critical political theory and moral development: on Kohlberg, Hampden-Turner, and Habermas. Theory Society *4:* 479–500 (1977).

Riegel, K.: Dialectical operations: The final period of cognitive development. Hum. Dev. *16:* 345–376 (1973).

Riegel, K.: The development of dialectical operations. Hum. Dev. *18:* No. 1–3 (1975; also Karger, Basel 1975).

Schwab, J. J.: Review of 'Education and the education of teachers', by R. S. Peters. Harv. Educ. Rev. *48:* 408–410 (1978).

Simpson, E. L.: Moral development research: a case study of scientific cultural bias. Hum. Dev. *17:* 81–106 (1974).

Sullivan, E.: A study of Kohlberg's structural theory of moral development: a critique of liberal social science ideology. Hum. Dev. *20:* 325–376 (1977).

Vygotsky, L. S.: Thought and lanuage (MIT Press, Cambridge 1962; 1st ed. 1934).

SUGGESTED READINGS

O'Connel, T. (1978). *Principles for a Catholic Morality,* Chapter 14, pp. 140–154. New York: Seabury.

Fuchs, J. (1970). *Human Values and Christian Morality.* Dublin: Gill and Macmillan.

Fuchs, J. (1983). *Personal Responsibility and Christian Morality.* Washington, D.C.: Georgetown University Press.

Part V

GUILT

.

Karl Rahner

22. "Sins" and Guilt

Karl Rahner, professor emeritus of theology, died in Munich in March 1984.

This section points away from the notion of sin as a violation of rules or laws and points more deeply to what sin and guilt really are—saying *no* to our true selves and to God's love, the sacred mystery in which we are rooted.

We don't like to hear the word 'sin' today. It sounds so old-fashioned. We feel that it places us back in our childhood days when we were expected to be good and to observe all kinds of rules which we didn't understand and about which we could do nothing except just that: be good children and obey promptly.

The word seems to suggest a God who issues commandments in order to test the quality of our obedience to his authority; it seems to be merely a common denominator for innumerable precepts which we cannot possibly observe and which we know only by studying the catechism (like a penal code) or by going through the sins listed in the preparation for confession in the prayer book. The word seems to have little in common with our experience of life: that we strive and therefore also err; that we must find *our* way, only slowly become mature (and then laugh at the stupidity of much that we once took seriously and dismiss it for good). The word (mostly used in the misleading plural: sins!) is like the governess's or pedantic schoolmaster's index finger, as they warn us not to break any of the rules in a system supervised by a strict, invisible censor (called God), who also assigns penalties for their infringement (evidently with singularly slight effect), so that everything may be in 'order'. And, on the other hand, what the mature person or one becoming mature otherwise (apart from suffering, disappointment, futility, death) experiences as the most profound incomprehensibility and absurdity, he prefers not to call 'sins', but guilt, for which there cannot really be any plural.

He is certainly aware of guilt, if he does not run away from the hideous incomprehensibility of his existence. If this really adult, mature person thinks that he cannot discover guilt in his life, then he has been granted an amazing, unmerited (even dangerous) grace which is not his by nature and which perhaps conceals from him what he really is by nature; or perhaps he represses his guilt, explains it away (psychologically, sociologically, or in one way or another). Or he has his guilt, he is still tied to it, even identical with it, and so of course has difficulty in admitting it to himself. Or he is aware of it at that depth of existence at which we and our knowledge of ourselves are still undivided, but cannot bring it home to himself as a reality when he tries to find it in the light of his mistaken idea of what is meant by sin and guilt.

Whatever the situation of individuals may be, there is such a thing as guilt. The personal experience of individuals, the testimony of the greatest interpreters of human existence, and the final interpretation given by Christian revelation (by proclaiming simply the miracle of forgiveness and really nothing else) bear witness to the reality of guilt. It is first and last not something which we, while remaining essentially good, have done at some particular point of time in our past life; but we are ourselves this guilt, when we freely say 'No' to ourselves (who are by nature directed to God), to the ultimate meaning of our existence, to the ineffable, sacred mystery in which we are unfathomably rooted, which seeks silently to speak to us as eternal love.

From OPPORTUNITIES FOR FAITH: Elements of a Modern Spirituality by Karl Rahner, translated by Edward Quinn, pp. 92–93. Reprinted by permission of the publisher, The Crossroad Publishing Company. © 1970 Verlag Herder KG, Freiburg-im-Breisgau; English translation copyright © 1974 S.P.C.K.

QUESTIONS

1. Do you see any relationship between Rahner's description of genuine guilt as related to a concept of self and Meacham's

discussion of the relation between morality and one's awareness of oneself?

2. Do you think that Rahner's concept of legalism is similar to the description of either Kohlberg's stage 4 or even of the post-conventional morality described by Gilligan and Murphy in Chapter 22?

SUGGESTED READING

Rahner, K. (1978). "Original Sin," in K. Rahner, *Foundations of Christian Faith: An Introduction to the Idea of Christianity* (pp. 106–115). New York: Seabury.

Louis Monden, S.J.

23. The Three Levels of Ethics

A native of Antwerp, Belgium, Louis Monden, S.J. received both his licentiate
in philosophy and his doctorate in sacred theology from the University of
Louvain, Belgium. He was a member of the theological faculty of Heverlee-
Louvain and professor of religion and psychology at John XXIII Seminary,
Louvain. At present he is editor of Hoogland Dokumentatate in Brussels.

Although he is not a developmental psychologist, his description of the three
levels of ethics in this selection can be compared to Kohlberg's levels of moral
development. In one sense, Kohlberg's pre-conventional level is somewhat
similar to Monden's level of instinct. The moral level of Monden also could
be seen to comprise the conventional and post-conventional levels of Kohlberg. The addition of the religious level emphasizes those aspects of love, personal relationship to God and awareness of forgiveness that Kohlberg does not
explore. The description of the three levels of guilt can also throw light on
Freud's view of guilt in the next section and on Hoffman's description of the
development of guilt.

We might use the word "ethics"—somewhat arbitrarily, to be
sure, but we cannot do without some well-defined terminology—for the whole of man's modes of being and of behaving in
their undivided totality. The ethical conduct of man may then
be considered on *three fundamental levels,* whereby the selfsame
terms of the ethical vocabulary receive a wholly different
meaning.[2]

THE LEVEL OF INSTINCT

When an animal's drive fails to reach its goal, because of
the resistance of things or the competition of another animal or
a human sanction, that drive may give rise to behavior which—
especially in domesticated animals, whose reflexes are heavily

conditioned by human contact—strongly resembles the conduct of a human being who feels or is guilty. In man too there is an experience of guilt and a sense of duty which, although strongly influenced by the intellect and rationalized with higher motives, stands essentially upon *the level of instinct.*

The *law* which directs this instinctive ethics comes not from within but from without, from the pressure of reality, and especially of society, which, by means of prohibitions and "taboos," builds a dam against the impulses of individual instinctivity. Although this pressure is introjected by the individual and turns into instinctive self-control, into a feeling of *obligation,* that "ought" is always felt as something alien to the person, even as something hostile to his instinctive impulses. Hence it is experienced with an ambivalence of rebellious resistance, neutralized by fear of sanctions or of failure and by the impression that the pressure is irresistible. That ambivalent feeling, which is not experienced as lucid insight but undergone as an instinctive warning, is, on this level, called *conscience.*

Guilt and *sin* of this kind consist in the material transgression of some prohibition or taboo. Whether the intention was good or not, the purpose wrong or nonexistent, the action performed freely or without freedom—all this has no bearing on guilt. The sin consists in the material fact of "transgression", this or that action, this or that object, is *ipso facto* sinful. The ensuing reaction is equally instinctive, although it may be rationalized with all kinds of moral considerations. It is a blind *feeling,* rather than a consciousness of *guilt;* it derives from the awareness not of having acted badly, irrationally, against one's conscience, but of having acted wrongly, faultily, against some order. It is an almost physical occult sense that one has strayed beyond a safe boundary and is now threatened with the vengeance of the mysterious power that guards it; a feeling of anxiety which makes one cower instinctively in expectation of the coming punishment and experience something almost like relief when it finally does come.

Contrition for sin too is, on this level, not an awareness of one's wickedness and a desire for amendment, i.e. for becoming one's good self again, but simply the instinctive urge to escape the consequences of the transgression. On this level contrition looks mostly for formulas, rites of reconciliation and magic gestures by means of which the angered powers may be placated, the transgression undone, the punishment avoided and the safety of legal limits regained. *Confession* of the fault, expression of a *firm resolve* to stay henceforth within the limits of the law, all this belongs to the conjuring rites. Both are sincerely meant, not however in the sense of a personal decision, but as an instinctive anxiety reflex: "I'll never dare do such a thing again, too bad I ever ran that risk."

THE MORAL LEVEL

We shall use the word "moral" here not in the general meaning of ethical conduct, but in the specific sense of the element in this ethical conduct which belongs to the level of the conscious and free self-realization of the human person. Hence "moral" refers to the most human aspect of the ethical. It is present where man, having reached adult conscious insight, fully realizes the conditions of his free and authentic self-development as a spirit in the world, in communion with his fellow men and in union with the absolute Spirit, God.

On this level the *law* is no longer a pressure from without. It is based ultimately on man's essential dependence on God. In practice it is experienced as autonomous, with an autonomy that does not reject every kind of dependence but emphasizes the fact that even man's profound dependence on God can manifest itself only through the structure and the growth of his own nature as a source of moral obligation. What man experiences as law is nothing but his own essential growth as a proffered possibility and as a task to be fulfilled; it is the direction towards total self-development which corresponds most closely to the structure of the inner self, put before the free act as an absolute demand. This absolute demand is moral *obligation:* man's freedom owes it to itself to be faithful to its authentic self-development. And *conscience* is the deepest self-consciousness of man, insofar as it acts as a power of discrimination deciding in every choice what will promote authentic self-realization and what will stand in its way. That conscience is not infallible, because it depends on the information it receives about a moral problem in a definite situation; hence it can err in good faith owing to insufficient data or the incorrect judgment of some situation. Yet the voice of conscience, even when erring in good faith, must unconditionally be obeyed.

There is moral *guilt* where the free will acts against conscience. It never consists in the matter of the action taken objectively. Only the free choice and the wrong direction taken by the will must be considered. Moral guilt is always freely chosen infidelity to authentic self-realization and the free yielding to a pseudo-value. The objectively wrong action which conscience considers good is not morally guilty. The objectively good action which conscience, in good faith, deems wrong is morally guilty. Likewise *punishment* for such an action is no longer feared from without, as the vengeance of a mysterious offended power. The guilty deed punishes itself, because it is a self-inflicted wound, a matter of growing in the wrong direction. Considered from without, the sinful course may look like the free unfolding of life and of one's own sovereign vitality; in fact it always means a denying of oneself, the teeming within one's soul of spiritual weeds or cancerous growths.

Hence on the level of morality *contrition* will always be the inner acknowledgement of an action as self-negation, the uttering of a verdict of guilty over one's own deviations, not as a resigned recording of some failure but as an active will to correct the deviation and as a steady *resolve* to restore and to make up for the missed occasions of self-development by a more vigorous moral growth in the future. The *confession* of one's guilt adds nothing to the value of the inner self-judgment. It may be one of the many means used for recovery, because it places one's self-condemnation and steady resolve in the concrete framework of one's moral development within a human community.

THE CHRISTIAN-RELIGIOUS LEVEL

The moral self-unfolding of man mentioned in the previous paragraph takes place mainly through the development of his personality in an adult, loving self-donation to others. On the moral level, however, ethical conduct does not find its norms directly in this self-donation, but in the degree of authenticity of human self-realization as expressed in that self-donation. Hence when that natural self-unfolding is raised to a totally new level of value, as it is gratuitously assumed into a divine intimacy of love, this intimacy itself must become the only norm of the new ethical conduct of the human partner in his dialog with God.

The *law* which guides this meeting with God is no longer the growth of one's own being, but the proffered invitation to rise above that level towards a new meeting in love, an invitation which is at once possibility, question, offer, and, in its own way, exigency for total donation. At first it looks as if the autonomy of self-decision has been given up once more for a law forced upon man from without. In fact there is no coercion from without, no giving up of one's own self-development, but a yielding in love to a God who is *intimior intimo meo* ("closer to me than I am to myself"), so that letting oneself go in this love entails a higher and deeper self-realization, a real divinization of man.

Whereas the outer pressure of taboo upon instinct entailed an inframoral heteronomy of the law, the heteronomy of the divine invitation to love is the basis of a supramoral ethics. This is true also of the *obligation* imposed by that law: moral duty is not suppressed by it, but assumed in a totally new "ought" which is even further removed from all coercion than moral obligation and might be called a "vocation" rather than an "obligation." The specific forms of this "ought" considerably transcend the moral forms; they lie in the domain of what might be designated as "counsel" or "beatitude." *Conscience* on this level will be love itself as a power of discriminating what can promote from what will hinder its growth. It is no longer a natural or rational insight—although moral insight continues to act in the religious conscience—but an affinity with the beloved, a communion in feeling and in thinking, a "connaturality" with him.

Here *guilt* and *sin* are less than ever a material action, nor are they even the impairing of one's own power of growth. They consist in saying No to love. Sin becomes man himself in a relation of refusal to God's love. Hence, on this religious level, a merely material transgression can never be a sin. A moral fault can, but owing to the religious relation it acquires a new dimension, because refusing to be oneself turns into refusing to be for the Other. Over and above the moral fault there is a specific religious refusal, a violation of divine love in itself, a kind of guilt which is now in the fullest meaning of that word a "sin." The *punishment* for that sin, too, is not a threat impending from without but the enduring invitation of love itself as the torment of him who rejects it.

On this level *contrition* too becomes a function of love: it is the awareness of our unfaithfulness to love, joined to our conviction that this love surpasses every infidelity, that "God is greater than our heart." Religious contrition is therefore infinitely more than a search for security from the avenging wrath of an offended power; much more, too, than self-condemnation and a will for restoration. It is an appeal to the *mercy* of the beloved, a certitude that love will accept the guilt which we confidently offer and turn it into a new increase of the love relationship. It is our boldness in converting the fault into a trustful offering of love. The answer to this contrition—for on this level of the meeting of persons a response always comes—is *forgiveness.* A word devoid of meaning on the instinctive and the ethical levels, on the religious level it means the creative restoration of love through the integration of the fault within its growth. It is not a gradual reparation which remedies the fault, but the resumption of the love relationship, the reawakening of love itself, out of the meeting of mercy and repentance. And precisely because this meeting is granted by God in a fully gratuitous manner, love can be restored more wonderfully than ever in one creative moment of mercy. The *confession* of the fault is the sign, the opening word of the dialog in which the encounter takes place. And penance or *reparation* is the making real, on the level of moral growth, of what has already become a reality on the religious level in the one creative moment of love.

The distinction between the three levels of the ethical might become clearer from a consideration of how one and the same concrete situation can be experienced on each of them.

A young mother has given birth to a deformed baby. All her instinctive love and possessiveness surges in rebellion. *Instinct*

says: "It is better not to let this child live. It can grow up only
for a life which will be a hell, it will not know one moment of
happiness." "Happiness" is understood here on the instinctive
level as health, beauty, success, acceptance, the possibility of
realizing one's plans. Underneath the instinctive compassion for
the child the voice of self-pity too may be heard: fear of all the
selfless love which such a child will demand, of the innumerable
humiliations which may be expected. Against the impulse of
instinct the only barrier is the law: it is forbidden, I may not do
it, they don't allow this, I will be punished for doing it. If, at a
given moment, the pressure of instinct prevails and the action is
performed against the pressure of external law, then everything
will depend on the reaction of society. If the courts and public
opinion are in the main hostile, the young mother breaks down
under her feeling of guilt. On the other hand, should public opinion show itself favorably disposed (and public opinion too will
almost unavoidably move on the level of instinct in its judgment about love and happiness) and force the law to approve—
or, at least, to acquit—then all feeling of guilt is gone. The brakes
are off: "Now it is allowed." One is even proud of having had
the courage to force the external law to open this gate, of having
breached the wall of social pressure by the sheer force of the
maternal drive. In all this there is not the slightest element of
moral judgment.

It is quite a different matter if the mother wishes to make
her decision on the *moral level.* In that case, independently of
any concern for legislation or eventual consequences, she will
ask herself: "Have I a right to interfere with this life which has
been entrusted to me? I am responsible for the meaning which
this young life will one day possess. Have I ever any right to say
that a human life has no meaning?" Her idea of human happiness, too, will no longer be merely instinctive, corresponding to
the public norms of wealth, success and social acceptance. She
will have to ask, "What are the ingredients of real happiness?
How can we explain the fact that people who seem to have none
of the things instinct considers essential for happiness call themselves happy, and others who seem to have all these things in
abundance commit suicide? Might not the meaning of human
life depend mainly on the meaning one gives to it—on the

meaning which, from the start, the love of the parents bestows on it? Is the action instinct trying to force on me a real gesture of mercy, or is it an attempt against what is authentically human?" Only the answer to this last question can be decisive, and if the young mother goes against it she will keep on feeling guilty even if all the courts acquit her and public opinion hails her as a heroine.

Finally, the young mother who is a Christian, who from the very start puts herself on the *religious level,* will not even have to deliberate. From the beginning of her pregnancy she has felt that the new life growing within her was a mandate and an invitation of God's love. Neither wealth nor success nor complete self-fulfillment is for her the meaning of human existence or the norm of happiness. To her every life means an invitation to grow in loving intimacy with God, and every human being, in the shelter of that depth of love, can find the strength to fulfill his own task and vocation in love and happiness. She knows that as a mother she is called to love that child too, with all her resources for sacrifice and suffering, in such a way that she may teach him to accept his painful yet beautiful destiny, and make him capable of authentic love and real human and divine happiness. For her the rejection of that mandate, however burdensome and difficult it may look, would be to reject God's invitation, to doubt the love which beckons and run away from the suffering involved in the task which is set before her.

Reprinted by permission of the publisher, Andrews and McMeel, Inc., from SIN, LIBERTY AND LAW, by Louis Monden, translated by Joseph Donceel, 1965, pp. 4–12.

BIBLIOGRAPHICAL NOTES

1. General bibliography: P. Anciaux, *The Sacrament of Penance* (New York, Sheed and Ward, 1962); P. Galtier, *Sin and Penance* (London, 1932); H. Rondet, *The Theology of Sin* (Notre Dame, Ind., Fides, 1960); P. Riga, *Sin and Penance* (Milwaukee, Bruce, 1962); A. van Speyr, *Confession* (New York, 1964); J. Sheerin, *The Sacrament of Freedom: A Book on Confession* (Milwaukee, Bruce, 1961); J. Oesterreicher, *The Israel of*

God (New York, Kenedy, 1961), ch. 2, "Sin, Pardon, Redemption"; M. Oraison, *Sin* (New York, Macmillan, 1962); Paul Palmer, *Sacraments and Forgiveness* (Westminster, Md., Newman, 1959) for source material; M. Scheler, "Repentance and Rebirth," in *On the Eternal in Man* (New York, Harper, 1960); P. Régnier, *Le sens du péché* (Paris, 1954); L. Monden, *Moraal zonder zonde?* (Bruges, 1955); H. Bacht, "Die Welt von heute und das Gespür für die Sünde," *Geist und Lebren,* 31 (1958), 7–16; L. Jerphanion, "Philosophie du repentir," *Nouv. Rev. Théol.,* 81 (1959), 392–399; *id., Théologie du péché* (Tournai, 1960); *id., Pastorale du péché* (Tournai, 1961); M. Zundel, *Morale et mystique* (Bruges, 1962); H. van Lier, *Le nouvel âge* (Tournai, 1962), pp. 205–222; P. Delhaye, *La conscience morale du chrétien* (Tournai, 1964); R. W. Gleason, *The World to Come* (New York, Sheed and Ward, 1958), pp. 13–42; J. Foster, "The Scapegoat and the Underdog: Ancient and Modern Sense of Guilt, Sin and the Community of Man," *Life of the Spirit,* 16 (1962), 430–443; P. De Letter, "The Sense of the Sin," *Clergy Monthly,* 26 (1962), 77–88; R. O'Connell, "Sense of Sin in the Modern World," *Way,* 2 (1962), 3–18.

See also the special issues devoted to the problems of confession and awareness of sin by: *Seelsorge,* 1958, Heft 2; *La Maison-Dieu,* nos. 55–56 (1958), *Christus,* January 1959, *Paroisse et liturgie,* October 1962, *Lumière et Vie,* no. 70 (1964).

2. See on this topic: E. Des Places, art. "Péché," in *Suppl. Dict. de la Bible,* vol. vii (1962), cols. 407–480; F. Manthey, "Religion als Erlebnis des Heiligen und Unheiligen," in *Theol. und Glaube,* 1964, 22–31.

Specifically concerning the feeling and the awareness of guilt, see: P. Régamey, "Avertissement des profondeurs," *La Vie Spir.,* 94 (1956), 133–166, C. Baudouin and L. Beirnaert, art. "Culpabilité," in *Dict. de Spiritualité,* vol. ii., cols. 2632–2654; J. M. Hollenbach, "Schuldgefühl und seelische Gesundheit," *Geist und Leben,* 48 (1958), 17–24; W. Bitter et al., *Angst und Schuld in theologischer und psychotherapeutischer Sicht* (Stuttgart, 1959); C. Nodet, "Psychanalyse et culpabilité," in *Pastorale du péché* (Tournai, 1961), pp. 237–266; G. Condreau, *Angst und Schuld als Grundprobleme der Psychotherapie* (Bern, 1962); G. Zilboorg, *Psychoanalysis and Religion* (New York, Farrar,

Straus, 1962); M. Eck, "L'éducation du sentiment de culpabilité," *Etudes,* 315 (1962), 330–342; P. Ricoeur, *Finitude et culpabilité* (Paris, 1962); F. Bourdeau, "La hantise d'être jugé," *La Vie Spir.,* 109 (1963), 716–726; D. Dunphy, "Guilt: Its Psychological Aspects and Moral Implications," *Priestly Studies,* 28 (1961), 2–28; C. F. Tageson, "Neurotic and Normal Guilt," *Way* (U.S.), 18 (1962), 39–47; E. O'Doherty, "Freedom, Responsibility and Guilt," *Studies,* 52 (1963), 363–372; A. Schneiders, *The Anarchy of Feeling* (New York, Sheed and Ward, 1963).

QUESTIONS

1. Contrast the three levels of ethics according to the way they differ on the topics of conscience, guilt, contrition and the need to confess.
2. Is the religious level a more integrated morality? How?

SUGGESTED READINGS

Bergson, H. (1956). *The Two Sources of Morality.* New York: Doubleday.

Kierkegaard, S. (1954). *Fear and Trembling.* Princeton: Princeton University Press.

Monden, L. (1965). *Sin, Liberty and Law.* New York: Sheed and Ward.

Tillich, P. (1964). *Morality and Beyond.* New York: Harper.

Sigmund Freud

24. Civilization and its Discontents

The life of Sigmund Freud is well known. The founder of psychoanalysis in Vienna, his work on the interpretation of dreams and his later works on religion and civilization have greatly influenced twentieth century thought and society.

Freud was one of the first to explore the psychological dimensions of guilt. It is important to realize that he is presenting a view of neurotic guilt, a form of guilt in which there is no real insight into the nature of the wrong done. This type of guilt emphasizes the need for punishment rather than an acceptance of responsibility. It is very similar to the guilt on the instinctual level which Monden described in the previous selection.

After proposing several ways by which he believes that guilt develops, Freud then shows the relationship between civilization and guilt, implying that the more civilized we become, the stronger our guilt becomes. To understand his views one must remember that Freud lived in a very different culture from ours.

Why do our relatives, the animals, not exhibit any such cultural struggle? We do not know. Very probably some of them—the bees, the ants, the termites—strove for thousands of years before they arrived at the State institutions, the distribution of functions and the restrictions on the individual, for which we admire them to-day. It is a mark of our present condition that we know from our own feelings that we should not think ourselves happy in any of these animal States or in any of the roles assigned in them to the individual. In the case of other animal species it may be that a temporary balance has been reached between the influences of their environment and the mutually contending instincts within them, and that thus a cessation of development has come about. It may be that in primitive man a fresh access of libido kindled a renewed burst of activity on the part of the destructive instinct. There are a great many questions here to which as yet there is no answer.

Another question concerns us more nearly. What means does civilization employ in order to inhibit the aggressiveness which opposes it, to make it harmless, to get rid of it, perhaps? We have already become acquainted with a few of these methods, but not yet with the one that appears to be the most important. This we can study in the history of the development of the individual. What happens in him to render his desire for aggression innocuous? Something very remarkable, which we should never have guessed and which is nevertheless quite obvious. His aggressiveness is introjected, internalized; it is, in point of fact, sent back to where it came from—that is, it is directed towards his own ego. There it is taken over by a portion of the ego, which sets itself over against the rest of the ego as super-ego, and which now, in the form of 'conscience', is ready to put into action against the ego the same harsh aggressiveness that the ego would have liked to satisfy upon other, extraneous individuals. The tension between the harsh super-ego and the ego that is subjected to it, is called by us the sense of guilt; it expresses itself as a need for punishment.[1] Civilization, therefore, obtains mastery over the individual's dangerous desire for aggression by weakening and disarming it and by setting up an agency within him to watch over it, like a garrison in a conquered city.

As to the origin of the sense of guilt, the analyst has different views from other psychologists; but even he does not find it easy to give an account of it. To begin with, if we ask how a person comes to have a sense of guilt, we arrive at an answer which cannot be disputed: a person feels guilty (devout people would say 'sinful') when he has done something which he knows to be 'bad'. But then we notice how little this answer tells us. Perhaps, after some hesitation, we shall add that even when a person has not actually *done* the bad thing but has only recognized in himself an *intention* to do it, he may regard himself as guilty; and the question then arises of why the intention is regarded as equal to the deed. Both cases, however, presuppose that one had

---

1. Cf. 'The Economic Problem of Masochism' (1924c), *Standard Ed.,* **19,** 166–7.

already recognized that what is bad is reprehensible, is something that must not be carried out. How is this judgement arrived at? We may reject the existence of an original, as it were natural, capacity to distinguish good from bad. What is bad is often not at all what is injurious or dangerous to the ego; on the contrary, it may be something which is desirable and enjoyable to the ego. Here, therefore, there is an extraneous influence at work, and it is this that decides what is to be called good or bad. Since a person's own feelings would not have led him along this path, he must have had a motive for submitting to this extraneous influence. Such a motive is easily discovered in his helplessness and his dependence on other people, and it can best be designated as fear of loss of love. If he loses the love of another person upon whom he is dependent, he also ceases to be protected from a variety of dangers. Above all, he is exposed to the danger that this stronger person will show his superiority in the form of punishment. At the beginning, therefore, what is bad is whatever causes one to be threatened with loss of love. For fear of that loss, one must avoid it. This, too, is the reason why it makes little difference whether one has already done the bad thing or only intends to do it. In either case the danger only sets in if and when the authority discovers it, and in either case the authority would behave in the same way.

This state of mind is called a 'bad conscience'; but actually it does not deserve this name, for at this state the sense of guilt is clearly only a fear of loss of love, 'social' anxiety. In small children it can never be anything else, but in many adults, too, it has only changed to the extent that the place of the father or the two parents is taken by the larger human community. Consequently, such people habitually allow themselves to do any bad thing which promises them enjoyment, so long as they are sure that the authority will not know anything about it or cannot blame them for it; they are afraid only of being found out.[2] Present-day society has to reckon in general with this state of mind.

---

2. This reminds one of Rousseau's famous mandarin. The problem raised by Rousseau has been quoted in full in Freud's paper on 'Our Attitude towards Death' (1915b), *Standard Ed.*, **14**, 298.

A great change takes place only when the authority is internalized through the establishment of a super-ego. The phenomena of conscience then reach a higher stage. Actually, it is not until now that we should speak of conscience or a sense of guilt.[3] At this point, too, the fear of being found out comes to an end; the distinction, moreover, between doing something bad and wishing to do it disappears entirely, since nothing can be hidden from the super-ego, not even thoughts. It is true that the seriousness of the situation from a real point of view has passed away, for the new authority, the super-ego, has no motive that we know of for ill-treating the ego, with which it is intimately bound up; but genetic influence, which leads to the survival of what is past and has been surmounted, makes itself felt in the fact that fundamentally things remain as they were at the beginning. The super-ego torments the sinful ego with the same feeling of anxiety and is on the watch for opportunities of getting it punished by the external world.

At this second stage of development, the conscience exhibits a peculiarity which was absent from the first stage and which is no longer easy to account for.[4] For the more virtuous a man is, the more severe and distrustful is its behaviour, so that ultimately it is precisely those people who have carried saintliness[5] furthest who reproach themselves with the worst sinfulness. This means that virtue forfeits some part of its promised reward; the docile and continent ego does not enjoy the trust of its mentor, and strives in vain, it would seem, to acquire it. The objection will at once be made that these difficulties are artificial ones, and it will be said that a stricter and more vigilant conscience is precisely the hallmark of a moral man. Moreover, when saints call themselves sinners, they are not so wrong, con-

---

3. Everyone of discernment will understand and take into account the fact that in this summary description we have sharply delimited events which in reality occur by gradual transitions, and that it is not merely a question of the *existence* of a super-ego but of its relative strength and sphere of influence. All that has been said above about conscience and guilt is, moreover, common knowledge and almost undisputed.

4. This paradox has been discussed by Freud earlier. See, for instance, Chapter V of *The Ego and the Id* (1923*b*), *Standard Ed.*, **19**, 54, where other references are given.

5. 'Heiligkeit.' The same term, used in the different sense of 'holiness', is discussed by Freud in some other passages. Cf. the paper on 'civilized' sexual morality (1908*d*), *Standard Ed.*, **9**, 187.

sidering the temptations to instinctual satisfaction to which they are exposed in a specially high degree—since, as is well known, temptations are merely increased by constant frustration, whereas an occasional satisfaction of them causes them to diminish, at least for the time being. The field of ethics, which is so full of problems, presents us with another fact: namely that ill-luck—that is, external frustration—so greatly enhances the power of the conscience in the super-ego. As long as things go well with a man, his conscience is lenient and lets the ego do all sorts of things; but when misfortune befalls him, he searches his soul, acknowledges his sinfulness, heightens the demands of his conscience, imposes abstinences on himself and punishes himself with penances.[6] Whole peoples have behaved in this way, and still do. This, however, is easily explained by the original infantile stage of conscience, which, as we see, is not given up after the introjection into the super-ego, but persists alongside of it and behind it. Fate is regarded as a substitute for the parental agency. If a man is unfortunate it means that he is no longer loved by this highest power; and, threatened by such a loss of love, he once more bows to the parental representative in his super-ego—a representative whom, in his days of good fortune, he was ready to neglect. This becomes especially clear where Fate is looked upon in the strictly religious sense of being nothing else than an expression of the Divine Will. The people of Israel had believed themselves to be the favourite child of God, and when the great Father caused misfortune after misfortune to rain down upon this people of his, they were never shaken in their belief in his relationship to them or questioned his power or righteousness. Instead, they produced the prophets, who held up their sinfulness before them; and out of their sense of guilt they created the over-strict commandments of their priestly reli-

---

6. This enhancing of morality as a consequence of ill-luck has been illustrated by Mark Twain in a delightful little story, *The First Melon I ever Stole.* This first melon happened to be unripe. I heard Mark Twain tell the story himself in one of his public readings. After he had given out the title, he stopped and asked himself as though he was in doubt: '*Was* it the first?' With this, everything had been said. The first melon was evidently not the only one. This last sentence was added in 1931.—In a letter to Fliess of February 9th, 1898, Freud reported that he had attended a reading by Mark Twain a few days earlier. (Freud, 1950a, Letter 83.)

gion.[7] It is remarkable how differently a primitive man behaves. If he has met with a misfortune, he does not throw the blame on himself but on his fetish, which has obviously not done its duty, and he gives it a thrashing instead of punishing himself.

Thus we know of two origins of the sense of guilt: one arising from fear of an authority, and the other, later on, arising from fear of the super-ego. The first insists upon a renunciation of instinctual satisfactions; the second, as well as doing this, presses for punishment, since the continuance of the forbidden wishes cannot be concealed from the super-ego. We have also learned how the severity of the super-ego—the demands of conscience—is to be understood. It is simply a continuation of the severity of the external authority, to which it has succeeded and which it has in part replaced. We now see in what relationship the renunciation of instinct stands to the sense of guilt. Originally, renunciation of instinct was the result of fear of an external authority: one renounced one's satisfactions in order not to lose its love. If one has carried out this renunciation, one is, as it were, quits with the authority and no sense of guilt should remain. But with fear of the super-ego the case is different. Here, instinctual renunciation is not enough, for the wish persists and cannot be concealed from the super-ego. Thus, in spite of the renunciaiton that has been made, a sense of guilt comes about. This constitutes a great economic disadvantage in the erection of a super-ego, or, as we may put it, in the formation of a conscience. Instinctual renunciation now no longer has a completely liberating effect; virtuous continence is no longer rewarded with the assurance of love. A threatened external unhappiness—loss of love and punishment on the part of the external authority— has been exchanged for a permanent internal unhappiness, for the tension of the sense of guilt.

These interrelations are so complicated and at the same time so important that, at the risk of repeating myself, I shall approach them from yet another angle. The chronological sequence, then, would be as follows. First comes renunciation of instinct owing to fear of aggression by the *external* authority.

---

7. A very much more extended account of the relations of the people of Israel to their God is to be found in Freud's *Moses and Monotheism* (1939a).

(This is, of course, what fear of the loss of love amounts to, for love is a protection against this punitive aggression.) After that comes the erection of an *internal* authority, and renunciation of instinct owing to fear of it—owing to fear of conscience.[8] In this second situation bad intentions are equated with bad actions, and hence come a sense of guilt and a need for punishment. The aggressiveness of conscience keeps up the aggressiveness of the authority. So far things have no doubt been made clear; but where does this leave room for the reinforcing influence of misfortune (of renunciation imposed from without) [p. 126], and for the extraordinary severity of conscience in the best and most tractable people [p. 125 f.]? We have already explained both these peculiarities of conscience, but we probably still have an impression that those explanations do not go to the bottom of the matter, and leave a residue still unexplained. And here at last an idea comes in which belongs entirely to psycho-analysis and which is foreign to people's ordinary way of thinking. This idea is of a sort which enables us to understand why the subject-matter was bound to seem so confused and obscure to use. For it tells us that conscience (or more correctly, the anxiety which later becomes conscience) is indeed the cause of instinctual renunciation to begin with, but that later the relationship is reversed. Every renunciation of instinct now becomes a dynamic source of conscience and every fresh renunciation increases the latter's severity and intolerance. If we could only bring it better into harmony with what we already know about the history of the origin of conscience, we should be tempted to defend the paradoxical statement that conscience is the result of instinctual renunciation, or that instinctual renunciation (imposed on us from without) creates conscience, which then demands further instinctual renunciation.

The contradiction between this statement and what we have previously said about the genesis of conscience is in point of fact not so very great, and we see a way of further reducing it. In order to make our exposition easier, let us take as our example

---

8. 'Gewissensangst.' Some remarks on this term will be found in an Editor's footnote to Chapter VII of *Inhibitions, Symptoms and Anxiety* (1926d), *Standard Ed.*, **20**, 128; *I.P.L.*, **28**, 42.

the aggressive instinct, and let us assume that the renunciation in question is always a renunciation of aggression. (This, of course, is only to be taken as a temporary assumption.) The effect of instinctual renunciation on the conscience then is that every piece of aggression whose satisfaction the subject gives up is taken over by the super-ego and increases the latter's aggressiveness (against the ego). This does not harmonize well with a view that the original aggressiveness of conscience is a continuance of the severity of the external authority and therefore has nothing to do with renunciation. But the discrepancy is removed if we postulate a different derivation for this first instalment of the super-ego's aggressivity. A considerable amount of aggressiveness must be developed in the child against the authority which prevents him from having his first, but none the less his most important, satisfactions, whatever the kind of instinctual deprivation that is demanded of him may be; but he is obliged to renounce the satisfaction of this revengeful aggressiveness. He finds his way out of this economically difficult situation with the help of familiar mechanisms. By means of identification he takes the unattackable authority into himself. The authority now turns into his super-ego and enters into possession of all the aggressiveness which a child would have liked to exercise against it. The child's ego has to content itself with the unhappy role of the authority—the father—who has been thus degraded. Here, as so often, the [real] situation is reversed: 'If I were the father and you were the child, I should treat you badly.' The relationship between the super-ego and the ego is a return, distorted by a wish, of the real relationships between the ego, as yet undivided, and an external object. That is typical, too. But the essential difference is that the original severity of the super-ego does not—or does not so much—represent the severity which one has experienced from it [the object], or which one attributes to it; it represents rather one's own aggressiveness towards it. If this is correct, we may assert truly that in the beginning conscience arises through the suppression of an aggressive impulse, and that it is subsequently reinforced by fresh suppressions of the same kind.

Which of these two views is correct? The earlier one, which genetically seemed so unassailable, or the newer one, which rounds off the theory in such a welcome fashion? Clearly, and by the evidence, too, of direct observations, both are justified. They do not contradict each other, and they even coincide at one point, for the child's revengeful aggressiveness will be in part determined by the amount of punitive aggression which he expects from his father. Experience shows, however, that the severity of the super-ego which a child develops in no way corresponds to the severity of treatment which he has himself met with.[9] The severity of the former seems to be independent of that of the latter. A child who has been very leniently brought up can acquire a very strict conscience. But it would also be wrong to exaggerate this independence; it is not difficult to convince oneself that severity of upbringing does also exert a strong influence on the formation of the child's super-ego. What it amounts to is that in the formation of the super-ego and the emergence of a conscience innate constitutional factors and influences from the real environment act in combination. This is not at all surprising; on the contrary, it is a universal aetiological condition for all such processes.[10]

It can also be asserted that when a child reacts to his first great instinctual frustrations with excessively strong aggressiveness and with a correspondingly severe super-ego, he is following a phylogenetic model and is going beyond the response that would be currently justified; for the father of prehistoric times was undoubtedly terrible, and an extreme amount of aggressiveness may be attributed to him. Thus, if one shifts over from individual to phylogenetic development, the differences between

---

9. As has rightly been emphasized by Melanie Klein and by other English writers.

10. The two main types of pathogenic methods of upbringing—over-strictness and spoiling—have been accurately assessed by Franz Alexander in his book *The Psychoanalysis of the Total Personality* 1927) in connection with Aichlorn's study of delinquency [*Wayward Youth,* 1925]. The 'unduly lenient and indulgent father' is the cause of children's forming an over-severe super-ego, because, under the impression of the love that they receive, they have no other outlet for their aggressiveness but turning it inwards. In delinquent children, who have been brought up without love, the tension between ego and super-ego is lacking, and the whole of their aggressiveness can be directed outwards. Apart from a constitutional factor which may be supposed to be present, it can be said, therefore, that a severe conscience arises from the joint operation of two factors: the frustration of instinct, which unleashes aggressiveness, and the experience of being loved, which turns the aggressiveness inwards and hands it over to the super-ego.

the two theories of the genesis of conscience are still further diminished. On the other hand, a new and important difference makes its appearance between these two developmental processes. We cannot get away from the assumption that man's sense of guilt springs from the Oedipus complex and was acquired at the killing of the father by the brothers banded together.[11] On that occasion an act of aggression was not suppressed but carried out; but it was the same act of aggression whose suppression in the child is supposed to be a source of his sense of guilt. At this point I should not be surprised if the reader were to exclaim angrily: 'So it makes no difference whether one kills one's father or not—one gets a feeling of guilt in either case!' We may take leave to raise a few doubts here. Either it is not true that the sense of guilt comes from suppressed aggressiveness, or else the whole story of the killing of the father is a fiction and the children of primaeval man did not kill their fathers any more often than children do nowadays. Besides, if it is not fiction but a plausible piece of history, it would be a case of something happening which everyone expects to happen— namely, of a person feeling guilty because he really has done something which cannot be justified. And of this event, which is after all an everyday occurrence, psycho-analysis has not yet given any explanation.'

That is true, and we must make good the omission. Nor is there any great secret about the matter. When one has a sense of guilt after having committed a misdeed, and because of it, the feeling should more properly be called *remorse*. It relates only to a deed that has been done, and, of course, it presupposes that a *conscience*—the readiness to feel guilty—was already in existence before the deed took place. Remorse of this sort can, therefore, never help us to discover the origin of conscience and of the sense of guilt in general. What happens in these everyday cases is usually this: an instinctual need acquires the strength to achieve satisfaction in spite of the conscience, which is, after all, limited in its strength; and with the natural weakening of the need owing to its having been satisfied, the former balance of power is restored. Psycho-analysis is thus justified in excluding

---

11. *Totem and Taboo* (1912–13), *Standard Ed.*, **13**, 143.

from the present discussion the case of a sense of guilt due to remorse, however frequently such cases occur and however great their practical importance.

But if the human sense of guilt goes back to the killing of the primal father, that was after all a case of 'remorse'. Are we to assume that [at that time] a conscience and a sense of guilt were not, as we have presupposed, in existence before the deed? If not, where, in this case, did the remorse come from? There is no doubt that this case should explain the secret of the sense of guilt to us and put an end to our difficulties. And I believe it does. This remorse was the result of the primodial ambivalence of feeling towards the father. His sons hated him, but they loved him, too. After their hatred has been satisfied by their act of aggression, their love came to the fore in their remorse for the deed. It set up the super-ego by identification with the father; it gave that agency the father's power, as though as a punishment for the deed of aggression they had carried out against him, and it created the restrictions which were intended to prevent a repetition of the deed. And since the inclination to aggressiveness against the father was repeated in the following generations, the sense of guilt, too, persisted, and it was reinforced once more by every piece of aggressiveness that was suppressed and carried over to the super-ego. Now, I think, we can at last grasp two things perfectly clearly: the part played by love in the origin of conscience and the fatal inevitability of the sense of guilt. Whether one has killed one's father or has abstained from doing so is not really the decisive thing. One is bound to feel guilty in either case, for the sense of guilt is an expression of the conflict due to ambivalence, of the eternal struggle between Eros and the instinct of destruction or death. This conflict is set going as soon as men are faced with the task of living together. So long as the community assumes no other form than that of the family, the conflict is bound to express itself in the Oedipus complex to establish the conscience and to create the first sense of guilt. When an attempt is made to widen the community, the same conflict is continued in forms which are dependent on the past; and it is strengthened and results in a further intensification of the sense of guilt. Since civilization obeys an internal erotic impulsion which causes human beings to unite in a closely-knit group, it can only achieve this aim through an ever-increasing reinforcement of the sense of guilt. What began in relation to the father is completed in relation to the group. If civilization is a necessary course of development from the family to humanity as a whole, then—as a result of the inborn conflict arising from ambivalence, of the eternal struggle between the trends of love and death—there is inextricably bound up with it an increase of the sense of guilt, which will perhaps reach heights that the individual finds hard to tolerate. One is reminded of the great poet's moving arraignment of the 'Heavenly Powers':—

> Ihr führt in's Leben uns hinein.
> Ihr lasst den Armen schuldig werden,
> Dann überlasst Ihr ihn den Pein,
> Denn iede Schuld rächt sich auf Erden.[12]

And we may well heave a sigh of relief at the thought that it is nevertheless vouchsafed to a few to salvage without effort from the whirlpool of their own feelings the deepest truths, towards which the rest of us have to find our way through tormenting uncertainty and with restless groping.

Having reached the end of his journey, the author must ask his readers' forgiveness for not having been a more skillful guide and for not having spared them empty stretches of road and troublesome *détours*. There is no doubt that it could have been done better. I will attempt, late in the day, to make some amends.

In the first place, I suspect that the reader has the impression that our discussions on the sense of guilt disrupt the framework of this essay: that they take up too much space, so that the

---

12. One of the Harp-player's songs in Goethe's *Wilhelm Meister*.

> To earth, this weary earth, ye bring us
> To guilt ye let us heedless go,
> Then leave repentance fierce to wring us:
> A moment's gult, an age of woe!
>
> Carlyle's translation.

The first couplet appears as an association to a dream in Freud's short book *On Dreams* (1901*a*), *Standard Ed.*, **5,** 637 and 639.

rest of its subject-matter, with which they are not always closely connected, is pushed to one side. This may have spoilt the structure of my paper; but it corresponds faithfully to my intention to represent the sense of guilt as the most important problem in the development of civilization and to show that the price we pay for our advance in civilization is a loss of happiness through the heightening of the sense of guilt.[13] Anything that still sounds strange about this statement, which is the final conclusion of our investigation, can probably be traced to the quite peculiar relationship—as yet completely unexplained—which the sense of guilt has to our consciousness. In the common case of remorse, which we regard as normal, this feeling makes itself clearly enough perceptible to consciousness. Indeed, we are accustomed to speak of a 'consciousness of guilt' instead of a 'sense of guilt'.[14] Our study of the neuroses, to which, after all, we owe the most valuable pointers to an understanding of normal conditions, brings us up against some contradictions. In one of those affections, obsessional neurosis, the sense of guilt makes itself noisily heard in consciousness; it dominates the clinical picture and the patient's life as well, and it hardly allows anything else to appear alongside of it. But in most other cases and forms of neurosis it remains completely unconscious, without on that account producing any less important effects. Our patients do not believe us when we attribute an 'unconscious sense of guilt' to them. In

---

13. 'Thus conscience does make cowards of us all . . .' That the education of young people at the present day conceals from them the part which sexuality will play in their lives is not the only reproach which we are obliged to make against it. Its other sin is that it does not prepare them for the aggressiveness of which they are destined to become the objects. In sending the young out into life with such a false psychological orientation, education is behaving as though one were to equip people starting on a Polar expedition with summer clothing and maps of the Italian Lakes. In this it becomes evident that a certain misuse is being made of ethical demands. The strictness of those demands would not do so much harm if education were to say: 'This is how men ought to be, in order to be happy and to make others happy; but you have to reckon on their not being like that.' Instead of this the young are made to believe that everyone else fulfils those ethical demands—that is, that everyone else is virtuous. It is on this that the demand is based that the young, too, shall become virtuous.

14. 'Schuldbewusstsein' instead of 'Schuldgefühl'. The second of these terms is the one which Freud has been using for the most part. They are synonyms apart from their literal meaning, and both are translated by the usual English 'sense of guilt' except on such special occasions as this.

order to make ourselves at all intelligible to them, we tell them of an unconscious need for punishment, in which the sense of guilt finds expression. But its connection with a particular form of neurosis must not be over-estimated. Even in obsessional neurosis there are types of patients who are not aware of their sense of guilt, or who only feel it as a tormenting uneasiness, a kind of anxiety, if they are prevented from carrying out certain actions. It ought to be possible eventually to understand these things; but as yet we cannot. Here perhaps we may be glad to have it pointed out that the sense of guilt is at bottom nothing else but a topographical variety of anxiety; in its later phases it coincides completely with *fear of the super-ego*. And the relations of anxiety to consciousness exhibit the same extraordinary variations. Anxiety is always present somewhere or other behind every symptom; but at one time it takes noisy possession of the whole of consciouness, while at another it conceals itself so completely that we are obliged to speak of unconscious anxiety or, if we want to have a clearer psychological conscience, since anxiety is in the first instance simply a feeling,[15] of possibilities of anxiety. Consequently it is very conceivable that the sense of guilt produced by civilization is not perceived as such either, and remains to a large extent unconscious, or appears as a sort of *malaise*,[16] a dissatisfaction, for which people seek other motivations. Religions, at any rate, have never overlooked the part played in civilization by a sense of guilt. Furthermore—a point which I failed to appreciate elsewhere[17]—they claim to redeem mankind from this sense of guilt, which they call sin. From the manner in which, in Christianity, this redemption is achieved— by the sacrificial death of a single person, who in this manner takes upon himself a guilt that is common to everyone—we have been able to infer what the first occasion may have been on which this primal guilt, which was also the beginning of civilization, was acquired.[18]

---

15. See Chapter VIII of *Inhibitions, Symptoms and Anxiety* (1926*d*), *Standard Ed.*, **20**, 132.—Feelings cannot properly be described as 'unconscious' (cf. *The Ego and the Id, Standard Ed.*, **19**, 22–3).

16. 'Unbehagen': the word which appears in the title of this work.

17. In *The Future of an Illusion* (1927*c*).

18. *Totem and Taboo* (1912–13) *Standard Ed.*, **13**, 153–5.

Though it cannot be of great importance, it may not be superfluous to elucidate the meaning of a few words such as 'super-ego', 'conscience', 'sense of guilt', 'need for punishment' and 'remorse', which we have often, perhaps, used too loosely and interchangeably. They all relate to the same state of affairs, but denote different aspects of it. The super-ego is an agency which has been inferred by us, and conscience is a function which we ascribe, among other functions, to that agency. This function consists in keeping a watch over the actions and intentions of the ego and judging them, in exercising a censorship. The sense of guilt, the harshness of the super-ego, is thus the same thing as the severity of the conscience. It is the perception which the ego has of being watched over in this way, the assessment of the tension between its own strivings and the demands of the super-ego. The fear of this critical agency (a fear which is at the bottom of the whole relationship), the need for punishment, is an instinctual manifestation on the part of the ego, which has become masochistic under the influence of a sadistic super-ego; it is a portion, that is to say, of the instinct towards internal destruction present in the ego, employed for forming an erotic attachment to the super-ego. We ought not to speak of a conscience until a super-ego is demonstrably present. As to a sense of guilt, we must admit that it is in existence before the super-ego, and therefore before conscience, too. At that time it is the immediate expression of fear of the external authority, a recognition of the tension between the ego and that authority. It is the direct derivative of the conflict between the need for the authority's love and the urge towards instinctual satisfaction, whose inhibition produces the inclination to aggression. The superimposition of these two strata of the sense of guilt—one coming from fear of the *external* authority, the other from fear of the *internal* authority—has hampered our insight into the position of conscience in a number of ways. Remorse is a general term for the ego's reaction in a case of sense of guilt. It contains, in little altered form, the sensory material of the anxiety which is operating behind the sense of guilt; it is itself a punishment and can include the need for punishment. Thus remorse, too, can be older than conscience.

Nor will it do any harm if we once more review the contradictions which have for a while perplexed us during our enquiry. Thus, at one point the sense of guilt was the consequence of acts of aggression that had been abstained from; but at another point—and precisely at its historical beginning, the killing of the father—it was the consequence of an act of aggression that had been carried out [p. 131]. But a way out of this difficulty was found. For the institution of the internal authority, the super-ego, altered the situation radically. Before this, the sense of guilt coincided with remorse. (We may remark, incidentally, that the term 'remorse' should be reserved for the reaction after an act of aggression has actually been carried out.) After this, owing to the omniscience of the super-ego, the difference between an aggression intended and an aggression carried out lost its force. Henceforward a sense of guilt could be produced not only by an act of violence that is actually carried out (as all the world knows), but also by one that is merely intended (as psycho-analysis has discovered). Irrespectively of this alteration in the psychological situation, the conflict arising from ambivalence—the conflict between the two primal instincts—leaves the same result behind [p. 132]. We are tempted to look here for the solution of the problem of the varying relation in which the sense of guilt stands to consciousness. It might be though that a sense of guilt arising from remorse for an evil *deed* must always be conscious, whereas a sense of guilt arising from the perception of an evil *impulse* may remain unconscious. But the answer is not so simple as that. Obsessional neurosis speaks energetically against it.

The second contradiction concerned the aggressive energy with which we suppose the super-ego to be endowed. According to one view, that energy merely carries on the punitive energy of the external authority and keeps it alive in the mind [p. 123]; while, according to another view, it consists, on the contrary, of one's own aggressive energy which has not been used and which one now directs against that inhibiting authority [p. 129]. The first view seemed to fit in better with the *history,* and the second with the *theory,* of the sense of guilt. Closer reflection has resolved this apparently irreconcilable contradiction almost too completely; what remained as the essential and common factor was that in each case we were dealing with an aggressiveness which had been displaced inwards. Clinical observation, moreover, allows us in fact to distinguish two sources for the aggressiveness which we attribute to the super-ego; one or the other of them exercises the strong effect in any given case, but as a general rule they operate in unison.

This is, I think, the place at which to put forward for serious consideration a view which I have earlier recommended for provisional acceptance.[19] In the most recent analytic literature a predilection is shown for the idea that any kind of frustration, any thwarted instinctual satisfaction, results, or may result, in a heightening of the sense of guilt.[20] A great theoretical simplification will, I think, be achieved if we regard this as applying only to the *aggressive* instincts, and little will be found to contradict this assumption. For how are we to account, on dynamic and economic grounds, for an increase in the sense of guilt appearing in place of an unfulfilled *erotic* demand? This only seems possible in a round-about way—if we suppose, that is, that the prevention of an erotic satisfaction calls up a piece of aggressiveness against the person who has interfered with the satisfaction, and that this aggressiveness has itself to be suppressed in turn. But if this is so, it is after all only the aggressiveness which is transformed into a sense of guilt, by being suppressed and made over to the super-ego. I am convinced that many processes will admit of a simpler and clearer exposition if the findings of psycho-analysis with regard to the derivation of the sense of guilt are restricted to the aggressive instincts. Examination of the clinical material gives us no unequivocal answer here, because, as our hypothesis tells us, the two classes of instinct hardly ever appear in a pure form, isolated from each other; but an investigation of extreme cases would probably point in the direction I anticipate.

I am tempted to extract a first advantage from this more restricted view of the case by applying it to the process of repression. As we have learned, neurotic symptoms are, in their essence, substitutive satisfactions for unfulfilled sexual wishes.

---

19. It has not been possible to trace this earlier recommendation.

20. This view is taken in particular by Ernest Jones, Susan Isaacs and Melanie Klein; and also, I understand, by Reik and Alexander.

In the course of our analytic work we have discovered to our surprise that perhaps every neurosis conceals a quota of unconscious sense of guilt, which in its turn fortifies the symptoms by making use of them as a punishment. It now seems plausible to formulate the following proposition. When an instinctual trend undergoes repression, its libidinal elements are turned into symptoms, and its aggressive components into a sense of guilt. Even if this proposition is only an average approximation to the truth, it is worthy of our interest.

QUESTIONS

1. Is genuine, mature guilt really expressed as a need for punishment?
2. Should one feel guilty because of the threat of the loss of love?
3. Do you agree with Freud that (a) the most important problem in the development of civilization is the sense of guilt, and that (b) the advance in civilization implies a greater sense of guilt?
4. Do you think that, if Freud lived in the last quarter of the twentieth century, he might have had a different view of guilt and the effect of civilization on a sense of guilt?

READINGS

Buber, M. (1958). "Guilt and Guilt Feelings." Cross Currents 9 (Summer).

Haring, B. (1961). *The Law of Christ.* Westminster: Newman Press.

Maguire, D. (1978). "Conscience and Guilt." In *The Moral Choice* (pp. 370–409). New York: Doubleday.

Part VI

PRAYER, SYMBOL AND SPIRITUALITY

Erich Neumann

25. Reflections on the Shadow

Born in Berlin, Erich Neumann left Germany after receiving his medical degree in 1933. He studied with C. G. Jung in 1934 and 1936 but his permanent home from 1934 on was Tel Aviv. He practiced there as an analytical psychologist until his death.

Neumann points out the conflict that all persons can experience: either to deny one's capacity for evil by projecting it onto a scapegoat or to submit oneself completely to the powers of darkness. But Jung and Neumann advocate that one accept one's shadow, or capacity for evil. This is actually an acceptance of the fact that one is a creature with all the limitations of creaturehood.

Appendix[1]

At first sight, it may appear that the shadow is no more than a problem of secondary interest and importance, since it is generally regarded as a figure belonging to the personal unconscious—that is to say, to the uppermost layer of those deep unconscious processes which analytical psychology has selected as its special field of study. The object of this paper, however, is to establish that the problem of the shadow is a *central* concern of modern psychology as such, and that the range of subjects which it involves are among the profoundest questions which analytical psychology has attempted to answer. It is not our purpose to recapitulate here what Jung has said about the shadow

---

1. This Appendix originally appeared as an article in *Der Psychologe* Vol. II *Heft* 7/8 July/August 1950. (This was a special number published on the occasion of Jung's seventy-fifth birthday.) It had been the author's intention to add this article to a second edition of the book in order to clarify the concept of the shadow.

in many passages in his writings;[2] it must suffice to recall that
the shadow is the unknown side of the personality, and that it
normally encounters the ego, the centre and representative of
the light side and of consciousness, in the form of a dark,
uncanny figure of evil—to confront whom is always a fateful
experience for the individual.

In mythology, the figures of the hostile brothers (for example, Osiris—Set, Balder—Loki, Abel—Cain, Jacob—Esau), the
antagonists such as Siegfried and Hagen, Faust and Mephisto,
Dr. Jekyll and Mr. Hyde, and the "Doppelgänger" figures of
fairy tale and poetry[3] are projections of the interdependence
between opposites which links the ego with the shadow. The
appearance of these figures in mythology is evidence in itself
that what is presented here for our discussion is a universal
human problem which completely transcends any purely personal problems of the individual.

At first, the figure of the shadow is experienced externally
as an alien and an enemy, but in the course of its progressive
realisation in consciousness it is introjected and recognised as a
component of one's own personality. Yet when the personal
shadow has been assimilated, the *archetypal shadow* (in the
form of the Devil or Adversary) still remains potent in the psyche. This archetypal shadow-figure has a specific meaning for
man as his antagonist in the process of development towards
consciousness. The same insight—that the psychological basis
for the phenomenon of the shadow is to be found in man's
development towards consciousness—was formulated by Jung
in the following terms.

"The enlargement of the light side of consciousness has the
necessary consequence that that part of the psyche which is less
light and less capable of consciousness is thrown into darkness
to such an extent that sooner or later a rift occurs in the psychic
system. At first, this is not recognised as such and is therefore

2. See especially *Psychological Types; The Relations between the Ego and the
Unconscious*, C.W.7; *Archetypes and the Collective Unconscious*, C.W.9 Part I; *Psychology and Religion*, C.W.11; *A Psychological Approach to the Dogma of the Trinity*,
C.W.11; and *Aion*, C.W.9 Part II, Ch. II.
3. Cf. Hoffman, Chamisso, Edgar Allan Poe, etc.

projected—i.e. it appears as a religious projection, in the form of a split between the powers of Light and Darkness."[4]

This "rift", which in a more or less obvious form runs through the psyche of every modern person, occurs when the processes of differentiation which lead to the development of consciousness endanger the means of communication with the dark side of the unconscious.[5] Man learns to identify himself as far as possible with the ego as the centre of the conscious mind; he learns to comply with the ethical demands presented to him by the collective and to identify himself to a large extent with the light world of moral values and of consciousness, and at the same time to do his best to rid himself of the so-called "antivalues" by the techniques of suppression and repression.[6]

Evidence of this "rift" in the psychic system is to be found in the fact that the split personality identifies itself with the powers of light, but leaves the powers of darkness (the shadow side) in projected form and then experiences and combats them in the shape of "the evil out there". This scapegoat psychology not only produces the most disastrous effects on the life of the collective (where it leads to wars and the extermination of groups holding minority opinions); it also gravely endangers the individual. It endangers him no less when he appears to have succeeded in ridding himself of his dark side than when he fails and is threatened or overwhelmed by the "powers of darkness". The condition of being threatened and overwhelmed by the dark element, which breaks through from the "other side", beyond the rift, is exemplified by the mental breakdowns with which modern depth psychology is so frequently confronted nowadays. The fact that these breakdowns are brought about by "the unconscious" means of course that it is the "dark side" which—for good or for ill—is asserting its claim to consideration. This implies that the mental sickness of modern man is largely due to his own condition of inner splitness; and to act as if the powers of darkness do not belong to his own psyche is no kind of solution to the problem. Man has to realize that he possesses a

---

4. Jung, *The Symbolism of the Spirit: The Spirit Mercurius*, C.W.13.
5. See the author's *The Origins and History of Consciousness*, Pt. ii.
6. Cf. pp. 34–35 of the volume in which this Appendix appeared.

shadow which is the dark side of his own personality; he is being compelled to recognize his "inferior function",[7] if only for the reason that he is so often overwhelmed by it, with the result that the light world of his conscious mind and his ethical values succumbs to an invasion by the dark side. The whole suffering brought upon man by his experience of the inherent evil in his own nature—the whole immeasurable problem of "original sin", in fact—threatens to annihilate the individual in a welter of anxiety and feelings of guilt.

It is precisely when the problem of the shadow has reached this critical point that a decisive new development occurs—a development which has made Jung's analytical psychology the bearer of a new consciousness of humanity for modern man. Freud still regarded sexuality pessimistically, from a reductive point of view, as a power from the dark side of the unconscious which would have to be "sublimated"; in his opinion, the assimilation of the unconscious led, at best, to "Civilization and its Discontents". Jung stands in direct contrast to this viewpoint. In spite of his unrivalled knowledge of the perils of the deep layer of the human psyche, he has a great and revolutionary faith in the creativity of human nature, and it is precisely the dark and ambiguous figure of the shadow which—according to analytical psychology—holds the key to a positive development that may be destined to lead the way to a new wholeness in modern man and to heal the disastrous "rift" in humanity.

Under the old order, the excessive demands made on human nature in the name of the Absolute and of its slogan *"Omne bonum a deo, omne malum ab homine"*[8] had led to a disastrous widening of the gulf between light and darkness in the psyche, and had left man with only two alternatives—either to be overwhelmed by his consciousness of the shadow, to acknowledge himself to be a sinner, and then to be "saved" by the intervention of religion—or else to make a radical attempt to rid himself of the dark side altogether. It is at this point that Jung appears as the healer of modern man and, in a truly superb

---

7. See Jung, *Psychological Types*, C.W.6.
8. "All good comes from God, all evil from man"; see Jung *Aion*, C.W.9 Pt. II, p. 46.

and revolutionary counter-movement, places himself on the side of humanity, on the side of the creature—and on the side of the shadow.

"This 'inferior' personality is made up of everything that will not fit in with, and adapt to, the laws and regulations of conscious life. It is compounded of 'disobedience' and is therefore rejected not on moral grounds only, but also for reasons of expediency . . . But this integration (of the inferior function) cannot take place and be put to a useful purpose unless one can admit the tendencies bound up with the shadow and allow them some measure of realization—tempered, of course, with the necessary criticism. This leads to disobedience and self-disgust, but also to self-reliance, without which individuation is unthinkable. The ability to 'will otherwise' must, unfortunately, be real if ethics are to make any sense at all."[9]

This disobedience, however, is not to be understood in terms of disobedience of society: its meaning is rather existential and primary—it is one of the basic structural components which make up the total human situation.

"Through the intervention of the Holy Ghost, however, man is included in the divine process, and this means that the principle of separateness and autonomy over against God—which is personified in Lucifer as the God-opposing will—is included in it too. But for this will there would have been no creation and no work of salvation either. The shadow and the opposing will are the necessary conditions for all actualization. An object that has no will of its own, capable, if need be, of opposing its creator, and with no qualities other than its creator's, such an object has no independent existence and is incapable of ethical decision . . . Therefore Lucifer was perhaps the one who best understood the divine will struggling to create a world and who carried out that will most faithfully. For, by rebelling against God, he became the active principle of a creation which opposed to God a counter-will of its own."[10]

The acceptance of man's shadow side does not only result in succour and healing; it includes an element of forgiveness and

---

9. Jung, *A Psychological Approach to the Dogma of the Trinity,* C.W.11, p. 198.
10. Ibid, p. 196.

absolution. Man learns more than simply to live on tolerable terms with himself; he must actually learn to live with his sin— though this, of course, must not be misunderstood as meaning to live "in" his sin. This brings us to the heart of the moral and psychological problem which the realisation of the shadow involves for human development, and which, in Jung's words, "should not be twisted into an intellectual activity, for it has far more the meaning of a suffering and a passion which implicate the whole man".[11]

In every case, the acceptance of the shadow is preceded by a mortal conflict, in which the ego struggles to the last to defend its own world of values; it is only through suffering that it finally arrives at an awareness of a new ethic, in which the ego and the conscious mind are no longer responsible for the sole and ultimate decision. At first, for both patient and therapist, the shadow is Evil—and Evil is that which is to be avoided.

"But we assiduously avoid investigating whether in this very power of evil God might have placed some special purpose which it is most important for us to know. One often feels driven to some such view when, like the psychotherapist, one has to deal with people who are confronted with their blackest shadow. At any rate, the doctor cannot afford to point, with a gesture of facile moral superiority, to the tablets of the law and say, 'Thou shalt not'. He has to examine things objectively and weigh up possibilities, for he knows, less from religious training and education than from instinct and experience, that there is something very like a *felix culpa*.[12] He knows that one can miss not only one's happiness but also one's final guilt, without which a man will never reach his wholeness."[13]

The acceptance of the problem of the shadow is the first part of a process of transformation in the personality which, whatever else it may include, always involves an enlargement of consciousness. This does not, however, by any means imply an irresponsible surrender to the shadow, which would result in a fatal

---

11. Jung, *The Spirit of Psychology*, C.W.8, p. 208.

12. "Happy fault", said of Adam's sin. From the Roman Missal, Holy Saturday Rite. The full text runs: *"O felix culpa, quae talem ac tantum meruit habere redemptorem!"* ("O happy fault, which merited so great and glorious a redeemer!")—(*Trans.*).

13. Jung. *Psychology and Alchemy*, C.W.12, pp. 29–30.

loss of consciousness. The change of attitude towards the shadow which is essential for the healing of the sick person, who is the representative of modern man in all his splitness and disintegration, has nothing in common with any megalomaniac condition of being "beyond good and evil". On the contrary, the acceptance of oneself as including a dark aspect and a shadow actually springs from a deep and humble recognition of the invincible creatureliness of man, which is a part of the purpose of his creation. Unlike the old unconscious dilemma—either surrender to the shadow and be overwhelmed, or else project it and lose it altogether—"acceptance of the shadow" is a solution which brings unconsciousness of the problem to an end. And that is in fact the point of the process.

Reprinted from DEPTH PSYCHOLOGY AND A NEW ETHIC, by Erich Neumann, translated by Eugene Rolfe, G.P. Putnam's Sons for the C.G. Jung Foundation for Analytic Psychology, 1969, pp. 137–143.

QUESTIONS

1. How does Neumann show that denial of one's own shadow or scapegoat psychology can lead to wars and to extermination of minority groups?
2. In another section of his book Neumann points out that it is wholeness (which includes acceptance of one's shadow) rather than perfection (or being without sin) that is the goal of human development. How does Neumann develop that same idea of wholeness in this article?
3. How does Neumann point to the relationship between the concept of the shadow and the notion of original sin?

SUGGESTED READINGS

Jung, C. G. (1951). *Aion.* Collected Works, Vol. 9. Part II (Chapter II). Princeton: Princeton University Press.
Jung, C. G. (1957). *The Undiscovered Self.* Boston: Little Brown.

Martin L. Hoffman

26. Development of Prosocial Motivation: Empathy and Guilt

Martin L. Hoffman is well known for his studies on moral development and more recently for his research on empathy. He is, at present, professor of psychology at the University of Michigan at Ann Arbor. He is more interested in the value of guilt as motivating persons toward altruistic action than he is in exploring neurotic guilt. In this selection he explores the nature of true interpersonal guilt which he sees as due to the conjunction of an empathic response to another's distress and an awareness that one is responsible for that distress. Then he discusses the cognitive dimension of guilt—a guilt quite different from that described by Freud (which was largely unconscious in its origins). Finally he examines the developmental levels of guilt and shows how educators and parents can help develop the genuine interpersonal guilt primarily by the process of induction which leads to the awareness of the consequences of one's actions on others. Although he points out the limits of his theory, it is clear that his linking of the cognitive component with the affective component goes beyond Kohlberg's emphasis on moral judgment.

GUILT

Let us examine this guilt response more closely. First, it should be clear that this type of guilt differs from the early conception of guilt in the literature as a conditioned anxiety response to anticipated punishment. Nor is it the same as the Freudian guilt, which is a remnant of earlier fears of punishment or retaliation that resulted in repression of hostile and other impulses, and which is triggered by the return of the repressed impulses to consciousness. (I suspect that these quasi-pathological conceptions account for the negative reputation guilt has acquired among psychologists.) What I am striving for is a concept of true, interpersonal guilt, which may be defined simply as the bad feeling one has about oneself because one is aware of actually doing harm to someone. Freud was aware of the necessity of this type of guilt, but neither he nor his followers have succeeded in integrating it into the main body of psychoanalytic theory.

GUILT AND REPARATIVE ALTRUISM

It is intuitively obvious and there is considerable evidence that most people from an early age feel guilt after harming someone (see review by Hoffman, in press, a). The positive social value of guilt is also indicated by the research showing that guilt arousal usually includes a disposition to help the victim. For example, in Murphy's (1937) nursery school observations there were several instances of one child's harming another. Usually they occurred in the context of a fight or argument, and the victim typically was helped by a bystander rather than by the aggressor. In the few instances of accidental harm, however, the responsible child typically did make a spontaneous attempt at reparation, although the act was sometimes delayed. Another example of the relation between guilt and prosocial action can be found in the research using projective story completion items involving moral transgressions by story characters the same age as the subjects (fifth graders, seventh graders, and adults). In this research, the guilt feelings attributed to the story characters were almost always followed by some sort of reparative behavior (Hoffman, 1975b; in press-a). In many instances the reparative act was followed by a reduction in guilt intensity. When reparation was precluded by the story conditions (it was too late for anything to be done), the guilt response was typically prolonged.

There is also evidence that guilt arousal may serve as a generalized motive for altruistic action beyond reparation to the victim. In numerous laboratory studies, done mainly in the late 1960s and early 1970s (e.g., Regan, 1971), adults who were led to believe that they had harmed someone showed a heightened willingness to help other people as well as the victim. These studies are limited, since they did not include a direct measure of guilt arousal, they showed only short-run effects (the altruistic deed immediately followed the guilt manipulation), and the subjects were all college students. In the story completion research, however, the evidence for guilt was explicit, and there was a suggestion of long-term effects: In some of the completions by children as well as adults, guilt appears to trigger a process of self-examination (e.g., "How could I have been so selfish?") and a reordering of one's value priorities, along with a resolution to act less selfishly in the future. Although by no means conclusive, the findings as a whole suggest, somewhat paradoxically, that guilt, which is usually the result of immoral or at least egoistic action, may subsequently operate as an altruistic motive.

If guilt over harming others is prevalent and socially beneficial, it seems unlikely that its motive base is typically as irrational as previous conceptions would suggest. The question is, what alternative, more realistic motive base is there? I have already suggested empathic distress, and my hypothesis is that true interpersonal guilt may be due to the conjunction of an empathic response to someone's distress and the awareness of being the cause of that distress.

DEVELOPMENT OF GUILT

It is too soon to advance a coherent theory, but I would like to discuss the cognitive prerequisites of guilt, to offer some preliminary speculations about the development of guilt and its parallels with empathy, and finally, to say something about a type of guilt that is neither Freudian nor based on the actual harm one has done to another. The aim of all this is to stimulate further research and theoretical discussion about this important, though neglected, concept.

First it must be noted that, like empathic distress, guilt has three components: affective, cognitive, and motivational. The affective dimension pertains to the painful feeling of disesteem for the self because of the harmful consequences of one's action; in the extreme, a sense of being a worthless person. The motivational dimension pertains to the fact that when one feels guilty, one also feels the urge to undo the damage or to make some form of reparation. The cognitive dimension, although having a lot in common with empathy, is far more complex and requires further discussion.

COGNITIVE DIMENSION OF GUILT

For a person to feel guilty requires an awareness of the harmful effects that one's behavior might have on others. One dimension of this awareness is the cognitive sense of others that is also important for empathy. For example, a child who does not know that others have independent inner states may not feel guilty over hurting their feelings. And, a child who is not yet aware of the self and the other as separate entities may even be uncertain as to who committed the harmful act—the victim or the self.

The cognitive dimension of guilt also includes the awareness that one has been the agent of the harm. This requires the ability to make causal inferences involving one's own actions— for example, the ability to infer from the temporal relation between one's act and a change in the other's state—that one's act was the cause of that change in state. Although research has been done on children's awareness of cause-effect relations in both the social and physical domains, there is very little research on cause-effect relations involving the child's own actions. What little research there is (for review see Hoffman, in press-b) suggests that children may begin to be aware that their actions can have simple physical effects on the external world before 1 year of age. Keeping both this and the social-cognitive levels discussed earlier in mind, we can make some reasonable speculations about the kinds of behaviors that might make the child feel guilty. The simplest case is when the child commits a physically harmful act. This is minimally demanding cognitively, because the consequences of the act are immediate and observable. Guilt over inaction, or omission, is more demanding cognitively because it requires the ability to imagine something that might have happened but did not, and to be aware of the consequences of that omission. That is, observers witness victims' distresses, imagine what they might have done to prevent or alleviate them, and realize that although they did not cause a distress, their inaction contributed to its continuation. Guilt over inaction must therefore be a later developmental acquisition. Perhaps even more demanding cognitively is guilt over contemplating a harmful act, or anticipatory guilt. Anticipatory guilt requires that one can not only establish connections between thoughts, intentions, and actions, but also that one can imagine both an act and its harmful social consequences when neither of these has yet occurred.

Another important cognitive dimension of guilt is the awareness that one has choice and control over one's behavior. Without this awareness there would be no grounds for feeling guilty. Here, too, there is very little research. The recent moral judgment research does show that children as young as 3 or 4 years will judge another child as being naughtier if what he or she did was intentional rather than accidental (e.g., Imamoglu, 1975). Although the actions judged were not the child's own, the findings do suggest that 4-year-olds may be sensitive to choice and control. What about younger children? Psychoanalytic writers have long suggested that there is a period of "omnipotence" in early infancy, before the differentiation of self and others, before "person permanence" (See Mahler, Pine & Bergman, 1975). This makes sense when we consider that at that age the infant's utterances of distress are typically acted upon fairly quickly by the mother. If the infants, as a result, feel that they control the world, then they may also have a rudimentary sense of controlling themselves since they are a part of the world. There is no evidence, however, that infants have any awareness of *choice.* The cry that controls the mother's behavior is very likely a natural response to discomfort, rather than an instrumental act of choice. It may not be until much later that children are aware of choice, and act on the basis of choice.

If there is an early period of omnipotence that is linked to a nondifferentiated state, then it seems likely that as one becomes aware of one's own separateness, one also becomes aware of the new and disturbing reality not only that other people's actions are mediated by *their* desires, not one's own, but also that one's actions are to some extent subject to control by others. With this insight, the delusion of omnipotence can no longer be maintained, and it may give way to a sense of helplessness and loss of control of one's own behavior. This, in time, is presumably followed by a more realistic awareness of having partial control and choice. Until the necessary research is done, it seems plausible tentatively to assume that there is an early developmental progression from a sense of omnipotence, to a sense of helplessness, and finally to an awareness of having some but not total control over one's actions.

A final cognitive dimension of guilt may appear sometime later in development, at least in most societies. This includes the awareness that there exists a moral norm against harming others and that one's act, or contemplated act, is discrepant from that norm. To the extent that one has been socialized to view oneself as an upholder of the norm, this discrepancy may be a threat to one's self-image, and the resulting negative affect may add to the intensity of the empathically based guilt. The awareness of a norm against harming others may thus contribute affectively as well as cognitively to the guilt response.

DEVELOPMENTAL LEVELS OF GUILT

I will not present a complete developmental model for guilt, as I did for empathy, but rather a brief preliminary scheme that utilizes the points made in the foregoing discussion. In this scheme the capacity for guilt develops in parallel with the levels of empathic distress described earlier.

First, a minimal requirement for feeling guilty over harming others is that one is psychologically separate from them. We may therefore not expect any signs of guilt until children have the faint beginnings of awareness of others as separate physical entities from themselves, which is around the end of the first year. Furthermore, in the earliest instances of guilt we may expect to see the most primitive kind of causal schema, which according to Heider (1958) is based on the simple contiguity of events. That is, children may feel that they are to blame just because of the temporal or geographical association of their actions with another person's signs of distress. Whether or not they actually caused the distress is irrelevant. Though they may be confused about who is the causal agent, they may nevertheless feel something like guilt, even if they are totally innocent. The guiltlike responses observed in a third of Zahn-Waxler *et al.*'s (1979) sample of 15–18-month-old infants may be illustrative of this level of guilt. For example, a child is playing with her mother. The mother looks sad for some reason. The child, who has done nothing wrong, looks sad and says, "I sorry, did I hurt you, Mommy?" In another example, a child is arguing with a sibling. The sibling is accidentally hurt. The child then alternates between continuing his aggressive behavior and comforting the sibling. He says he is sorry, kisses the sibling's hand, and then hits his own head. These examples illustrate the young child's empathic distress and his or her confusion about causality. Perhaps more importantly, they also suggest a rudimentary sense of being responsible for an act, which predates some of the cognitive requisites of guilt mentioned earlier—for example, a sense of having choices. Why should children feel that they are to blame? I suggest that they feel culpable because of their sense of omnipotence, which, together with their cognitive limitations, leads them to view all things associated with their actions as caused by them. To summarize, an early, nonveridical sense of being the causal agent may combine with empathic distress to produce a rudimentary feeling of guilt.

A note of caution before we proceed. The examples just cited may reflect a primitive guilt feeling in the child, as suggested. It is also possible, however, that the child feels empathic distress and says "I'm sorry" and yet the words do not reflect a feeling of culpability, but rather a simple parroting of what others have said in similar situations. A careful examination of the child's words, along with accompanying changes in his or her facial expression and any other behavioral indexes of guilt, may be necessary to resolve this issue. The child's hitting him- or herself on the head may be more convincing evidence for guilt feelings than conventional expressions like "I'm sorry," although it is possible that the child has seen others engage in this behavior.

In any case, sometime later in development when children are aware of the impact of their actions, the stage may be set for the development of true interpersonal guilt. This development should proceed along lines corresponding roughly to the levels of social-cognitive development discussed earlier. Thus the earlier true guilt should occur when the child has engaged in some simple physical action that has harmed someone such as knocking another child down, hitting that child, or breaking the child's toy. The cues from the victim indicating he or she is hurt, usually a cry or a pained look, will elicit a guilt feeling, though it may be fleeting. Instances of this abound in the nursery school. For example, a boy takes a toy from another, who cries. The child who took the toy responds with a seemingly genuinely sad look on his face and returns the toy, sometimes with a comforting gesture. We do not know why he responds that way. It might be to avoid a scolding by the teacher, but the child's manner is often that of a contrite and sympathetic, not fearful, child, and it seems plausible that he might feel guilty. Interesting instances of delayed reparation can also be found, which suggest guilt. An example is the girl who offered to give a ride on a swing to someone she accidentally knocked down 15 minutes earlier.

Once the child begins to be aware that others have their own inner states—by 2 or 3 years, as noted earlier—guilt over hurting people's feelings should become a possibility. At about the same time, the child may also begin to show evidence of having the cognitive requisites of guilt over inaction. Finally, when the child becomes aware that other people have their own existence and personal identity—in late childhood or early adolescence— he or she can begin to feel guilty over the harmful effects of his or her action or inaction beyond the immediate situation. In its earliest manifestation, such guilt may be felt when one imagines discrete instances of distress in the victim, although eventually it may also be felt when one is aware of the harmful effects that one's actions may have on the victim over time.

"EXISTENTIAL GUILT"

There is another type of guilt that I have discussed at length elsewhere (Hoffman, 1976b; 1980; in press-a) and should be mentioned at least briefly in any work on altruism: Namely, people may at times feel culpable because of the vast differences in well-being between themselves and others. The most obvious example is survivor guilt. More important for present purposes because of its possible developmental implications is the feeling reported by some of the affluent 1960s social activists who were guilty over how privileged they were in life as compared to others. I call this existential guilt, to distinguish it from true guilt, since the person has done nothing wrong but feels culpable because of circumstances beyond his or her control. It obviously has something of the quality of guilt over inaction, however, as illustrated by some of the activists in Keniston's (1968) sample who felt that because of their privileged position they should be able to do something to alleviate the condition of less fortunate people; and if they did nothing they were therefore responsible for perpetuating this condition. For some, who believed that actions by their relatives or members of their social class contributed to the plight of the less advantaged, existential guilt appeared to shade into an actual feeling of guilt over commission, a sort of guilt by association.

Existential guilt may be heavily influenced by cultural and situational factors, since it requires not only the perception that one is relatively advantaged but also the belief that there is no justification for this. Privilege in the past was often justified by religious doctrine or ideas about racial superiority. These have lost much of their force in our society, and even the idea that one deserves what one earns is no longer tenable for the increasing number of young people who live on loans or gifts from relatives. Thus, although existential guilt may be the most advanced developmentally because of its cognitive complexity, it may be confined to one's culture, social status, and historical period.

RELATION BETWEEN GUILT
AND EMPATHIC DISTRESS

I will now summarize this highly speculative developmental scheme for guilt, highlighting its parallels with empathic distress. First, before becoming aware of others as separate physical entities, children respond to simple expressions of pain by others with empathic distress and also at times with a rudimentary guilt feeling, even though they may lack a keen sense of being the causal agent. Once they know that others are separate entities, they experience empathic distress when observing someone who is physically hurt, and their emphatic distress may be transformed into guilt if their own actions were responsible for the hurt. Similarly, once aware that others have inner states, the empathic distress one experiences in the presence of someone having painful or unhappy feelings may be transformed into guilt if one's actions were responsible for those feelings. Finally, once aware of the identity of others beyond the immediate situation, one's empathic response to their general plight may be transformed into guilt if one feels responsible for their plight, or if one's attention shifts from their plight to the contrast between it and one's own relatively advantaged position.

Although empathic distress is here viewed as a prerequisite for the development of guilt, it seems likely that guilt may eventually become largely independent of its empathic origin. In some situations—for example, those in which the victim is visibly sad or hurt—guilt may continue to be accompanied by empathic distress. In other situations, however, the victim and his or her hurt may be less salient than other things—for example, the actor's behavior or motivation. In these cases, the actor may feel guilt without empathy. And, in most instances of anticipatory guilt, there may rarely be empathic arousal except in the unusual case in which one imagines the other's response to one's planned action especially vividly. In general, then, at some point in development, the awareness of being the causal agent of another's misfortune may be enough to trigger guilt feelings without empathy. Thus, although empathic distress may be a necessary factor in the *development* of guilt, it may not, subsequently, be an inevitable accompaniment of guilt.

It seems likely, moreover, that once the capacity for guilt is attained, especially guilt over omission or inaction, the weight of influence may be the other way around. That is, guilt may become a part of all subsequent responses to another's distress, at least in situations in which one might have helped but did not. From then on, even as an innocent bystander, one may rarely experience empathic distress without some guilt. The line between empathic distress and guilt thus becomes very fine, and being an innocent bystander is a matter of degree. To the degree that one realizes that one could have acted to help but did not, one may never feel totally innocent. Empathy and guilt may thus be the quintessential prosocial motives, since they may transform another's pain into one's own discomfort and make one feel partly responsible for the other's plight whether or not one has actually done anything to cause it.

Evidence for the connection between empathy and guilt is scanty and largely circumstantial. It includes the fact that children typically respond empathically to others in distress, taken together with the finding (to be discussed later) that discipline techniques that point up the victim's distress and the child's role in causing it appear to contribute to guilt development. There is also some experimental evidence (Thompson & Hoffman, 1980). The subjects—first, third, and fifth grade children—were shown stories on slides, which were also narrated by the experimenter, in which a story character does harm to another person. For example, a boy who accidentally bumps into another boy, scattering his newspapers, does not stop to help because he is in a hurry. After each story, two guilt measures were administered. One is simple: The subject is asked how he or she would feel if he or she were the story character who committed the transgression. The other is a projective item: The subject completes the story, and guilt scores are derived from the amount of guilt attributed to the culprit. Before administering the guilt measures, half the subjects were asked to tell how they think the *victim* in each story felt. The subjects in this empathy arousal condition produced higher guilt scores than a control group who were not asked to think about the victim. These results do not bear directly on the origin of guilt, but they suggest that guilt may at least be intensified by arousal of empathy for the victim of one's actions.

THE ROLE OF SOCIALIZATION

The discussion so far has dealt with the natural processes of empathy and guilt development assumed to occur under ordinary conditions in most cultures because of the tendency of humans to respond vicariously to others. People also have egoistic needs, however, which must not be overlooked, and socialization, which in part reflects the larger themes in society, may build upon the child's empathic or egoistic proclivities in varying degrees. I have suggested elsewhere (Hoffman, 1970b) that there may be little conflict between empathic and egoistic socialization in early childhood, even in individualistic societies like ours. At some point in life the two may begin to clash, however, sometimes dramatically, as one becomes aware that the society's resources are limited and that one's access to them is largely contingent on how well one competes with others. Parents know this, and it may affect their child-rearing goals. For this and other reasons (e.g., their patience with the child, their own personal needs, and the stresses under which they operate), wide variations in child-rearing practices, hence in children's capacity for empathy and guilt, can be expected. What follows are speculations about these socialization effects.

EMPATHY

There is little research on socialization and empathy, but if we assume that helping another in distress reflects an empathic response—which seems reasonable in view of the findings relating empathy to helping—then we can find modest support for speculations based on our theoretical model.

First, we would expect people to be more likely to empathize with someone else's emotion if they have had direct experience with that emotion themselves. It follows that socialization that allows children to experience a variety of emotions, rather than protecting them from these emotions, will increase the likelihood of their being able to empathize with different emotions. That is, it will expand their empathic range. The only evidence to date for this hypothesis is that preschool children who cry a lot themselves appear to be more empathic than children who do not often cry (Lenrow, 1965). There is a theoretical limitation to this hypothesis: Certain extremely painful situations might be repressed, resulting in an inability to empathize with the emotions involved.

A second expectation can be derived from the idea that empathy is a largely involuntary response. By involuntary we mean that if a person pays attention to the victim, he or she usually will have an empathic response. It follows that socialization experiences that direct the child's attention to the inner states of other people should contribute to the development of empathy. We should therefore expect that in situations in which the child has harmed others, the parent's use of discipline techniques that call attention to the victim's pain or injury or encourage the child to imagine him- or herself in the victim's place—inductive techniques—should help put the feelings of others into the child's consciousness and thus enhance the child's empathic potential. The positive correlation between inductive techniques and helping in older children has long been known (see review by Hoffman, 1970a), and the same thing has recently been reported in children under 2 years (Zahn-Waxler et al., 1979).

We would expect role-taking opportunities to help sharpen the child's cognitive sense of others and increase the likelihood that he or she will pay attention to others, thus extending the child's empathic capability. We must remember, however, that role taking is an ego skill potentially useful in manipulating as well as helping others. Role-taking opportunities in positive social contexts should therefore be a more reliable contributor to empathy and helping than role-taking opportunities in competitive contexts. The research thus far seems to provide modest support for this expectation: Role-taking training in prosocial contexts has been found to increase helping behavior in children and adults; the research on role taking in competitive contexts, all of it correlational, unfortunately, appears to show a lack of relation between role taking and helping (see review by Hoffman, in press-a).

Finally, we would expect that giving children a lot of affection would help keep them open to the needs of others and empathic, rather than absorbed in their own needs. And, we would also expect that exposing the child to models who act altruistically and express their sympathetic feelings would contribute to the child's acting empathically rather than making counterempathic attributions about the cause of people's distress. Both these expectations have been borne out by the research (see review by Hoffman, in press-a).

It thus appears that empathy and helping may be fostered by relatively benign, nonpunitive socialization experiences. These experiences may be effective because empathy develops naturally, as I suggested, and is to some extent present at an early age. Empathy may thus serve as a potential ally to parents and others with prosocial child-rearing goals for the child— something to be encouraged and nurtured, rather than punished as egoistic motives must sometimes be. And, besides benefiting from the child's existing empathic tendencies, these same socialization experiences may also help enhance those empathic tendencies. In other words, there may be a mutually supportive interaction between naturally developing empathy and these socialization experiences.

GUILT

Socialization should be especially important in guilt development for the following reason. Guilt feelings are not only aversive, as is empathic distress, but they are also highly deprecatory and threatening to the child's emerging self-image. We may therefore expect children to be motivated to avoid guilt. And they can often succeed in this, because most situations in which children harm others are ambiguous in one way or another as regards who, if anyone, is to blame. That is, children rarely harm others intentionally and without provocation, in which case it would be easy to assign blame. The ambiguity is most apparent when one has harmed another accidentally— whether in rough play or in independent pursuit of one's own interests. But ambiguity also exists in fights and arguments, where it may seem as reasonable to assign blame to the other as to blame the self. In competitive situations one might conceivably feel guilt about wanting to be victorious over the other, about wanting the other to lose, but then one knows that the other is similarly motivated, and so there may be no grounds for guilt. Besides blaming others, or blaming no one, children can use perceptual guilt-avoiding strategies such as turning away from the victim. It seems to follow that even when children have the necessary cognitive and affective attributes for guilt, they often will not experience it unless an external agent is present who somehow compels them to attend to the harm done to the victim and to their own role in the victim's plight. This is exactly what parents often do when the child does harm to someone, and it seems reasonable to expect that the type of discipline used in these situations will have an effect on the development of a guilt disposition in children.

Indeed, the discipline research does show, fairly consistently, that parents who frequently use discipline techniques in which the salient component is induction, that is, techniques in which the parent points up the harmful effects of the child's behavior on others—combined with a lot of affection outside the discipline encounter—have children who tend to experience guilt feelings when they have harmed others (Hoffman, 1970a). Parents who frequently use power assertion—which includes force, deprivation of material objects or privileges, or the threat of these—are apt to have children who tend to respond with fear of retaliation or punishment, rather than guilt. (The frequent use of love withdrawal, in which the parent simply gives direct but nonphysical expression to his anger or disapproval of the child for engaging in undesirable behavior, does not seem to relate to guilt, although such a relationship might be expected from a psychoanalytic perspective.)

My theoretical explanation of these findings, presented elsewhere (see especially Hoffman, in press-b), will be summarized briefly. First, although the research describes discipline techniques as fitting one or another category, when examined empirically most discipline techniques have power-assertive and love withdrawing properties, and some also contain elements of induction. The first two comprise the motive-arousal component of discipline techniques that may be necessary to get the child to stop what he or she is doing and attend. Having attended, the child will often be influenced cognitively, and affectively by the information contained in the inductive component, when it is present. Second, if there is too little arousal the child may ignore the parent; too much arousal, and the resulting fear, anxiety, or resentment may prevent effective processing of the inductive content, as well as direct the child's attention to the consequences of his or her action for the self. Techniques having a salient inductive component ordinarily achieve the best balance, and direct the child's attention to the consequences of his or her action for the victim. Third, the child may process the information in the inductive component; and the cognitive products of this processing constitute knowledge about the moral norm against harming others. Processing this information should also often enlist the capacity for empathy that the child brings to the discipline encounter. The child thus may feel badly due to the other's distress rather than, or, in addition to, anticipated punishment to the self. Fourth, since inductions also point up the fact that the child caused the victim's distress, these techniques may often result in the temporal conjunction of empathic distress and the attribution of personal responsibility for the other's distress that may be needed to transform empathic distress into guilt. (This analysis is most applicable to those instances in which the victim of the child's act exhibits clear signs of being sad and downcast, hurt, or otherwise distressed. If the victim is angry and retaliates, the child may feel anger or fear rather than empathic distress and guilt.)

Fifth, the cognitive products of the information processing that occurs in discipline encounters are hypothesized as being semantically organized and encoded in memory. They are then activated in future discipline encounters, modified, and cumulatively integrated with similar information from other inductions over time. The associated guilt feelings are also activated in these future situations. The source of the information—the discipline encounters settings—is organized separately in a shallower, nonsemantic mode (Craik & Lockhart, 1972) or encoded in "episodic" memory (Tulving, 1972). Consequently, it interferes minimally with the semantic organization, and may be soon forgotten, Sixth, owing to the child's active role in processing the information in inductions, as well as the differential memory for idea content and setting, the child may eventually experience the moral cognitions and guilt feelings generated in discipline encounters as deriving from the self.

I also suggested that once guilty feelings are aroused in discipline encounters, the ideas about the harmful consequences of one's actions that gave rise to them may be suffused with guilty affect and become "hot cognitions" whose affective and cognitive features are inseparable. These hot cognitions may then be encoded in memory and eventually experienced in temptation situations or moral encounters as an affective-cognitive unity. Another interesting possibility is that although the guilty feelings derive from the ideas about harmful consequences, they may be encoded separately, through a special process or channel reserved for affects. If so, then in later temptation situations the guilty feelings may be evoked without any conscious awareness of the ideas about consequences that gave rise to them. (This may sound like the Freudian notion of guilt, but it is different because it is not based on repression.) Stated most generally, this theory suggests that it is (*a*) the appropriate mix of parental power, love, and information; (*b*) the child's processing of the information in discipline encounters and afterwards; and (*c*) the cognitive and affective products of that processing that determine the extent to which the child feels guilty when he or she has harmed another, contemplates acting in a way that might harm another, or does not help another when it is appropriate to do so. Thus the child's empathic and cognitive capabilities that I described earlier may be mobilized for the first time in discipline encounters, with guilt feelings as the result, and the resulting guilt capability may then be generalized to other situations.

CONCLUDING REMARKS

A theoretical model of empathic arousal, its developmental course, its transformation into guilt, and its implications for altruistic motivation has been presented. The model differs from others in the prosocial area in its stress both on emotion and on the interaction between affective and cognitive processes within a developmental framework. It may be useful to point up in general outline the main characteristics of the model. First, the emotion in question, whether empathic distress or guilt, has a cognitive as well as an affective component. The affective component pertains to the arousal and motivational properties of the emotion. The cognitive component pertains to the shaping and transformation of the affective experience that results from the actor's awareness that the event is happening to someone else, and the actor's causal attributions about the event and its impact on the other person. Second, the affective and cognitive components are seen as developing largely through distinctly different processes. Third, the two components are constantly interacting, and, furthermore, despite the differences in the processes underlying their development, they tend to be experienced not as much as separate states but as a fusion. That is, empathic distress and guilt are what may be called "hot cognitions." Fourth, at all four developmental levels, the experience of these emotions is assumed to include a motivational disposition toward prosocial action.

Although as yet loose and tentative, the model appears to provide a broad integrative framework for ordering existing developmental knowledge about the motivation to consider others. A true assessment of the model, however, awaits the test of hypotheses derived specifically from it. It should also be noted that the model has certain limitations. Although empathy and guilt may explain why people act morally and feel bad when they harm someone, no affect theory by itself can explain how children learn to negotiate and achieve a balance between this moral motive and the egoistic motives that may also be aroused in situations. And as I suggested, although one's empathic proclivities may make one more receptive to certain moral values, empathy alone cannot explain how people formulate complex moral ideologies and apply them in situations.

Another limitation of an empathy-based morality may be revealed in situations in which moral judgments must be made, especially when several behaviors are to be compared or competing claims evaluated. Although the model predicts that a mature empathizer responds in terms of a complex network of information including knowledge of the other's life condition, and is thus sensitive to subtle differences in the severity and quality of the consequences that different actions might have for different people, mature empathizers may still show a bias in favor of certain persons, for example, those perceived as similar to themselves. It may be impossible to make objective moral judgments in such complex situations without recourse to moral principles that transcend particular individuals and that may be reduced to one universally accepted principle. Unfortunately, there is no universally accepted principle and as a result competing principles may apply in a given situation (e.g., fairness requires allocating resources according to need *versus* fairness requires allocating according to effort or productivity). The principle one chooses may then simply reflect one's personal values, and judging on the basis of principle may be as vulnerable to bias as relying on empathy.

Without a universal moral principle, it may be beneficial to look for connections between empathy and principles having some consensus in our society. Since empathy is a response to another's state, it may be reasonable to expect empathy to develop into a motive to act in accord with the welfare of others, and, furthermore, to expect this motive to acquire an obligatory quality and be transformed into a verbalized principle for judging the behavior of others as well as guiding one's own actions. The link between empathy and other principles like fairness or justice may be less direct because they often involve competing claims. Even these principles have a welfare-of-others component, and so it may seem reasonable to hypothesize that when empathic children are exposed to these principles they are more likely to adopt them and express them in behavior than are nonempathic children.

The simple moral motives discussed here, then, may link up developmentally with the complex cognitive processes involved in building prosocial moral ideologies and establishing moral priorities. The investigation of this link would seem to be a worthy topic for developmental research.

Reprinted from THE DEVELOPMENT OF PROSOCIAL BEHAVIOR, edited by Nancy Eisenberg, pp 297–313, © 1982 by Academic Press, Inc.

REFERENCE NOTES

1. Aronfeed, J., & Paskal, V. Altruism, empathy, and the conditioning of positive affect. Unpublished manuscript, University of Pennsylvania, 1965.

2. Radke-Yarrow, M., & Zahn-Waxler, C. Roots, motives and patterning in children's prosocial behavior. Presented at the International Conference on the development and maintenance of prosocial behavior, Jablonna, Poland, June 1980.

3. Strayer, J. Empathy, emotions, and egocentrism. Presented at meetings of the International Congress of Psychology, Leipzig, Germany, July 1980.

4. Main, M., Weston, D. R., & Wakeling, S. "Concerned attention" to the crying of an adult actor in infancy. Presented at meetings of the Society for Research in Child Development, San Francisco, March, 1979.

5. Sawin, D. B. Assessing empathy in children: A search for an elusive construct. Presented at meetings of the Society for Research in Child Development, San Francisco, March 1979.

6. Lieman, B. Affective empathy and subsequent altruism in kindergartners and first graders. Presented at meetings of the American Psychology Association, Toronto, Sepetember 1978.

REFERENCES

Aderman, D., Brehm, S. S., & Katz, L. B. Empathic observation of an innocent victim: The just world revisited. *Journal of Personality and Social Psychology,* 1974, *29,* 342–347.

Bandura, H., & Rosenthal, L. Vicarious classical conditioning as a function of arousal level. *Journal of Personality and Social Psychology,* 1966, *3,* 54–62.

Barnett, M. A., King, L. M., Howard, J. A., & Dino, G. Empathy in young children. *Developmental Psychology,* 1980, *16,* 243–244.

Borke, H. Interpersonal perception of young children: Egocentrism or empathy? *Developmental Psychology,* 1971, *5,* 263–269.

Cialdini, R. B., Darby, B. L., & Vincent, J. E. Transgression and altruism: A case for hedonism. *Journal of Experimental Social Psychology,* 1973, *9,* 502–516.

Craik, F. I. M., & Lockhart, R. S. Levels of processing: A framework for memory research. *Journal of Verbal Learning and Verbal Behavior,* 1972, *11,* 671–684.

Feshbach, N. D., & Feshbach, S. The relationship between empathy and aggression in two age groups. *Developmental Psychology*, 1969, *1*, 102–107.

Feshbach, N. D., & Roe, K. Empathy in six- and seven-year-olds. *Child Development*, 1968, *39*, 133–145.

Heider, F. *The Psychology of interpersonal relations*. New York: Wiley, 1958.

Hoffman, M. L. Parent discipline and the child's consideration of others. *Child Development* 1963, *34*, 573–588.

Hoffman, M. L. Moral development. In P. Mussen (Ed.), *Handbook of child psychology*. New York: Wiley, 1970. (a)

Hoffman, M. L. Conscience, personality, and socialization techniques. *Human Development*. 1970, *13*, 90–126. (b)

Hoffman, M. L. Developmental synthesis of affect and cognition and its implications for altruistic motivation. *Developmental Psychology*, 1975, *11*, 607–622. (a)

Hoffman. M. L. Sex differences in moral internalization. *Journal of Personality and Social Psychology*, 1975, *32*, 720–729. (b)

Hoffman, M. L. Empathy, role-taking, guilt and development of altruistic motives. In T. Lickona (Ed.), *Moral development and behavior: Theory, research and social issues*. New York: Holt, Rinehart & Winston, 1976.

Hoffman, M. L. Moral internalization: Current theory and research. In L. Berkowitz (Ed.), *Advances in experimental social psychology*, Vol. 10. New York: Academic Press, 1977, pp. 86–135. (a)

Hoffman, M. L. Empathy, its development and prosocial implications. In C. B. Keasey (Ed.), *Nebraska Symposium on Motivation*, (Vol. 25). Lincoln: University of Nebraska Press, 1977, pp. 169–218, (b)

Hoffman. M. L. Adolescent morality in development perspective. In J. Adelson (Ed.), *Handbook of adolescent psychology*, New York: Wiley, 1980, pp. 295–344.

Hoffman, M. L. Is altruism part of human nature? *Journal of Personality and Social Psychology*, 1981, *40*, 121–137.

Hoffman, M. L. Empathy, guilt, and social cognition. In W. F. Overton (Ed.), *Knowledge and development*. Hillsdale, N. J.: Erlbaum, in press. (a)

Hoffman, M. L. Affective and cognitive processes in moral internalization: An information processing approach. In E. T. Higgins, D. Ruble, & S. W. Hartup (Eds.), *Developmental social cognition: A socio-cultural perspective.* New York: Cambridge University Press, in press. (b)

Hoffman, M. L. Measurement of empathy. In C. Izard (ed.), *Measurement of emotions in infants and children.* New York: Cambridge University Press, in press. (c)

Hoffman, M. L. Affect and moral development. In D. Cicchetti (Ed.), *New directions in child development.* San Francisco: Jossey-Bass, in press. (d)

Humphrey, G. The conditioned reflex and the elementary social reaction. *Journal of Abnormal and Social Psychology,* 1922, *17,* 113–119.

Imamoglu, E. O. Children's awareness and usage of intention cues. *Child Development,* 1975, *46,* 39–45.

Kagan, S., & Madsen, M. Cooperation and competition of Mexican, Mexican-American, and Anglo-American children of two ages under four instructional sets. *Developmental Psychology,* 1971, *5,* 32–39.

Kameya, L. I. *The effect of empathy level and role-taking training upon prosocial behavior.* Unpublished doctoral dissertation, University of Michigan, 1976.

Kaplan, L. J. The basic dialogue and the capacity for empathy. In N. Freedman & S. Grand (Eds.), *Communicative structures and psychic structures.* New York: Plenum, 1977.

Keniston, K. *Young radicals.* New York: Harcourt, 1968.

Klein, R. Some factors influencing empathy in six and seven year old children varying in ethnic background (Doctoral dissertation, University of California, Los Angeles, School of Education, 1970). *Dissertation Abstracts International,* 1971, *31,* 396A. (University Microfilms No. 71-3862)

Krebs, D. L. Empathy and altruism. *Journal of Personality and Social Psychology,* 1975, *32,* 1124–1146.

Lenrow, P. B. Studies in sympathy. In S. S. Tomkins & C. E. Izard (Eds.), *Affect, cognition and personality.* New York: Springer, 1965.

Lerner, M. J., & Simmons, C. Observer's reaction to the innocent victim: Compassion or rejection? *Journal of Personality and Social Psychology,* 1966, *4,* 203–210.

Levine, L E., & Hoffman, M. L. Empathy and cooperation in 4-
year-olds. *Developmental Psychology,* 1975, *11,* 533–534.

Lipps, T. Das Wissen von fremden Ichen. *Psychologische Unter-
suchungen,* 1906, *1,* 694–722.

Mahler, M. S., Pine, F., & Bergman, A. *The psychological birth
of the human infant.* New York: Basic Books, 1975.

Marcus, R. F., Telleen, S., & Roke, E. J. Relation between cooperation and empathy in young children. *Developmental Psychology,* 1979, *15,* 346–347.

Murphy, L. B. *Social behavior and child personality.* New York:
Columbia University Press, 1937.

Regan, J. W. Guilt, perceived injustice and altruistic behavior.
Journal of Personality and Social Psychology, 1971, *18,*
124–132.

Sagi, A., & Hoffman, M. L. Empathic distress in newborns.
Developmental Psychology, 1976, *12,* 175–176.

Schacter, S., & Singer, J. E. Cognitive, social and physiological
determinants of emotional state. *Psychological Review,*
1962, *69,* 379–399.

Simner, M. L. Newborn's response to the cry of another infant.
Developmental Psychology, 1971, *5,* 136–150.

Stotland, E. Exploratory investigations of empathy. In L. Berkowitz (Ed.), *Advances in experimental social psychology,*
(Vol. 4). New York: Academic Press, 1969.

Stotland, E., Mathews, K. E., Sherman, S, E., Hansson, R., &
Richardson, B. Z. *Empathy, fantasy and helping.* Beverly
Hills, Calif.: Sage, 1979.

Thompson, R., & Hoffman, M. L. Empathy and the arousal of
guilt in children. *Developmental Psychology,* 1980, *15,* 155–
156.

Tulving, E. Episodic and semantic memory. In E. Tulving & W.
Donaldson (Eds.), *Organization of memory,* New York:
Academic Press, 1972, pp. 381–403.

Zahn-Waxler, C., Radke-Yarrow, M., & King, R. A. Childrear-
ing and children's prosocial initiations towards victims of
distress. *Child Development,* 1979, *50,* 319–330.

QUESTIONS

1. How does Hoffman show that guilt can be a strong motivator of helping behavior?
2. What are the cognitive prerequisites of genuine interpersonal guilt?
3. Describe the developmental levels of guilt.
4. How can existential guilt move some of the young privileged toward working for social change?
5. What can adults do to foster healthy interpersonal guilt which can result in helping behavior?

SUGGESTED READINGS

Hoffman, M. L. (1976). "Empathy, Role-Taking, Guilt and Development of Altruistic Motives. In T. Lickona (ed.), *Moral Development and Behavior: Theory, Research and Social Issues.* New York: Holt, Rinehart & Winston.

Hoffman, M. L. (1984). "Empathy, Guilt, and Social Cognition." in W. F. Overton (ed.), *Knowledge and Development.* Hillsdale: Erlbaum.

27. Individual and Collective Symbols

Psychotherapist, teacher and scientific writer, Jolande Jacobi lived for many years in Zurich where she was closely associated with Carl Jung. She was a founder and member of the board of directors of the C. G. Jung Institute of Zurich and worked closely with Jung. This selection on symbols points to the fact that religious and/or peak experiences, arising as they do from the depth of the unconscious, can only be expressed through symbol, since the reality they express is too great for any rational definition. There can be many different symbols for one archetypal pattern. So, too, the individual symbols of mystics and the official symbols of religions, while differing in the concrete expression, all point to a common underlying archetypal pattern.

Not all archetypes or archetypal materials are equally suited to the formation of symbols. Along with the many venerable symbols that the human spirit has formed in the course of the millennia, there are others which arise from the symbol-forming capacity of each individual psyche, but which are based on universal and fundamental archetypal forms and which, according to their expressive power and richness of content, have been taken over by mankind as a whole or by certain larger or smaller groups.

"The living symbol formulates an essential unconscious factor, and the more generally this factor prevails, the more general is the effect of the symbol; for it touches the corresponding chord in every psyche."[64]

Many of these individual symbols are short-lived, limited to an individual or a few individuals. They help to clarify the ineffable, to throw bridges between obscure intimations and ideas that can be fully apprehended, so mitigating the isolation of the individual. But only when the universal archetypal pattern has shone through from behind the individual symbol and become accepted by the people as a whole, only when it has become a "collective symbol" in the manner of the innumerable symbols of mythology and religion with which we are familiar, can it fully exert its liberating and saving effect. An individual symbol, understood as a parallel to a universal symbol,[65] i.e., carried back to the "primordial pattern" common to them both, enables the individual psyche to preserve its unique form of expression and at the same time to merge it with the universally human, collective symbol.

Thus when a symbol emerges from the darkness of the psyche, it always has a certain character of illumination; often it may be charged with the full numinosity of the archetype that has become visible in it and act as a *fascinosum* which threatens to rend the individual apart unless he can integrate it with a collective symbol. How menacing and terrifying was the "face" that appeared to St. Niklaus von der Flüe in his vision,[65a] the face that he regarded as the face of God, and how many weeks of tormented struggle were needed before he could transform it into a collective symbol, namely a vision of the collectively accepted Trinity, and so understand it! In the course of time every symbol undergoes a development of meaning, yet all the variations and stages of this development and unfolding disclose invariable, basic traits.

Symbols are never consciously devised; they arise spontaneously. They are not rational or a product of rational thinking or of the will, but rather result from "a psychic process of development, which expresses itself in symbols."[66] This is particularly evident in the case of religious symbols. They are not thought up; rather, they are "spontaneous products" of unconscious psychic activity; they have grown gradually in the course of the centuries; they have a "revelatory character."[67] And for this reason Jung writes:

"Experience shows that religions are in no sense conscious constructions but that they arise from the natural life of the unconscious psyche and somehow give adequate expression to it. This explains their universal distribution and their enormous influence on humanity throughout history, which would be incomprehensible if religious symbols were not at the very least truths of man's psychological nature."[68] And further: "Religions are psychotherapeutic systems in the truest sense of the word. . . . They express the whole range of the psychic problem in powerful images; they are the avowal and recognition of the soul, and at the same time the revelation of the soul's nature."[69]

If we consider the collective unconscious metaphorically as the "universal soul" of human history, the universal as well as the individual aspects of this process of development may be found in any number of symbol sequences revealing parallel "patterns" (because they are based on the same archetypal pattern). In analytical treatment, therefore, according to Jung, every symbol should be considered in its collective as well as its individual context of meaning and as far as possible should be understood and interpreted on the basis of both.

Every human group, family, people, nation, etc., may produce the symbols it requires from out of its common unconscious. Individual and collective symbols are formed in outwardly different ways, but ultimately both are based on an identical structural pattern or archetype.[70] The points of contact between the individual religious symbols of numerous mystics and the official symbols of the various religions can be attributed to this common underlying pattern. The danger that this represents for the religions (i.e., the possibility of shattering their traditional forms) and the measures taken against it (excommunication, for example) acquire a broader meaning in this connection.

"Hence 'at bottom' the psyche is simply 'world.' . . . The more archaic and 'deeper,' that is the more *physiological,* the symbol is, the more collective and universal, the more 'material' it is. The more abstract, differentiated, and specific it is and the more its nature approximates to conscious uniqueness and individuality, the more it sloughs off its universal character. Having finally attained full consciousness, it runs the risk of becoming a mere *allegory* which nowhere oversteps the bounds of conscious comprehension, and is then exposed to all sorts of attempts at rationalistic and therefore inadequate explanation."[71]

The "archetype of the maternal," for example, is pregnant with all the aspects and variations in which "motherliness" can manifest itself, e.g., the sheltering cave, the belly of the whale, the womb of the church, the helpful fairy or the wicked witch, the ancestress, the Magna Mater, or (on the level of individual life) one's own personal mother. Similarly "the father" is first of all an all-embracing god-*image*,[72] the epitome of everything fatherly, a dynamic principle which lives as a powerful archetype in the soul of the child.[73]

Innumerable symbols are superimposed, as it were, on the one archetypal "pattern." But the closer the stratum from which they derive comes to our familiar objective and concrete world, the more these symbols lose their symbolic character. In the personal unconscious they take the form of "screen figures," i.e., 26gns, and ultimately on the "highest" individual level they become the exact copy of a factual and consciously intended content.[74] A similar thought is expressed by Goethe: "True symbolism occurs where the particular represents the more general, not as dream and shadow, but as living, momentary revelation of the unfathomable."[75]

The most impressive examples are provided by the mythologies of all peoples. The fairy tales and fables, whose basic motifs recur among most peoples, belong to a related category. Some are more primordial and naïve than the mythologems, others are more artfully and consciously elaborated. Jung also declares that the religious dogmas and symbols are empirically demonstrable correspondences to the archetypes of the collective unconscious and, from a psychological point of view, are based on them.[76]

"But, although our whole world of religious ideas consists of anthropomorphic images that could never stand up to rational criticism, we should never forget that they are based on numinous archetypes, i.e., on an emotional foundation which is unassailable by reason. We are dealing with psychic facts which logic can overlook but not eliminate."[77]

Jung, in his investigations, pointed to the Christian dogmas as "basic truths of the Church, which apprise us of the nature of intrapsychic experience in an almost inconceivably perfect way." All scientific theories are necessarily abstract and rational, "whereas dogma expresses an irrational whole by means of imagery."[78] It is something that has grown in the soul, not, as many sceptics suppose, something that has been worked out intellectually. Dogmas "are the repositories of the secrets of the soul, and this matchless knowledge is set forth in grand symbolical images."[79] This accounts for their living and often astonishing effect on the souls of so many men.

But mythology, as a living reflection of world creation, is the form of manifestation, the "primordial guise" assumed by the archetypes in the process of becoming symbols. Since the basic forms of the archetypes are common to all nations and times, it should not surprise us to find amazing parallels in the myths that have arisen autochthonously in every corner of the earth. There is a primordial kinship between the great traditional mythologies with their mythologems and the archetypes with their symbols, which have condensed into "individual mythologies" in the individual human psyche. Who can say when the two first met? For the divine images of the great mythologies are nothing other than projected intrapsychic factors, nothing other than personified archetypal powers, in which human existence rises to the grandeur of the type and is concretized in its aspects. One of the profoundest students of these relationships, K. Kerényi, who has devoted several volumes to the problem, writes very aptly:

"In mythology the shaping is pictorial. A torrent of mythological pictures streams out. . . . Various developments of the same ground theme are possible side by side or in succession, just like the variations of a musical theme. For, although what 'streams out' always remains in itself pictorial, the comparison with music is still applicable, certainly with definite *works* of music, i.e., something objective, that has become an object with a voice of its own, that one does justice to not by interpretation and explanation but above all by letting it alone and allowing it to utter its own meaning."[80]

Archetypes, mythologems, and music are woven from the same stuff, from the primordial archetypal material of the living world, and every future view of the world and of man will also emanate from this "matrix of life experience."

NOTES

64. *Psychological Types,* p. 605 (modified).

65. Cf. "Transformation Symbolism in the Mass" (C. W. 11).

65a. To avoid any possible misunderstanding, I should like to make it clear that, in keeping with the whole tenor of this book, the visions of St. Niklaus von der Flüe are discussed only in their psychological aspect. The character of revelation accorded them by the Roman Catholic Church is not questioned in any way or even taken into consideration.

66. Jung, Commentary on *The Secret of the Golden Flower,* p. 96.

67. "The Soul and Death" (C. W. 8), par. 805.

68. Ibid.

69. "Zur gegenwärtigen Lage der Psychotherapie" (1934). ["The State of Psychotherapy Today," C. W. 10. Here tr. R.F.C.II.]

70. Cf. the "transformation symbolism" in the Catholic Mass, in nature, and in the mythologems and dreams of individual modern men, whose basic pattern is often strikingly similar.

71. "The Psychology of the Child Archetype" (C. W. 9, i), par. 291.

72. In order to avoid any misunderstandings on this score, it should be stated expressly that this observation applies only to the "image" of God as it appears in the psyche and has no bearing on His essence. As Théodore Bovet so aptly puts it in his *Die Ganzheit der Person in der ärtzlichen Praxis* (1940), p. 116: "Science can never encounter God; its conceptual system is adapted only to the shadows cast by His light."

73. "Mind and Earth," in *Contributions,* p. 124. [C. W. 10.]

74. Cf. "Der philosophische Baum," in *Von den Wurzeln des Bewusstseins,* p. 378: "The psychoid form underlying an archetypal idea retains its character at all stages, though empirically it is capable of endless variation. Even if the outward form of the Tree has undergone many changes in the course of time, the richness and life of a symbol express themselves more in

change of meaning." [C. W. 13; here tr. R.F.C.II.] (Cf, p. 53 f., above.)

75. Goethe, *Maximen und Reflexionen,* N. 314.
76. *Psychology and Alchemy* p. 17.
77. "Answer to Job" (C. W. 11), par. 556.
78. "Psychology and Religion" (C. W. 11), par. 81.
79. "Psychology of the Transference" (C. W. 16). p. 193.
80. Kerényi, "Prolegomena" to *Essays on a Science of Mythology,* p. 4.

QUESTIONS

1. How does Jacobi account for both the similarities and the differences between different mythologies?
2. If symbols are not consciously devised, how and why do they arise?
3. Do symbols help to define God or to find God?

SUGGESTED READINGS

Jacobi, J. (1959). *Complex/Archetype/Symbol in the Psychology of C. G. Jung.* Princeton: Princeton University Press.

Jung, C. G. (1929). "On the Relation of Analytical Psychology to Poetry." in C. G. Jung, *The Spirit in Man, Art and Literature. Collected Works,* Vol. 15, paras. 97–132. Princeton: Princeton University Press.

Neumann, Erich (1971). *Art and the Creative Unconscious.* Princeton: Princeton University Press.

Abraham H. Maslow

28. Comments on "Religions, Values, and Peak-Experiences"

Abraham Maslow was for some years chairman of the department of psychology at Brandeis University in Massachusetts. Former president of the American Psychological Association, he was one of the foremost spokesmen for the third force (or humanistic) psychologies. This selection is the new preface to the revised edition of his well-known *Religions, Values and Peak Experiences*. In the first edition he implied that one could not have peak experiences (experiences of the one, true, transcendent) if one were a member of an institution. As the 1960's progressed, he realized that there was a need for a balance between, or an integration of, direct experience and the need for order and organization. He explicitly disagrees with Freud who saw religious persons as neurotic. Instead he states that religion is compatible at higher levels of personal development with rationality and social passion. His view of human nature includes the religious or transcendent dimension as an essential component which can be developed only through and in society.

Since *Religions, Values, and Peak-Experiences* was first written, there has been much turmoil in the world and, therefore, much to learn. Several of the lessons I have learned are relevant here, certainly in the sense that they are helpful supplements to the main thesis of the book. Or perhaps I would call them warnings about overextreme, dangerous, and one-sided *uses* of this thesis. Of course this is a standard hazard for thinkers who try to be holistic, integrative, and inclusive. They learn inevitably that most people think atomistically, in terms of either-or, black-white, all in or all out, of mutual exclusiveness and separativeness. A good example of what I mean is the mother who gave her son two ties for his birthday. As he put on one of them to please her, she asked sadly, "And why do you hate the other tie?"

I think I can best state my warning against polarization and dichotomizing by a historical approach. I see in the history of many organized religions a tendency to develop two extreme wings: the "mystical" and individual on the one hand, and the legalistic and organizational on the other. The profoundly and authentically religious person integrates these trends easily and automatically. The forms, rituals, ceremonials, and verbal formulae in which he was reared remain for him experientially rooted, symbolically meaningful, archetypal, unitive. Such a person may go through the same motions and behaviors as his more numerous coreligionists, but he is never *reduced* to the behavioral, as most of them are. Most people lose or forget the subjectively religious experience, and redefine Religion as a set of habits, behaviors, dogmas, forms, which at the extreme becomes entirely legalistic and bureaucratic, conventional, empty, and in the truest meaning of the word, antireligious. The mystic experience, the illumination, the great awakening, along with the charismatic seer who started the whole thing, are forgotten, lost, or transformed into their opposites. Organized Religion, the churches, finally may become the major enemies of the religious experience and the religious experiencer.

But on the other wing, the mystical (or experiential) also has its traps which I have not stressed sufficiently. As the more Apollonian type can veer toward the extreme of being reduced to the merely behavioral, so does the mystical type run the risk of being reduced to the merely experiential. Out of the joy and wonder of his ecstasies and peak experiences he may be tempted to *seek* them, *ad hoc,* and to value them exclusively, as the only, or at least the highest goods of life, giving up other criteria of right and wrong. Focused on these wonderful subjective experiences, he may run the danger of turning away from the world and from other people in his search for triggers to peak experiences, *any* triggers. In a word, instead of being temporarily self-absorbed and inwardly searching, he may become simply a selfish person, seeking his own personal salvation; trying to get into "heaven" even if other people can't, and finally even perhaps *using* other people as triggers, as means to his sole end of higher states of consciousness. In a word, he may become not only selfish but also evil. My impression, from the history of mysticism, is that this trend can sometimes wind up in meanness, nastiness, loss of compassion, or even in the extreme of sadism.

Another possible booby trap for the (polarizing) mystics throughout history has been the danger of needing to escalate the triggers, so to speak. That is, stronger and stronger stimuli are needed to produce the same response. If the *sole* good in life becomes the peak experience, and if all means to this end become good, and if more peak experiences are better than fewer, then one can *force* the issue, push actively, strive, and hunt, and fight for them. So they have often moved over into magic, into the secret and esoteric, into the exotic, the occult, the dramatic and effortful, the dangerous, the cultish. Healthy openness to the mysterious, the realistically humble recognition that we don't know much, the modest and grateful acceptance of gratuitous grace and of just plain good luck—all these can shade over into the antirational, the antiempirical, the antiscientific, the antiverbal, the anticonceptual. The peak experience may then be exalted as the best or even the *only* path to knowledge, and thereby all the tests and verifications of the *validity* of the illumination may be tossed aside.

The possibility that the inner voices, the "revelations," may be mistaken, a lesson from history that should come through loud and clear, is denied, and there is then no way of finding out whether the voices within are the voices of good or of evil. (George Bernard Shaw's *Saint Joan* confronts this problem.) Spontaneity (the impulses from our best self) gets confused with impulsivity and acting out (the impulses from our sick self) and there is then no way to tell the difference.

Impatience (especially the built-in impatience of youth) dictates shortcuts of all kinds. Drugs, which can be helpful when wisely used, become dangerous when foolishly used. The sudden insight becomes "all" and the patient and disciplined "working through" is postponed or devalued. Instead of being "surprised by joy," "turning on" is scheduled, promised, advertised, sold, hustled into being, and can get to be regarded as a commodity. Sex-love, certainly one possible path to the experience of the sacred, can become mere "screwing," i.e., desacralized. More and more exotic, artificial, striving "techniques" may escalate further and further until they become *necessary* and until jadedness and impotence ensue.

The search for the exotic, the strange, the unusual, the uncommon, has often taken the form of pilgrimages, of turning away from the world, the "Journey to the East," to another country or to a different Religion. The great lesson from the true mystics, from the Zen monks, and now also from the Humanistic and Transpersonal psychologists—that the sacred is *in* the ordinary, that it is to be found in one's daily life, in one's neighbors, friends, and family, in one's back yard, and that travel may be a *flight* from confronting the sacred—this lesson can be easily lost. To be looking elsewhere for miracles is to me a sure sign of ignorance that *everything* is miraculous.

The rejection of a priestly caste that claimed to be exclusive custodians of a private hotline to the sacred was, in my opinion, a great step forward in the emancipation of mankind, and we have the mystics among others—to thank for this achievement. But this valid insight can also be used badly when dichotomized and exaggerated by foolish people. They can distort it into a rejection of the guide, the teacher, the sage, the therapist, the counselor, the elder, the helper along the path to self-actualization and the realm of Being. This is often a great danger and always an unnecessary handicap.

To summarize, the healthily Apollonian (which means integrated with the healthily Dionysian) can become pathologized into an extreme, exaggerated, and dichotomized compulsive-obsessional sickness. But also the healthily Dionysian (which means integrated with the healthily Apollonian) can become pathologized at its extreme into hysteria, with all *its* symptoms.[1]

Obviously, what I am suggesting here is a pervasively holistic attitude and way of thinking. The experiential must be not only stressed and brought back into psychology and philosophy as an opponent of the merely abstract and abstruse, of the *a priori,* of what I have called "helium-filled words." It must then also be *integrated* with the abstract, and the verbal, i.e., we must make a place for "experientially based concepts," and for "experientially filled words," that is, for an experience-based rationality in contrast to the *a priori* rationality that we have come almost to identify with rationality itself.

The same sort of thing is true for the relations between experientialism and social reform. Shortsighted people make them opposites, mutually exclusive. Of course, historically this has often happened and does today still happen in many. But it need not happen. It is a mistake, an atomistic error, an example of the dichotomizing and pathologizing that goes along with immaturity. The empirical fact is that self-actualizing people, our best experiencers, are also our most compassionate, our great improvers and reformers of society, our most *effective* fighters against injustice, inequality, slavery, cruelty, exploitation (and also our best fighters *for* excellence, effectiveness, competence). And it also becomes clearer and clearer that the best "helpers" are the most fully human persons. What I may call the Bodhisattvic path is an *integration* of self-improvement and social zeal, i.e., the best way to become a better "helper" is to become a better person. But one necessary aspect of becoming a better person is *via* helping other people. So one must and can do both simultaneously. (The question "Which comes first?" is an atomistic question.)

In this context I would like to refer to my demonstration in the Preface to the revised edition of my *Motivation and Personality* (95) that normative zeal is *not* incompatible with scientific objectivity, but can be integrated with it, eventuating in a higher form of objectivity, i.e., the Taoistic.

What this all adds up to is this: small "r" religion is quite compatible, at the higher levels of personal development, with rationality, with science, with social passion. Not only this, but it can, in principle, quite easily integrate the healthily animal, material, and selfish with the naturalistically transcendent, spiritual, and axiological.

For other reasons also, I now consider that my book *Religions, Values, and Peak-Experiences* (85) was too imbalanced toward the individualistic and too hard on groups, organizations, and communities. Even within the last six or seven years we have learned not to think of organizations as *necessarily* bureaucratic, as we have learned more about humanistic, need-fulfilling kinds of groups, from, e.g., the research in Organization Development and Theory-Y management, the rapidly accumulating experience with T-groups, encounter groups, and personal-growth groups, the successes of the Synanon community, of the Israeli Kibbutzim, etc. (See my listing of the Eupsychian Network, an appendix in the revised edition [89] of my *Toward a Psychology of Being*.)

As a matter of fact, I can say much more firmly than I ever did, for many empirical reasons, that basic human needs can be fulfilled *only* by and through other human beings, i.e., society. The need for community (belongingness, contact, groupiness) is itself a basic need. Loneliness, isolation, ostracism, rejection by the group—these are not only painful but also pathogenic as well. And of course it has also been known for decades that humanness and specieshood in the infant is only a potentiality and must be actualized by the society.

My study of the failure of most Utopian efforts has taught me to ask the basic questions themselves in a more practicable and researchable way. "How good a society does human nature permit?" and, "How good a human nature does society permit?"

Finally, I would now add to the peak-experience material a greater consideration, not only of nadir experiences, the psycholytic therapy of Grof (40), confrontations with and reprieves from death, post-surgical visions, etc., but also of the plateau experience.[2] This is serene and calm, rather than poignantly emotional, climactic, autonomic response to the miraculous, the awesome, the sacralized, the Unitive, the B-Values. So far as I can now tell, the high-plateau experience always has a poetic and cognitive element, which is not always true for peak experiences, which can be purely and exclusively emotional. It is far more voluntary than peak experiences are. One can learn to see in this Unitive way almost at will. It then becomes a witnessing, an appreciating, what one might call a serene, cognitive blissfulness which can, however, have a quality of casualness and lounging about it.

There is more an element of surprise, and of disbelief, and of aesthetic shock in the peak experience, more the quality of having such an experience for the *first time*. I have pointed out elsewhere that the aging body and nervous system is less capable of tolerating a really shaking peak-experience. I would add here that maturing and aging means also some loss of first-time-ness, of novelty, of sheer unpreparedness and surprise.

Peak and plateau experiences differ also in their relations to death. The peak experience can often meaningfully itself be called a "little death," a rebirth in various senses. The less intense plateau-experience is more often experienced as pure enjoyment and happiness, as let's say, a mother sitting quietly looking, by the hour, at her baby playing and marveling, wondering, philosophizing, not quite believing. She can experience this as a very pleasant, continuing, contemplative experience rather than as something akin to a climactic explosion, which then ends.

Older people, making their peace with death, are more apt to be profoundly touched, with (sweet) sadness and tears at the contrast between their own mortality and the eternal quality of what sets off the experience. This contrast can make far more poignant and precious what is being witnessed, e.g., "The surf will be here forever and you will soon be gone. So hang on to it; appreciate it; be fully conscious of it. Be grateful for it. You are lucky."

Very important today in a topical sense is the realization that plateau experiencing can be achieved, learned, earned by long hard work. It can be meaningfully aspired to. But I don't know of any way of bypassing the necessary maturing, experiencing, living, learning. All of this takes time. A transient glimpse is certainly possible in the peak experiences which may, after all, come sometimes to anyone. But, so to speak, to take up residence on the high plateau of Unitive consciousness, that is another matter altogether. That tends to be a lifelong effort. It should not be confused with the Thursday evening turn-on that many youngsters think of as *the* path to transcendence. For that matter, it should not be confused with *any* single experience. The "spiritual disciplines," both the classical ones and the new ones that keep on being discovered these days, all take time, work, discipline, study, commitment.

There is much more to say about these states which are clearly relevant to the life of transcendence and the transpersonal, and to experiencing life at the level of Being. All I wish to do here with this brief mention is to correct the tendency of some to identify experiences of transcendence as only dramatic, orgasmic, transient, "peaky," like a moment on the top of Mt. Everest. There is also the high plateau where one can *stay* "turned-on."

To summarize in a few words, I would say it this way: Man has a higher and transcendent nature, and this is part of his essence, i.e., his biological nature as a member of a species which has evolved. This means to me something which I had better spell out clearly, namely, that this is a flat rejection of the Sartre-type of Existentialism, i.e., its denial of specieshood, and of a biological human nature, and its refusal to face the existence of the biological sciences. It is true that the word "Existentialism" is by now used in so many different ways by different people, even in contradictory ways, that this indictment does not apply to all who use the label. But just *because* of this diversity of usage, the word is now almost useless, in my opinion, and had better be dropped. The trouble is that I have no good alternative label to offer. If only there were some way to say simultaneously: "Yes, man is in a way his own project and he does make himself. But also there are limits upon what he can make himself into. The 'project' is predetermined biologically for all men; it is to become a man. He cannot adopt as his project for himself to become a chimpanzee. Or even a female. Or even a baby." The right label would have to combine the humanistic, the transpersonal, and the transhuman. Besides, it would have to be experiential (phenomenological), at least in its basing. It would have to be holistic rather than dissecting. And it would have to be empirical rather than *a priori,* etc.

The reader who is especially interested in continuing developments along the lines of this book may be referred to the recently established (1969) *Journal of Transpersonal Psychology* (P. O. Box 4437, Stanford, California 94305) and to the older weekly *Manas* (P. O. Box 32112, El Sereno Station, Los Angeles, California 90032).

NOTES

1. Colin Wilson's "Outsider" series will furnish all the examples necessary.
2. This is a very brief anticipation of a more detailed study of "plateau experiences" (R. Johnson, Asrani), and the "Easy State" (Asrani), which I hope to write soon.

QUESTIONS

1. What was Maslow's original view of organized religion?
2. Why did he change his mind? What are the Apollonian and the Dionysian components he speaks of?
3. What is his final view of the relationship of organized religion to healthy personal growth?

SUGGESTED READINGS

Egan, H. (1982). *What Are They Saying About Mysticism?* Ramsey: Paulist Press.

Johnston, W. (1978) *The Inner Eye of Love: Mysticism and Religion.* San Francisco: Harper & Row.

Maslow, A. H. (1968). *Toward a Psychology of Being.* New York: Van Nostrand.

Maslow, A. H. (1970). *Religions, Values and Peak Experiences.* New York: Viking.

Maslow, A. H. (1971). *The Farther Reaches of Human Nature.* New York: Penguin.

Walter Houston Clark

29. Mysticism as a Basic Concept in Defining the Religious Self

Now retired, Walter Houston Clark lives in Newton Center, Massachusetts. He has had a long and distinguished career as professor of the psychology of religion most recently at Fuller Theological Seminary in California and at Andover Newton Theological School in Newton. This selection describes the phenomenon or experience of mysticism and does not consider the essence of mysticism. Clark emphasizes the relational aspect of his definition of religion which includes a mystical encounter with God. In this sense, his view is similar to that of Jung who speaks of the relationship with "an extra-mundane reality" (Chapter 7 in this book). It differs, however, from Fowler's notion of faith which is cognitive and not relational. Like Jung, too, Clark sees the similarity between Maslow's peak experiences and artistic and mystical experiences. Finally he shows the differences and the similarities between the primitive undifferentiated awareness of the infant and adult mystical awareness. The latter is experienced as a rebirth which enables the mystic to feel one with the whole of humanity.

MYSTICISM AND PSYCHOLOGY

Certainly mysticism cannot be ignored either by those responsible for the well-being of religious institutions, whether Catholic or non-Catholic, or by those concerned with the religious nurture of the young. The psychologist of religion must consider it as he seeks to define and describe his area of study. If he is to pretend that his discipline is in any sense a science, he remembers that the first step in the systematizing of any field is to order one's observations and so describe them that they can be studied scientifically. One can never hope to be as exact in describing the field of religion as in describing the world of nature because religion is so much less tangible. Consequently, there is much

310

dispute among even experts in the field as to what religion really is. This is an unhappy state of affairs for a would-be-science. But since there is little that can be done about it, the next best thing is for each student to define what he takes to be religion so that others may know to what phenomena his conclusions may pertain. It is with this ultimate aim in mind, that I concern myself with mysticism. It seems to me to be the essential principle underlying the religious consciousness.

American psychologists have spent a kind of fifty-year sojourn in Egypt in bondage to the behaviorists. This has paid exceedingly meager dividends from the point of view of learning anything very important about personality. Fortunately, many of the behaviorists themselves have become seduced by Freudianism sufficiently to enrich their superficial obsession with mere human behavior through the insights of Freudian subjectivism. This has even led, by devious paths, to some tentative return to the concept of the self, first popularized in the psychology of William James. This development is a happy omen for psychologists of religion. However, they will be in no position to exploit this development without descriptions of the religious self to act as guidelines. There are a few American psychologists who have approached the problem. For example. G. W. Allport in his perceptive book *Becoming*[1] speaks of what he calls *the proprium,* the luminuous core of the personality that must be activated for any kind of single-minded, passionate pursuit such as religion. This idea has been well used by Orlo Strunk, Jr., in his little volume *Religion: A Psychological Interpretation,*[2] which constitutes the best discussion of the religious self that we appear to have. But it is still desirable to describe much more exactly the religious self as opposed to other aspects of the self, so far as this is possible. Here it is important to recognize that religion has many forms, and almost any of these forms might be seized on by somebody and made the essential principle of the religious life and so the core concept of the religious self. Each approach will doubtless have something to commend it, and it must be understood that no one can pretend to

---

1. New Haven; Conn.: Yale University Press, 1955.
2. New York: Abingdon Press, 1962.

be definitive in this controversial field. But in this article I propose to argue the case for mystical experience, not as an all-inclusive category that will cover all aspects of the religious self, but as its core concept.

RELIGIOUS EXPERIENCE

Most forms of what passes for religious behaviour are not clearly to be distinguished from secular experience. William James included in religion any human activity that was directed toward a "religious object." This is one way of defining religion. I propose to differ in that I am saying that *there must be something unique in the quality of the experience itself that makes it religious.* This quality is the mystical. One may give all his time and energy to the business affairs of a church, but unless this service is not in some way enlightened by *a sense of the Beyond,* a mystical encounter with God, then it is hard to see how it is psychologically different from the handling of a secular business. A theologian with an extreme acuteness of intellect may give his life to the intellectual consideration of the attributes of God, but unless he himself has had some immediate experience of God, it is hard to see how his intellectual pursuit is psychologically different from that of a secular philosopher who spends his time, say, in a consideration of the attributes of the State. It is the fact that most theologians are redeemed through some firsthand knowledge of God himself that their works become religious and reflect true Wisdom rather than the mere playing with ideas. Otherwise, they can be thought of as religious only in a very secondary or even tertiary sense, and not in the essential sense in which I am now speaking.[3]

But in mysticism we have an experience that is unique and is consistently reported as qualitatively different from all other human experiences. It is found wherever religion is found, sometimes in very primitive form, but nevertheless still different and unique. It has even been reported by atheists and agnostics,

---

3. For a discussion of this point see W. H. CLARK *Psychology of Religion.* N.Y.: Macmillan, 1958, Chapter 1, or Orlo STRUNK, Jr., *op. cit.*

for example by Arthur Koestler. He was a dedicated Communist and therefore an atheist when he underwent not indeed a Christian mystical experience but one that involved genuine mysticism. He was in one of Franco's prisons expecting execution when he sustained the remarkable experience he recounts in the chapter "The hours by the window" in his autobiographical *The Invisible Writing.*[4] The episode initiated his period of disenchantment with Communism, and he left the movement for good about two years later. Such experiences of cosmic unity are nearly always identified as in some way religious whether or not the subject uses the terminology of any particular faith to describe what he has undergone. They are usually felt in some way to be a direct apprehension of Truth, though this may not be identified verbally as God.

THE CORE OF MYSTICISM

Psychologists will find one of the most recent and valuable titles containing a careful comparative and phenomenological description of mysticism to be *Mysticism and Philosophy*[5] by the Princeton University philosopher W. T. Stace. He has gathered his data carefully from a wide variety of cultures and faith traditions in all centuries. While not all scholars would necessarily agree with him at every point, he has listed common characteristics in what he calls "the universal core" of mysticism. He divides mystical experience into two types, "extrovertive mysticism," the lesser of the two, in which unity is sensed, but outward reality nevertheless maintains the separateness of objects; and "introvertive mysticism," in which all differentiation dissolves into one unity. In describing introvertive mysticism, Stace lists: 1) The unitary consciousness; 2) Timelessness and spacelessness; 3) Sense of objectivity or reality; 4) Blessedness, peace; 5) Feeling of the holy, sacred, or divine; 6) Sense of paradoxicality; 7) Alleged by mystics to be ineffable. These characteristics, the universal core of mystical experience, which he says

---

4. Boston: Beacon Press, 1955.
5. Philadelphia: Lippincott, 1960, especially Chapter 2.

is natural and non-creedal, he distinguishes from the various interpretations of mysticism, which will differ from faith to faith. God, for example, tends to be much more sharply distinguished in the Judeo-Christian and Mohammedan faiths than He is in Buddhism. This does not mean, however, that the latter is atheistic—at least in the usual sense—as many Western writers have claimed.

Parenthetically we may ask whether the characteristics listed by Stace are not very similar to those described by A. H. Maslow or Marghanita Laski,[6] both of whom mention mystical experience but neither of whom sees mysticism as more than a part of a much larger whole, a special kind of "peak experience" or "ecstasy." There is no doubt that there is a close kinship between mystical experience and deeply creative experiences of a different kind, such as the ecstasies of a poet or an artist, or even certain kinds of mathematical or scientific illumination. Laski discusses sexual love as a source of ecstasy. However, it would seem that secular forms of ecstasy may often be psychologically identical with mysticism. At the very least, the mystic is the poet or the artist of the religious life, so that what distinguishes a profound experience with the mark of religion may be its *interpretation,* which is to say its *theology.* Thus, in the last analysis, it would be the experiencer who would determine what religion is. This, of course is one way to approach religion, but it is not the one I am proposing. There is not space for me to discuss this complex problem further. I will return to Stace's characteristics.

I have verified these seven characteristics among contemporary mystics who have been willing to supply me with information about their religious experiences, notably by a counselee whose experience illustrates all of the seven features. Her first mystical experience occurred and was described before Stace's book appeared and so was not influenced by it. The event led to a sharp change in her values and eventually to her resigning a professorship in order to prepare herself for a religious vocation.

---

6. Maslow, *Toward a Psychology of Being.* Princeton, N.J.: Van Nostrand, 1962— LASKI, *Ecstasy: A Study of Some Secular and Religious Experiences.* Bloomington, Ind.: University of Indiana Press, 1961.

One can also find some of these features suggested in a case where the mysticism developed under non-directive therapy described by Carl Rogers as "The case of Mrs. Oak."[7] Another case in an incorrigible criminal will be found briefly described in the first chapter of Standal and Corsini's *Critical Incidents in Psychotherapy.*[8] These cases support the contention of Stace that mystical experience is unique and wholly different from any ordinary human experience. In this way mysticism seems to fit our requirement that whatever our basic concept of the religious self is, it should be well differentiated from non-religious approaches to the self.

These three cases also illustrate another frequent concomitant of mystical experience inasmuch as all three exhibited radical and profound changes in values and behavior. Churches teach that this is the normal and to-be-expected accompaniment of the making of any faith commitment—or even when this is made for us, as in Baptism. However, social scientists have had a great deal of difficulty detecting any close correspondence between church affiliation and superior ethical behavior—at least apart from some kind of shattering confrontation with the Divine that also brings one face-to-face with oneself and involves profound commitment.[9] This kind of confrontation or solution of one's problem of identification is often brought about through mystical experience. I question whether any profound experience identified as religious is wholly without some mystical feature, whether acknowledged by the individual or not.

MYSTICISM AND SCIENTIFIC PSYCHOLOGY

In spite of this tremendous power to change personality, most psychologists, at least in America, have been almost wholly without curiosity about the place of mysticism in person-

---

7. ROGERS C. R. and DYMOND, R. F., *Psychotherapy and Personality Change.* Chicago: U. of Chicago Press, 1954.

8. Englewood Cliffs, N.J.: Prentice Hall, 1959.

9. See, for example, THORNDIKE E. L., *Your City,* N.Y.: Harcourt Brace, 1939, or WARNER, W. Lloyd, *Democracy in Jonesville,* N.Y.: Harpers, 1949.

ality. One can scan the index of textbook after textbook, both in the general field of psychology and that of personality without finding a single reference to mystical experience. Freud and depth psychology will usually be given very generous treatment, but any remarks about mysticism, if made at all, are apt to be disparaging. Yet Aldous Huxley has called mysticism the only method yet discovered for "the radical and permanent transformation of personality."[10]

Doubtless much of this neglect is due to the desire of psychologists to be considered scientists, and it must be admitted that mystical experience makes a very elusive subject for the pursuit of scientific studies. Scientists have a predilection for data either that they already pretty well understand, or that gives clear indications of yielding its secrets to scientific methodology, or that fits into scientific theory. Insecure as to their status as scientists, psychologists particularly are apt to eschew any study that does not promise clearcut results. It is largely for this reason that they have wasted so much time and money in their obsessive interest in the superficial aspects of personality. Aside from suggestive speculations of Jungian oriented psychologists, there are few theories to explain these sometimes amazing mystical transformations.

Perhaps the most satisfying that I have come across are the theories developed by Dr. Henry Elkin, a psychotherapist of New York City.[11] He sees the self developing from the primordial, undifferentiated state of unified bliss that constitutes the world as it must appear to the newly born child, at least until an unkind reality rudely interrupts the bliss. This original state of mind becomes the prototype of mystical experience and in some sense is reawakened in the mystical ecstasy of the adult. From this state there develops, perhaps aided by the terrifying experience of the infant's finding himself helpless and dependent, first a generalized sense of the world that lies beyond himself, to him the *wholly other,* and then gradually, as features of this *other* detach themselves from the amorphous mass of his perceptions,

----

10. *Grey Eminence*, N.Y.: Meridian Books, p. 306.
11. "On the origin of the self", *Psychoanalysis and the Psychoanalytic Review*, 45 (4) (Winter) 1958–1959, pp. 57–76.

he begins to sense the *differentiated other.* This then becomes his phenomenological world of objects and people. Along with this are developed his attitudes and emotions. Depending on whether he has been treated with love by those who care for him or merely manipulated as if he were an object to be used, he learns to react toward others in a similar way. The world may be a home in which he finds his place through fellowship and love, or, on the other hand, a place where other people are to be exploited.

Mystical experience in the adult according to Elkin, then, is in some sense a re-awakening of the primordial state. Partly it is a sort of regression in which the individual may risk psychosis through fixation at this infantile level, and also perhaps through releasing dangerous primordial urges or complexes sleeping in the unconscious. But because the individual takes with him in his strange voyage back to infancy the whole apparatus of the painfully acquired development which has made him an adult, the mystical experience of unity differs in important ways from the original experience of the infant. Often the mystics spontaneously have referred to their experience as a "re-birth." This suggests that in some way the individual has an opportunity to re-experience his development. Brought up to exploit others so that any kind of trust or love relationship is practically impossible, the mystic may so cogently feel his unity with that of all mankind that suddenly he finds within himself that which seems to him *a miraculous new power to relate to others.* No longer is his cooperation with society based on a shrewd sense of give and take with the hope of getting the best of the bargain himself. For the first time in his life he may so cogently have realized his identity with all mankind that compassion and love are possible for him, and he becomes capable of identifying with a fellowship or community instead of being only the reluctant member of a collectivity. For such a one the Church becomes the Blessed Community instead of merely the means of securing celestial favors. Something like this seems to have occurred within the psyche of the rebellious and wretched criminal already alluded to in the reference to Standal and Corsini. It is in this way that at least the dim outlines of the psychical processes appear that can explain the sudden and radical transformations of personality that often follow on a profound mystical experience.

AN OBJECTION

But it may be objected that the mystical consciousness is too unusual an occurrence to be useful as the core concept of the religious self. Is this not too much of a Medieval phenomenon to serve a purpose suited to modern religious life? In answer we can make two replies.

First, if we discover only a few cases in which mystical experiences mediate these transforming changes in human nature, we can suspect the possibility that this can take place in all. The changes that took place in Socrates, St. Teresa of Avila, Blaise Pascal, or even in Carl Rogers' Mrs. Oak took place at a deep level of personality. Elkin's theories suggest that in such cases the memory traces of early infancy are involved. If this is so, when the mystic speaks of "re-birth," or Jesus tells Nicodemus that he must return to his mother's womb, they may not be speaking quite so symbolically as we usually assume. And if mysticism depends in any important way on the infant's experience following birth, it may very well be a universal potentiality within the reach of all.

Second, we may see an analogy to the esthetic which will strengthen the case for the universality of this potentiality. No matter how scarce true artists in the creative sense are, we know that it would be a very twisted and inhuman personality in whom some preference for the beautiful were wholly absent, even though it might be nothing more than a preference for green grass over the asphalt pavements of a dirty inner city. In much the same way, if we only look for it, and though some people have to be taken off their guard to disclose it, we can sense some primitive concern for the spiritual and mystical in almost everyone. The Communists seem to have had a signal lack of success in suppressing all religion in their country, and their shrill tirades on the evils of religion sound suspiciously like protesting too much. Then there is the fact that we all can sense a strange kind of power behind the personality of a true mystic, and also our natures "reverberate" in moving ways to the words of mystics, as with Plato's Allegory of the Cave in *The Republic,* the poetry of *The Book of Job,* or Christ's words to Nicodemus.

Reprinted by permission of the publisher, Loyola University Press, from FROM RELIGIOUS EXPERIENCE TO A RELIGIOUS ATTITUDE, edited by A. Godin, 1965, pp. 31–38.

QUESTIONS

1. What does Clark mean by the term "mysticism"?
2. How does Clark show that even atheists and agnostics can have mystical experiences?
3. How does the mystical experience result in a new power to relate to others?
4. Does Clark think that the mystical experience which transforms human nature is possible for all persons?

SUGGESTED READINGS

Batson, C. and Ventis, W. (1982). *The Religious Experience: A Social-Psychological Perspective.* New York: Oxford.

Clark, W. H. (1958). *Psychology of Religion.* New York: Macmillan.

Rahner, K. (1967/1974). "The Experience of Grace." In K. Rahner, *Theological Investigations,* Vol. III, pp. 86–89. London: Darton, Longman and Todd.

Strunk, O. (1962). *Religion: A Psychological Interpretation.* Nashville: Abingdon.

Edward Kinerk, S.J.

30. Toward a Method for the Study of Spirituality

At present Fr. Kinerk is rector of the Jesuit Novitiate, St. Stanislas Kostka, in Denver, Colorado. He is a well-known spiritual director and has given many Ignatian retreats. This last selection defines clearly what is meant by spirituality and spiritual growth. By showing that spirituality is the expression of personal growth toward authenticity and total authenticity entails complete self-transcendence in love, Fr. Kinerk synthesizes the insights of the other selections in this section.

WHAT IS SPIRITUALITY?

Everyone has a notion of spirituality, but efforts to pin it down in definition can be frustrating. It is everywhere yet nowhere; its scope is so vast—potentially as vast as the sum and depth of all human experience—that workable content virtually disappears.

Spirituality has been described as "life-style." If we realize that this means more than length of hair and particular preferences for food and clothing, this *definition* is actually quite good. A person's spirituality is the way in which he or she lives in accordance with basic values. The famous Swiss theologian, Hans Urs von Balthasar, has given this a more philosophical formulation: "The way in which [an individual] acts and reacts habitually throughout his life according to his objective and ultimate insights and decisions."[5] The strength of such a definition lies in its completeness; its weakness is that it is too complete. We are left afloat on a sea of private human experience with no markers to make this or that dimension of experience stand out. These definitions are good because they include everything, but they are not workable because they distinguish nothing. And without distinctions analysis is impossible.

What should we look for in a workable definition? First of all, a definition of spirituality for the purpose of study should limit the material to what is *expressed*. Nothing can be studied unless it is communicated in some way. It is true that spirituality must deal with the mysterious depths of the human person in relationship to God and that this mystery often defies conceptualization. However, it is usually open to communication through symbolization; and this, too, is a form of expression. Spirituality studies expressions, and these expressions can be conceptual or symbolic: they can be words, or they can be art, music, architecture, or indeed any form of human activity. Of course, an individual's full experience of his or her relationship with God can never be *adequately* expressed, not even symbolically. This is simply a difficulty which the study of spirituality must accept; we can only examine what is expressed and yet we know that the expression is never exhaustive of the reality.

Secondly, a definition of spirituality should contain the idea of *personal growth*. There is no spirituality for an animal, nor do we ever speak of God's spirituality.[6] What distinguishes the human condition is growth beyond self, self-transcendence. There is a restlessness which is a constant striving to move from the less authentic to the more authentic. This is why spirituality gravitates so readily to psychology, and it is precisely the point at which the greatest care must be exercised not to confuse the two.[7]

Finally, as indicated earlier, a workable definition must contain markers: terms in the definition which orient the material by distinguishing what is important from what is unimportant. Without some means of making distinctions the material of spirituality presents an undivided sameness inimical to study. Markers differentiate that material; and this, in turn, facilitates questions for analysis. The particular selection of markers will necessarily be somewhat arbitrary. Here I have chosen to view any spirituality primarily from the standpoint of expressions of the *authentic* and expressions of the *inauthentic*.

A spirituality, then, is the expression of a dialectical personal growth from the inauthentic to the authentic. There are three ingredients in the definition: expression, dialectical personal growth, and authentic-inauthentic. *Expression* need not be clarified further. *Growth* has been called *dialectical* to underscore the fact that all spiritual growth is a simultaneous "yes" to one thing and a "no" to something else. Each step toward the *authentic* demands a corresponding rejection of the inauthentic.[8] The Gospel of Luke manifests this dialectical character in its expression of the beatitudes: every benediction has its corresponding curse (Lk 6:20-26).

Inauthentic and *authentic* are the markers referred to above. The total authenticity of a human person would be his or her complete self-transcendence in love. Conversely, total inauthenticity would be complete self-alienation, self-centeredness in hate. For our purposes, however, expressions of the authentic and inauthentic will normally be but partial representations of these absolute states. In a famous line from the *Imitation of Christ,* for example, compunction is an expression of the authentic while vain knowledge is an expression of the inauthentic;[9] they are signposts along the way. Furthermore, specific expressions of the authentic and the inauthentic are not always univocal, even within the same spirituality. In the *Cloud of Unknowing,* meditation on Christ's passion can be either an expression of the authentic or the inauthentic, depending on the stage of one's contemplative development.[10]

NOTES

5. Hans Urs von Balthasar, "The Gospel as Norm and Test of All Spirituality in the Church," from *Spirituality in the Church,* Christian Duquoc, editor, *Concilium,* vol 9 (Paulist, 1965), p. 7.

6. Process theologians may take exception to this. In a dipolar notion of God one might be able to speak of God's spiri-

tuality: "God in his consequent aspect receives into himself that which occurs in the world, so that it becomes the occasion for newer and richer, as well as better, concretions in the ongoing movement of divine activity," W. Norman Pittenger, "Process Thought: A Contemporary Trend in Theology," *Process Theology,* Ewert H. Cousins, editor (Newman, 1971), p. 27. Even if one were to accept this position, it would be quite difficult to move from the idea of a spirituality of God to its description.

7. It is very easy for spiritual direction to become psychological counseling. Of course, sometimes this is desirable because it is counseling which is needed, but often we slide into a counseling framework simply because it seems to have more substance than spiritual direction. This again reveals the necessity of definition and methodology proper to spirituality.

8. Lonergan views this as a fundamental characteristic of religious development. See *Method,* p. 110.

9. "I would rather feel compuction of heart for my sins than merely know the definition of compunction," Thomas a Kempis, *The Imitation of Christ,* edited with an introduction by Harold C. Gardiner (Image, 1955), Book I, chapter 1.

10. *The Cloud of Unknowing,* by an anonymous four-teenth-century Englishman, edited and introduced by William Johnston (Image, 1973), chapter vii.

QUESTIONS

1. Can one's relationship with God ever fully be expressed either symbolically or conceptually?
2. Why should a definition of spirituality contain the idea of personal growth?
3. What is the difference between spiritual direction and psychological counseling?
4. What then is spirituality?
5. What is the total authenticity of a human person? Why is human authenticity so described?

SUGGESTED READINGS

Duquoc, C. (ed.) (1965). *Spirituality in the Church. Concilium,* Vol. 9. Ramsey: Paulist.

Johnston, W. (1981). *The Mirror Mind: Spirituality and Transformation*. San Francisco: Harper & Row.

Santa-Maria, M. L. (1983). *Growth Through Meditation and Journal Writing: A Jungian Perspective on Christian Morality*. Ramsey: Paulist.